Photography and China

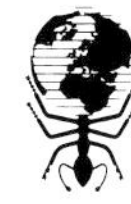

exposures

EXPOSURES is a series of books on photography designed to explore the rich history of the medium from thematic perspectives. Each title presents a striking collection of images and an engaging, accessible text that offers intriguing insights into a specific theme or subject.

Series editors: Mark Haworth-Booth and Peter Hamilton

Also published

Photography and Africa Erin Haney

Photography and Anthropology Christopher Pinney

Photography and Archaeology Frederick N. Bohrer

Photography and Australia Helen Ennis

Photography and China Claire Roberts

Photography and Cinema David Campany

Photography and Death Audrey Linkman

Photography and Egypt Maria Golia

Photography and Flight Denis Cosgrove and William L. Fox

Photography and Ireland Justin Carville

Photography and Italy Maria Antonella Pelizzari

Photography and Japan Karen M. Fraser

Photography and Literature François Brunet

Photography and Science Kelley Wilder

Photography and Spirit John Harvey

Photography and Travel Graham Smith

Photography and the USA Mick Gidley

Photography and China

Claire Roberts

reaktion books

For Nick

Published by Reaktion Books Ltd
33 Great Sutton Street
London EC1V 0DX
www.reaktionbooks.co.uk

First published 2013

Printed and bound in Hong Kong

British Library Cataloguing in Publication Data
Roberts, Claire, 1959–
Photography and China. – (Exposures)
1. Photography – China – History. 2. Photographers – China – History.
I. Title II. Series
770.9'51-DC23

ISBN 978 1 86189 911 8

Contents

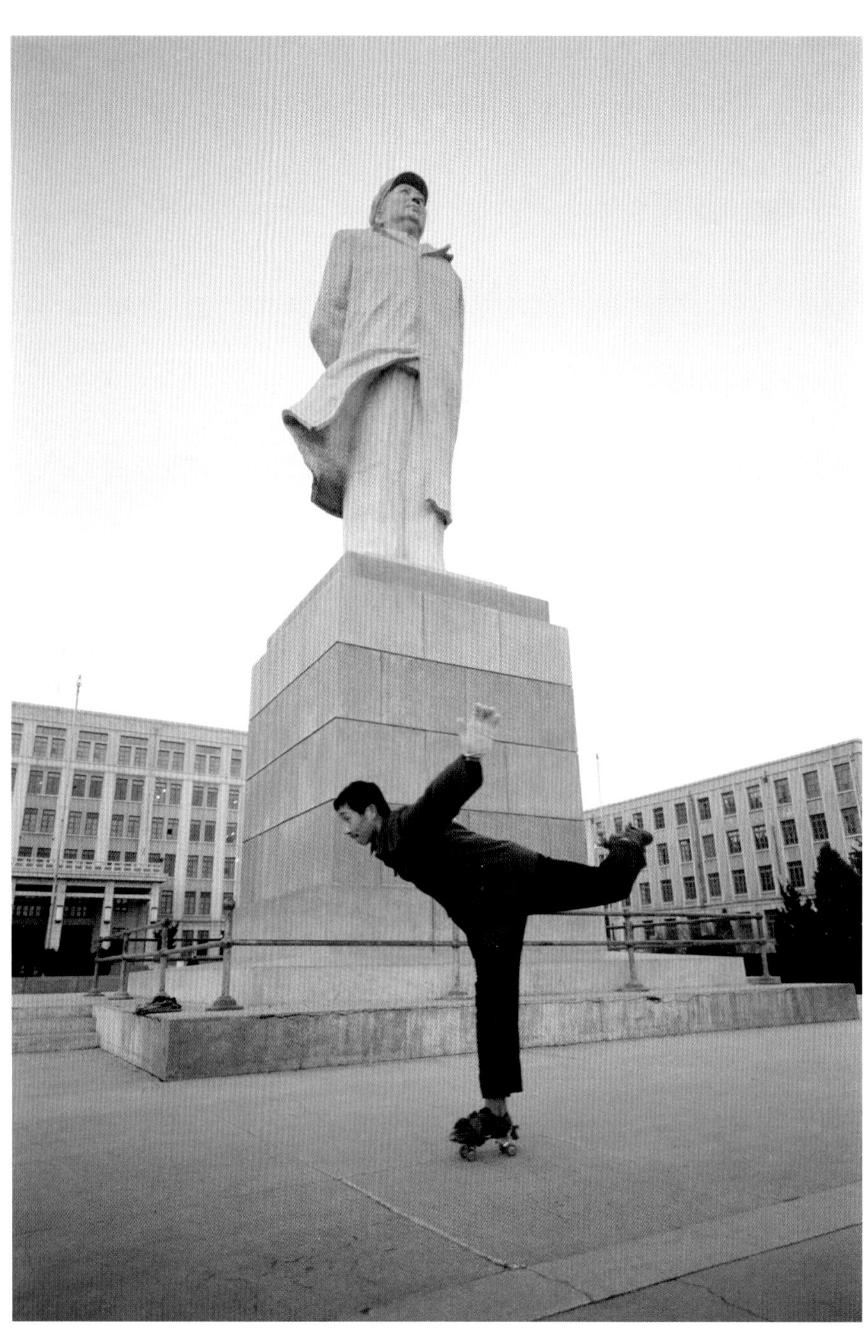

Introduction

In China photography has played an extraordinary role in the transformation of visual culture, touching on many aspects of people's lives. Unlike traditional forms of expression, such as brush-and-ink painting, the new technology offered a powerfully modern, seemingly objective representation of reality mediated through the lens. This situation was not unique to China, but in China photography developed in distinctive ways and that story of response and creative adaptation is the subject of this book.

Prior to photography, distant parts of the world were known to armchair travellers through drawings, paintings and textual description. Understandings were refracted in translation and transmission. The earliest identified photographs of China were taken in the 1840s by visiting military personnel, diplomats, traders and wanderers, who sought to document what they saw in the interests of geopolitical ambition and trade, and to satisfy the curiosity of people back home. With the advent of photography, Chinese people and places were exposed to the outside world as never before.

Chinese artists working in Macao, Hong Kong and Guangzhou (Canton), gateways of the China trade, had long catered to the foreign demand for souvenir paintings and cheap portrait renditions, adopting techniques of oil painting on canvas and board, gouache, and watercolour on ivory. They recognized the commercial potential of photography, learning the craft from visiting Western practitioners or from translations of Western texts. Over time photography was adapted to local mores and customs and was embraced as a medium that offered

1 Liu Heung Shing, *A Student Skates Past Mao's Giant Statue at Dalian Technology University, Liaoning Province*, 1981, gelatin silver print.

commercial, promotional and artistic agency. Through a process of cultural encounter and transfer, like painting in its absorption of introduced materials and techniques, photography became a Chinese medium, used for a wide variety of public and private purposes.

This book explores the introduction of photography to China, how the medium was understood in technological and cultural terms, and how it has been applied. It is a story about East–West exchange and the dynamic dialogue arising from foreign incursion and Chinese sojourning overseas, involving a medium that has always been at the heart of technological, economic and cultural change. The story is entwined with the history of the Chinese world itself, never more turbulent than in the period documented by photography, a narrative of extreme twists and turns, progress and retreat, deep continuity and ongoing transformation. The narrative begins with daguerreotypes of the 1840s and concludes with present-day digital images, highlighting the work of mainland Chinese, Hong Kong and Taiwanese photographers who have used photographic media for news, commerce and propaganda, as well as personal and artistic expression. While my primary focus is the work of Chinese photographers, reference will also be made to the work of some key non-Chinese photographers in acknowledgment of photography's history as an international medium and the important role that such photographers have played in creating images of China for an international public.

While many books have been written about photography and China, there is no overview in English of the subject from the 1840s to the present, nor a sustained discussion of individual photographs covering this time span that draws attention to the perspective of the photographer. This book offers a series of thematic essays that consider selected photographs, yet in a wide-ranging and perhaps provocative way. Space and image limitations have imposed restrictions on the narrative. The photographs, arrayed in gallery-like sequences, have been chosen for their visual presence, historic significance and power to illuminate an aspect of the narrative. Owing to problems of identification and dating associated with much of the early photography in China, and the importance of the perspective of the photographer, I have privileged the work of Chinese photographers and subjects, and preferred photographs where the detail of who made them, of what subject, when, where and why can be reliably surmised. I have also chosen unusual examples, and works by less well-known studios and photographers for breadth and depth, in a short book where much, regrettably, must be left out. A further aim is to bring the names of some key Chinese studios and practitioners to the attention of a broader readership as part of a reconsideration of the role that photography has played in the cultural life of China since the 1840s.

I have highlighted certain themes, including the adaptation of photography to Chinese philosophical and aesthetic concepts, particularly through dialogue with the different kinds of representation found in varieties of Chinese painting. I explore photography as an entrepreneurial, revolutionary and innovative medium, and as a means of 'transmitting spirit' (*chuan shen*). I recognize its flow and exchange with the world outside China at different levels and points in time, including the present era of rapid image and information sharing via the internet and mobile devices. It is as a result of these currents and creative energies that contemporary Chinese photography flourishes as one of the most vibrant art forms of our time.

Archival research has taken me to China (where access to many collections remains a challenge) and North America, the United Kingdom and Europe (where much historical material has been preserved), but there is a lot still to be discovered, understood and made available in this infinitely rich field. In writing this book I acknowledge the pioneering work of many others including An Ge, Bao Kun, Terry Bennett, Cai Tao, Chen Hsueh Sheng, Chen Shen, Hu Zhichuan, Ma Yunzeng, Qian Zhangbiao and Peng Yongxiang, Chen Xiaobo, Jeffrey Cody and Frances Terpak, Gu Di, Gu Yi, Gu Zheng, Jin Yongquan, Richard Kent, Edwin Kin-keung Lai, H. S. Liu, Oliver Moore, Nicholas Pearce, Rong Rong, Karen Smith, Régine Thiriez, Clarke Worswick, Wu Hung, Roberta Wue, Yang Xiaoyan and Zhang Wei. I hope that this modest volume will inspire more comprehensive studies of Chinese photography, adding to the understanding of this important field of Chinese visual culture.

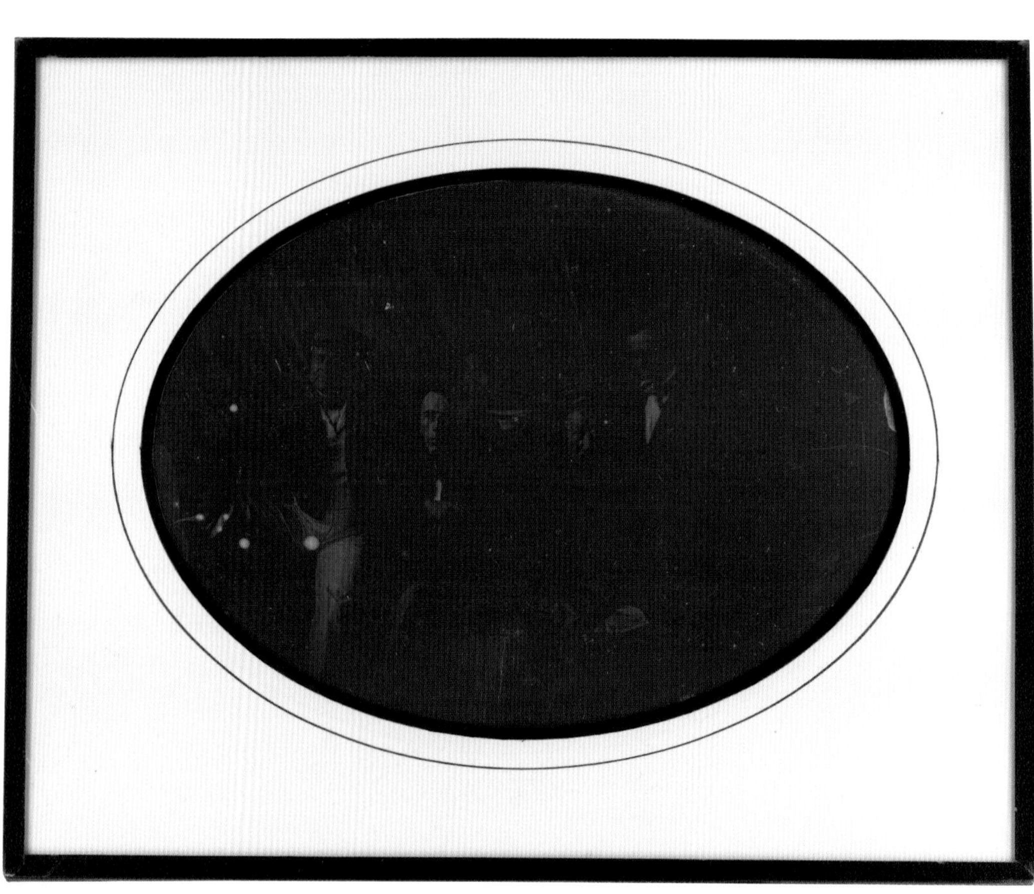

One

China Exposed

Photography reached China soon after Louis Daguerre's announcement of the new technique in France in 1839. The following decade marked a low ebb in China's long imperial history, as defeat by the British in the First Opium War (1839–42) and later conflicts forced treaties on China that gave Westerners residency rights in a string of coastal and river ports and opened the country to international trade. In the historical narrative of today's China, the humiliation inflicted by those 'unequal treaties' marks the beginning of the country's uneasy transformation into a strong and modern nation, a twenty-first-century power.

The Treaty of Nanking, signed by British and Chinese representatives on 29 August 1842, established treaty ports in Guangzhou, Xiamen, Fuzhou, Ningbo and Shanghai, ceded the island of Hong Kong to Britain, and exacted monetary compensation. No photographs recorded the occasion (there are extant engravings), but the signed treaty document was subsequently reproduced in London using the newly devised calotype photographic process (a rival to the daguerreotype, also announced in 1839), which was licensed to the portrait painter Henry Collen, recording what in hindsight proved a crucial event in world history.[1] Two years later a Frenchman, Jules Itier (1802–1877), produced a commemorative portrait of French and Chinese officials gathered to sign the Treaty of Whampoa (Huangpu near Canton) on 24 October 1844, which granted France similar rights to Britain's. Itier, a senior customs official and member of the French trade embassy to China, and a keen amateur scientist, was using the daguerreotype technique announced by his countrymen

2 Jules Itier, Qiying and members of the French embassy on board *L'Archimède*, 24 October 1844, daguerreotype.

only five years earlier: 'not an instrument which serves to draw nature; but a chemical and physical process which gives her the power to reproduce herself'.[2]

The photograph is one of a series taken on the deck of the French Navy corvette *L'Archimède*, using the sail as a backdrop. Qiying (1790–1858), the viceroy in negotiations that had resulted in the Treaty of Nanking, signed with the British two years earlier, is seated alongside the French ambassador Théodore de Lagrené. To his left is the ship's captain. The interpreter stands to the right of Qiying and the secretary of the legation, at the rear. Qiying sits upright and stares directly at the camera, his posture and demeanour in stark contrast to the French, who adopt more casual poses. Half of Qiying's face is in shadow, but his expression is serious, befitting his status as representative of the emperor, and reflecting the solemnity of the occasion for China.

The photograph is an example of the important role that decorum plays in Chinese portraiture and the seriousness with which portraiture in general was regarded. Itier also took single portrait shots of Qiying and another official, which were exchanged for a fan inscribed with calligraphy.[3] The ritual of gift exchange has a long history in China and photographic portraits would come to play an important role in Chinese diplomacy, being used by officials, diplomats and merchants, functioning as a visual calling card or aide-memoire, as was customary in Europe and America.

The oval mount gives the impression of a fantastic scene glimpsed through the porthole of a ship. The remarkable one-off image, created from the action of light-sensitive chemicals on a polished silver-coated copper plate, looks as though it has been conjured from the darkness. Darker around the edges, the figures seem to float like apparitions. The plate is smeary, pitted and scratched, reminding us of the difficulty of working with a new and complex medium in which both skill and chance played a part.

On his return to France, Itier published a record of his travels, *Journal d'un voyage en Chine en 1843, 1844, 1845, 1846*, that included engravings made from the daguerreotypes. Itier was one of a number of early photographers whose involvement with foreign trade missions or military forays provided an opportunity to produce images of a part of the world that had previously been known only through drawings, paintings and textual description. China had been imagined at a remove and often with a degree of distortion. For early practitioners of photography in China, such as the American painter and daguerreotypist George R. West (*c*. 1825–1859), who accompanied the American diplomatic mission to China in 1844, and Giacomo Caneva (1813–1865), who travelled with an Italian trade delegation to silk-producing areas in 1859, the new medium, based on the science of optics, promised a truer and more useful form of representation.

An important element of Ambassador de Lagrené's discussions with Qiying in 1844 was the French request for the Catholic Church to be allowed back into China. The French delegation included members of the Society of Jesus including Father Adrien-Hyppolyte Languillat (1808–1878).[4] After more than a century of Jesuit presence in China, the imperial court had prohibited Christianity in 1724. The French government wanted to reopen the country to missionary activity as a way of expanding French cultural influence. Missionaries had played a significant role in the introduction of Western scientific, technological and artistic concepts to the court, using modern Western learning as a conduit for their faith. Lagrené's discussions were lengthy but ultimately productive. In 1846 the Daoguang Emperor issued an edict legalizing the practice of Christianity in China.

A group of salt print portraits of Jesuits, including Monseigneur Languillat, are among the earliest photographs of missionaries in China (illus. 3).[5] The salt print, or calotype, was developed by British inventor William Henry Fox Talbot in the late 1830s, using a paper or glass negative coated with light-sensitive salts from which multiple positive prints could be made. In 1857 Languillat was consecrated Vicar Apostolic of Zhili, Hebei province, a position that he occupied until 1865. The photograph of Languillat may have been taken by Brother Casimir Hersant (1830–1895) who arrived in 1859 and is recorded as having taken other portraits of the bishop.[6] From the time of their arrival in southern China in 1583, the Jesuits studied the language and adopted Chinese customs, including dress. Languillat wears the garb of a Chinese scholar-official, a privilege that was granted to missionaries. Kneeling before him

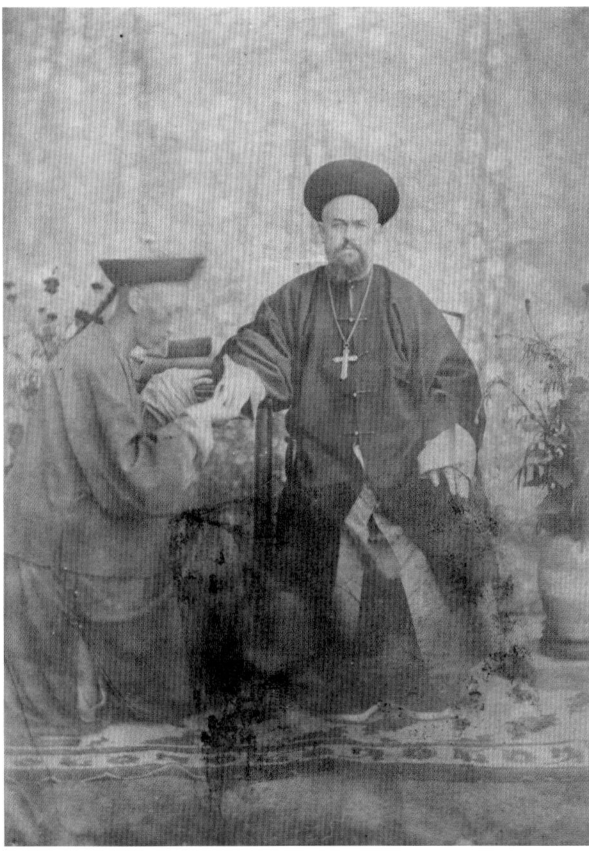

3 *Monseigneur Adrien-Hyppolyte Languillat*, c. 1856, salted paper print, photographer unknown.

is a convert who touches his hand (kissing the bishop's ring was a sign of respect), and a bible rests on the table to his side. The formality of the image and Languillat's full frontal engagement with the camera, influenced by representations of religious or authority figures, conveys the mission's seriousness of purpose. Like many missionaries working in China Languillat endured hardship and was killed during an anti-foreign rampage in Shanghai in 1878.

Like this image, most early photographs taken in China are difficult to attribute and date.[7] They were taken by professionals and amateurs stationed in the newly created zones where foreign business and diplomatic and missionary activity were conducted. The photographers were motivated by a sense of purpose and a desire to share and benefit from images of their encounters.

Chinese practitioners were quick to respond. An early figure whose life and work contributes to but also problematizes the history of photography in China, as Oliver Moore has shown, is Zou Boqi (1819–1869), a teacher and scholar of science (mathematics, astronomy and cartography) from Nanhai, southwest of Canton.[8] Zou's writings, published posthumously in 1873, and discoveries of equipment on his former property that suggest instruction if not experimentation, have led him to be celebrated in China as the 'inventor' of the first Chinese camera. Like his European and American counterparts, Zou was fascinated by optics. *Science*

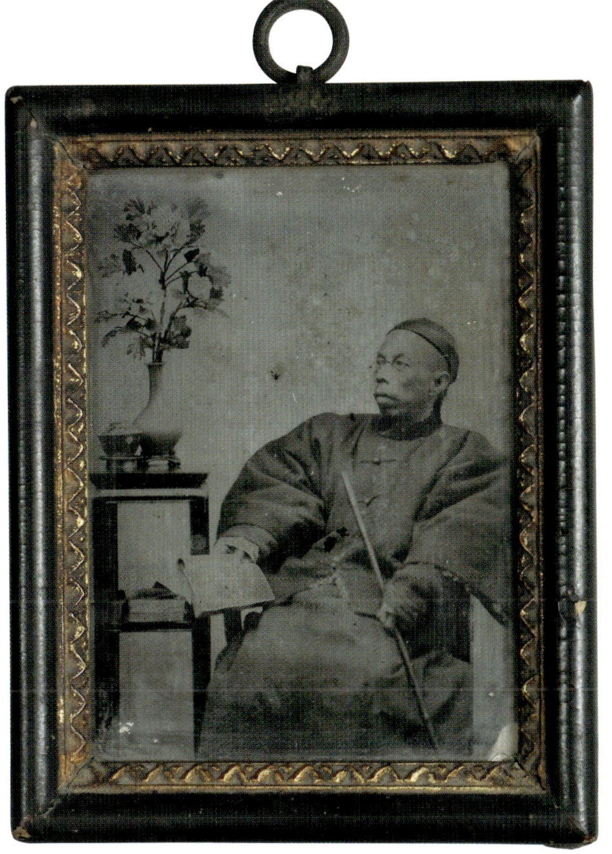

4 Self-portrait of *Zou Boqi*, c. 1863–6, collodion positive on glass.

Updates outlines the history of optics in China and contains information about lenses used in microscopes and telescopes, and *Notes on a Mechanism for Capturing Images* details the functioning of the camera obscura and a plate camera. Zou's writings represent the development of work by Chinese scholars including Zheng Fuguang (*b*. 1780), whose treatise based on Western optical geometry was published in 1846, and earlier figures such as Shen Gua (1033–1097). Zou would have had access to Western ideas and technologies entering China through Guangzhou and Hong Kong, and through Jesuit missionaries who were scientists as well as men of God. On 19 October 1839 *The Canton Press*, a weekly English-language newspaper, published an article about the newly invented daguerreotype camera, and in 'Miscellaneous Notes on Guangdong' the Hunan scholar Zhou Shouchang describes the process of portrait photography following his visit in 1846, indicating that the practice was not an isolated activity.[9]

In 1962 the descendants of Zou Boqi donated a glass-plate portrait of Zou to the Guangzhou Museum, which has since been designated a 'grade one national treasure'.[10] The Chinese scholar of science Dai Nianzu dates the photograph to 1863–6. A poem titled 'Self-portrait', said to have been written by Zou as he approached the age of 50, includes the lines 'There was no particular reason for the self-portrait, but summoning it is like communing with my spirit', prompting Chinese scholars to regard the photograph as a self-portrait.[11] In the poem Zou suggests the mystery of photography and the wonder with which it was apprehended at that time.

In the photograph Zou poses with an open book in one hand and a teaching cane in the other. The vase of peonies, covered porcelain teacup and books indicate his status as a man of learning. The three-quarter view, careful studio lighting and cropping of the body accentuate the feeling of intimacy and perspectival space, and suggest that it was taken in a photographic studio, possibly that of a Westerner.

Zou's posture and demeanour may be compared to that of Luo Yili (1802–1852) in another photograph of the period, also said by Chinese scholars to be a self-portrait.[12] Luo, by contrast, squarely faces the camera, bare-chested, with one foot resting on the chair. The distinctive table appears in other early portraits, too, and suggests that those photographs

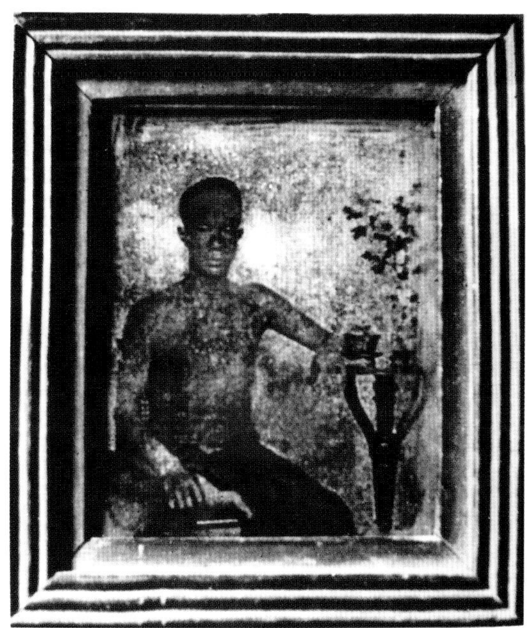

5 Self-portrait of *Luo Yili*, c. 1850–52, collodion positive on glass.

were taken by Luo Yili, or that the portrait of Luo was taken in one of Guangdong's commercial studios.[13] The portrait is an image of studied casualness and manliness, not unlike some painted self-portraits of scholar-artists from around the same time. Its possible intention was to convey the vigour and confidence of an individual, and by association the empire, during a time of national humiliation and trauma occasioned by foreign incursion and war. It is as if the sitter and the photographer are testing the camera's ability to record what is most real – a person's flesh and blood. These two early commemorative photographs of Chinese subjects are refreshingly idiosyncratic, and point to the importance of personal agency. They suggest a dynamic interaction between subject and photographer, whoever they are, to achieve a desired result, thus extending our understanding of 'self-portrait'. The portraits, both on glass, are mounted in protective wooden frames with an authentic patina and hanging loops which suggest that they hung for many years as physical and spiritual ancestral presences in their respective family homes.

Despite the paucity of evidence for the dates and circumstances of these early photographs, Zou's understanding of the principles of the medium is significant and establishes an early link between China, modern scientific enquiry and photography. A distinction has to made, however, between Zou Boqi and most other early Chinese practitioners of the new technique, whose interest in photography was primarily commercial.

A remarkable five-plate panorama of Hong Kong harbour taken by the Italian-British photographer Felice A. Beato (1834–1906) in March 1860 records the large and menacing presence of the British and French military fleet en route to north China. Beato was with the British forces to document the Anglo-French military expedition that would conclude the Second Opium War (1856–60). With its expansive field of vision, the panorama provided proof of progress in establishing a colonial presence on the island, the might of allied naval power, and the potential for expanding commercial interests suggested by the mountainous topography of Kowloon and southern China.

Beato had photographed the aftermath of conflicts in the Crimea (1855–6) and in India (1858) prior to arriving in Hong Kong. He sailed with the British forces to northern China to document hostilities that resulted in the looting and burning of the Yuan Ming Yuan imperial palace, the Garden of Perfect Brightness, outside, Peking (Beijing). His images of the captured fort at Dagu, where many Chinese soldiers lost their lives, are among the earliest photographs of a military campaign in China. They are permeated with what David Harris refers to as the 'ideology of empire'.[14] They are also a reminder of how images are constructed. Beato, who was on the victors' side, took the liberty of adjusting the position of dead bodies to improve the composition. Photography for him, as so often in China subsequently, was about spectacle. Beato was practiced in the art of image creation and mindful of his audience and their expectations. The Dagu photographs are about death and vanquishment, and the eerie sensation of an absence of life.

Beato prepared captions for his images and sold photographs to serving officers singly or in albums, and later to people far from China who were curious about international affairs. As the technique for photogravure had not yet been developed, Beato's photographs formed the basis of engravings and lithographs in the *Illustrated London News* and other published accounts of the war.

From a Chinese perspective, one of Beato's most significant images is a portrait of Prince Gong (Yixin, 1833–1898), the sixth son of the Daoguang Emperor, taken on 2 November 1860, a few days after the signing of the Convention of Peking that concluded the war with Britain and France (illus. 7). Beato's photograph taken on the day of the signing of the British treaty had failed due to a lack of light. The treaty provided war indemnity to Britain and France, allowed diplomats residency rights in Peking, granted missionaries freedom of religious activity, ceded the mainland territory of Kowloon to Britain, opened Tianjin as a trading port and legalized the opium trade. The photograph of the prince, like another where he faces away from the camera, captures him in an

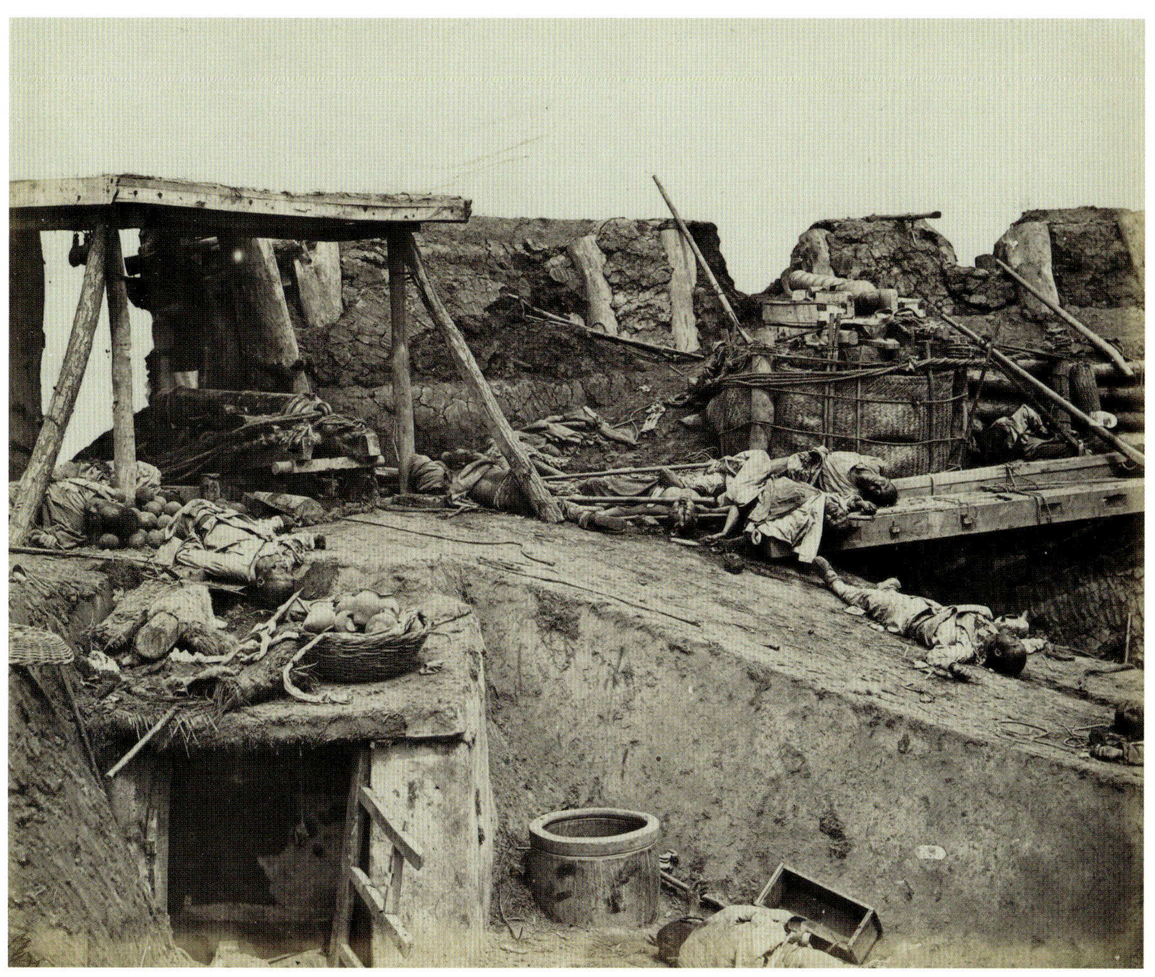

6 Felice Beato, *Interior of the English Entrance to the North [Dagu] Fort on 21st August 1860*, 1860, albumen print.

uncomfortable moment, as if taken against his will. These rare views of an imperial family member representing China at a time of national humiliation formed part of the growing currency of images of famous and newsworthy personages that circulated throughout the world.

Individuals and companies exploited commercial opportunities afforded by war and took advantage of advances in photographic technology. In 1859 the London firm Negretti and Zambra published a series of stereographs of Hong Kong and Guangzhou taken by the Swiss

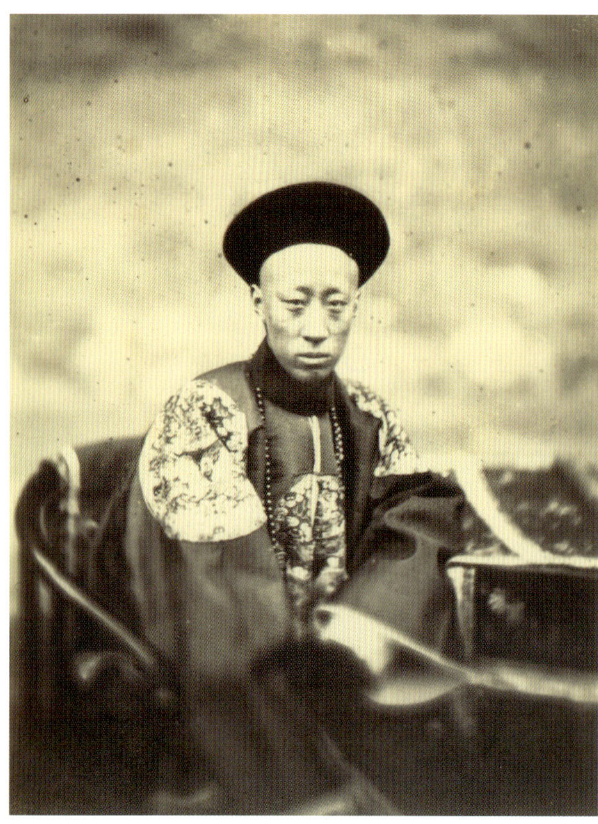

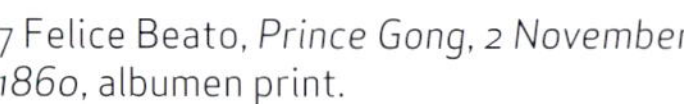

7 Felice Beato, *Prince Gong, 2 November 1860*, albumen print.

photographer Pierre Joseph Rossier (*c.* 1829–1897), who had been sent there to create a supply of images. They are the first commercial views of China to be sold in the West and include panoramas, street views, architecture and portraits. The stereograph was a popular novelty. Two slightly different images, taken side by side to mimic human sight and mounted on a card or plate, were viewed in a stereoscope (invented some years earlier), causing the flat image to be transformed into three dimensions. Sold singly or as themed sets functioning as a virtual 'tour of the world', with captions or an accompanying guidebook, stereographs became a parlour entertainment that transported European and American viewers into remote and fantastic worlds from the comfort of their own locales.

8 (front), 9 (back) Pierre Joseph Rossier, *'Panorama of Canton. Taken from Magazine Hill, now the head quarters of the Allied troops. No. 3'*, 1858–9, albumen print stereograph.

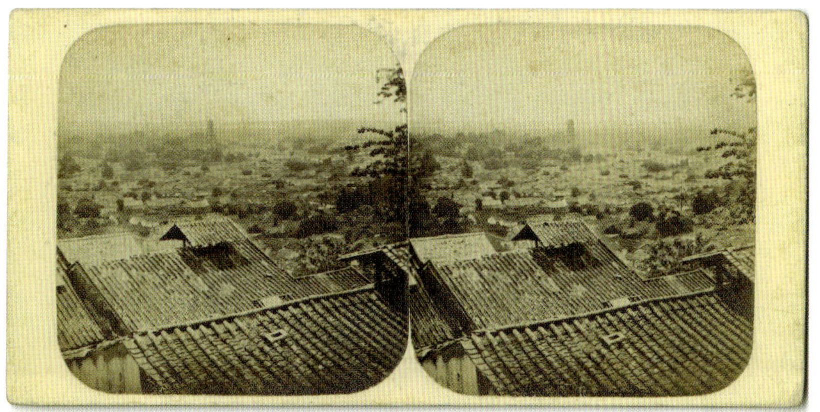

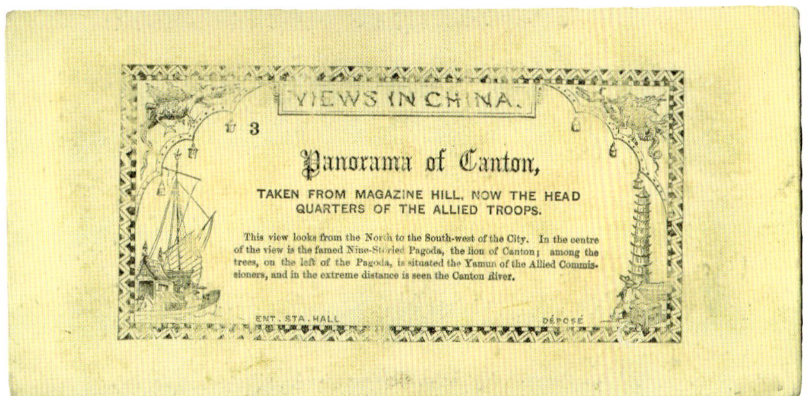

As foreign involvement with China grew, so did the English-language press in China. *The China Directory*, an annual compendium for expatriates, began publication in 1860 and rapidly expanded from a slim volume to a hefty tome as a consequence of the 'opening of new ports and the influx of foreigners'. In 1862 the American photographer Milton Miller placed a notice in the *Directory* advising readers that he had taken over the premises of American photographers Weed & Howard in Hong Kong:

Likenesses from Miniature to Life Size, Views of Houses, & c., executed at short notice. As his stay at the above place is limited, those wishing his services will please call early. A Collection of Views of various places for sale.

Many early commercial photographic studios in China were short lived. It was hard to make a living. Photographers took the kinds of images that were in demand – formal portraits, commissioned views, and souvenirs of Chinese and expatriate life. While Miller is today known for his fine portraits of generic Chinese 'types', he also took photographs of government ministers, officials and compradors, works most likely to help grease the wheels of business and to assist corporations to identify the people with whom they were dealing.[15] By the 1870s there were many skilled Chinese photographers operating in Hong Kong too. The introduction of the wet collodion process in the early 1850s, which allowed for multiple prints from a glass plate, providing fine detail with much faster exposure times, improved on the limitations of the daguerreotype and the calotype, and was not patented, making it attractive and readily available to Chinese practitioners. The Scottish photographer John Thomson (1837–1921, active in China 1868–72) spoke of Chinese photographers in Hong Kong as having 'taken kindly' to the art and commended their work.[16] A photograph of Queen's Road taken by the British photographer William Pryor Floyd (*c.* 1834–1900) in the late 1860s or early 1870s shows the exterior of his own Victoria Photographic Gallery surrounded by Chinese competitors. Most of the signs are written in English, indicating that the majority of customers were foreigners connected with maritime trade. Chinese businesses responded to local demand and offered ship portrait painting services and maritime chart copying, in addition to portrait painting and photography. Artists painted in oil on canvas, or in gouache, or watercolour on paper or ivory as required, and became adept at copying from miniature paintings and engravings, and later from photographs, enlarging subjects and bringing them to life in colour.

A striking glass stereograph by John Thomson gives us the impression of a China-trade artist at work (illus. 11). The figure is positioned to accentuate the customary hairstyle for men, a shaved forehead and long

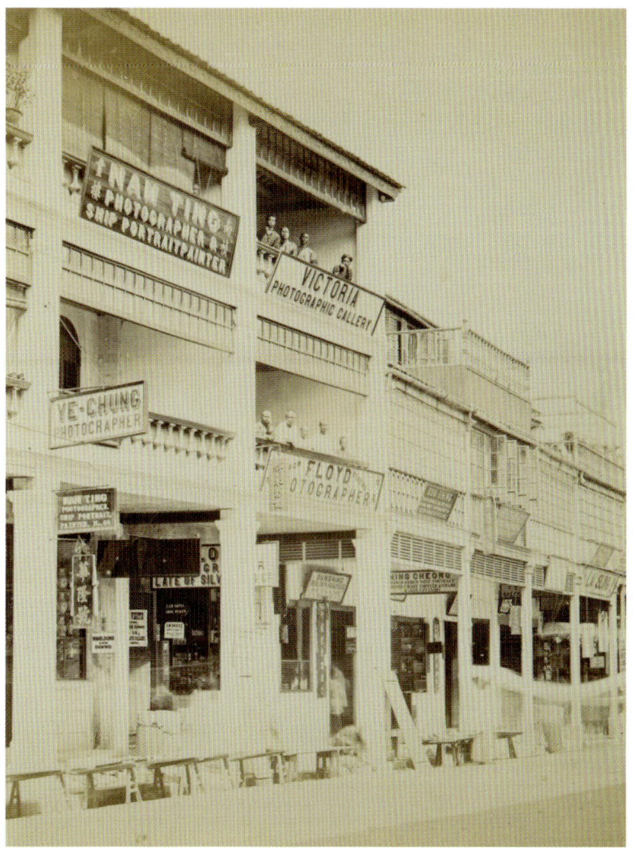

10 William Pryor Floyd, *Chinese House, Queen's Road, Hong Kong*, c. 1867–8, albumen print.

plaited queue. The back wall is hung with typical examples of China trade paintings intended for the foreign market including paintings of women with exotic hairstyles wearing silk robes, similar to photographs created by Thomson, Milton Miller and others, highlighting the cross-fertilization of visual genres (illus. 12). Titled *A Hong-Kong Artist*, the photograph was included in Thomson's deluxe four-volume folio publication *China and Its People*, published in 1873–4, printed with new collotype technology. Despite his stated aim to produce 'an accurate impression of the country', the images were cropped for printing, in this case preventing the viewer from seeing the faux set-up in his studio, where it was possible to create an ideal image.

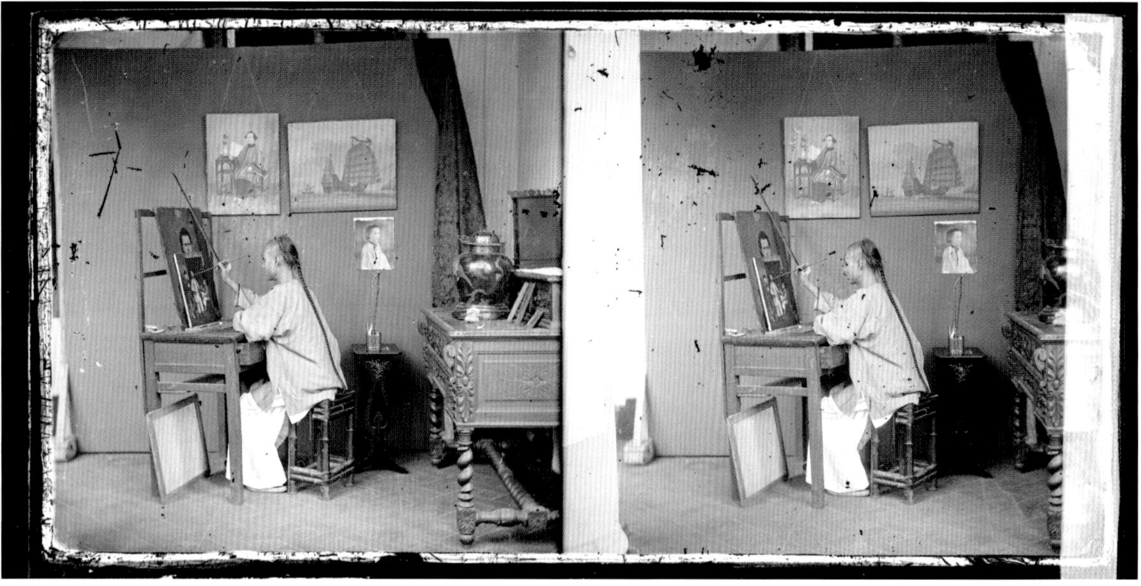

11 John Thomson, *A Hong Kong Artist*, 1869, glass photonegative, wet collodion stereograph.

During his long sojourn in China, Thomson travelled extensively and took hundreds of fine photographs of people and places. He worked out of Hong Kong, Macao and treaty ports along the coast and upriver, including Tianjin, not far from Peking. His photographs present Chinese subjects according to popular themes of 'native types' and genre scenes established by artists much earlier but, as Roberta Wue has observed, his 'intelligent curiosity led to the creation of more nuanced, less stereotyped images of Chinese life'.[17]

The best known of the early Chinese photographic studios in Hong Kong was Afong, established by Lai Afong in 1859. For many years the studio was located in Queens Road Central, a prime position in the growing business district of the colony. From the mid-1860s onwards, competition between photographers in Hong Kong was fierce and photographers did all they could to attract customers. Some studios offered cheaper prices and a faster service or employed Western assistants and photographers, reminding us of the cross-cultural interactions that occurred in businesses such as photographic studios. Emil Riisfeldt (1846–1893) worked in the Afong studio for some six months in 1871–2, and the British photographer

D. K. Griffith (*c*. 1841–?) worked there from 1878 to 1883. While the content of the photographs produced by the Afong studio was largely dictated by the needs of expatriate and transient foreign customers, those images are among the earliest visual documents of Hong Kong and China recorded by a commercial Chinese photographer.

Thomson knew Afong and in 1872 commented on his 'exquisite taste', referring to his ability to cater to a foreign aesthetic.[18] It was perhaps for this reason that he was able to promote himself as 'Photographer to H.E Sir Arthur Kennedy, Governor of Hong Kong and H.I.H. The Grand Duke Alexis'. In 1872 Arthur Kennedy (1809–1883) was appointed Governor of

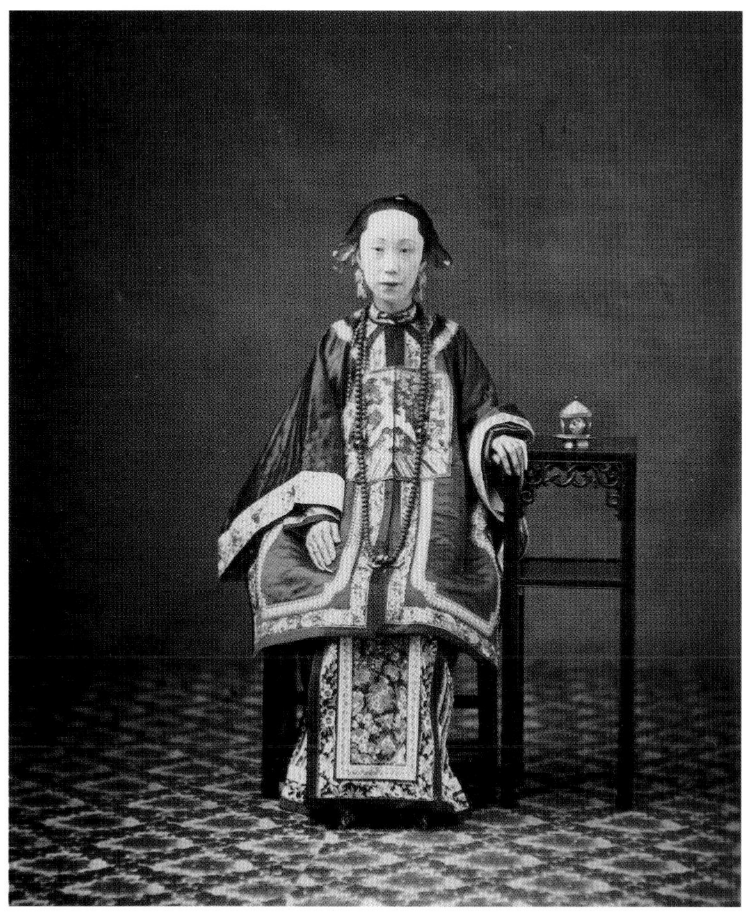

12 Milton M. Miller, *A Lady of Rank, Shanghai*, 1860–69, albumen print.

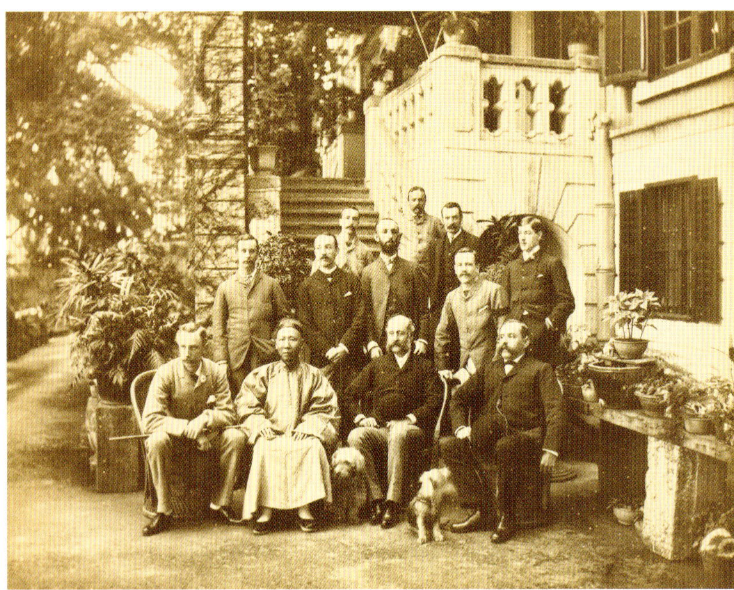

13 Afong studio, *'English [clerks] of Russell & Co., Hong Kong'*, c. 1885, albumen print.

Hong Kong and in that same year Grand Duke Alexei Alexandrovich of Russia (1850–1908) stopped in Hong Kong during a goodwill trip to Japan. Portrait photographs of such celebrities circulated in the form of small, portable *cartes de visite* and became collectible. Further evidence of the studio's standing is the inclusion of 'Photographs of different local scenes in the Colony' by 'Mr J. D. Griffiths and by Mr A. Fong' in the 1886 Colonial and Indian Exhibition in London.[19]

The Afong studio undertook commissions for resident expatriates, including diplomats and traders. One assignment was a series of photographs of the Delano family property 'Rose Hill' on Victoria Peak, Hong Kong. Warren Delano (1809–1898), grandfather of US president Franklin Delano Roosevelt, was a partner in the shipping firm Russell & Co., one of the earliest and most successful American companies to engage in the China trade (tea, silk and opium).[20] In 1859 Delano returned to Hong Kong for a second time and in 1862 took up residence at Rose Hill with his wife and children. Delano's daughter Dora married William Howell Forbes, a junior partner in the firm, and continued to live at Rose Hill until about 1900. A large group photograph taken outside Rose Hill is mounted on a card with 'Afong Photographer Hong Kong' printed on the reverse.[21] The photograph, thought to have been taken in 1885, records a gathering of Russell & Co. executives and their Chinese comprador.

By the 1880s foreign photographers were moving on from Hong Kong, leaving the field to the Chinese studios. When a photographer went out of business the stock was generally sold, invariably becoming part of the buyer's inventory and traded under the name of the new studio, or just plain pirated. The practice compounds the difficulty of identification. Even when a studio is named, we cannot be certain if the photograph was in fact taken by that studio, and even less who took the photograph. The only available evidence may be our interpretation of the image that has come down to us.

One of the most popular Chinese photographic studios in Hong Kong from the 1860s to the 1880s was Pun-Lun. Established by the Cantonese brothers Wan Chik-hing and Wan Leong-hoi, the studio specialized in *cartes de visite*. These were small photographs mounted on sturdy board the size of a calling card that from 1853 swept the world as the first mass-produced portrait photographs. Up to eight different frames could be accommodated on a single glass plate, making such works cheap to produce. They were usually created and sold by the dozen, and their size made them practical, durable and collectible. Portraits of Chinese or Westerners, sometimes with a label, message or autograph on the front or back, indicate their use as a souvenir, keepsake or a personalized expression of appreciation in business dealings. In addition to commissioned portraits the studio created formulaic studio shots of Chinese 'types', such as women and people engaged in various trades (illus. 14). Like many studios at the time, Pun-Lun printed 'Photographer & Ivory Painter' in English on the reverse of his *cartes de visite*, suggesting that, while embracing the new technology of photography, the studio retained its painting skills too, giving customers a choice for their miniature souvenir.

As the number of photographers in Hong Kong and Canton increased, businesses moved north to explore new markets. Around 1863 Xie Fen, one of the founders of Ye Chung in Hong Kong, moved up the coast to Fuzhou (Foochow) where he operated a studio for a number of

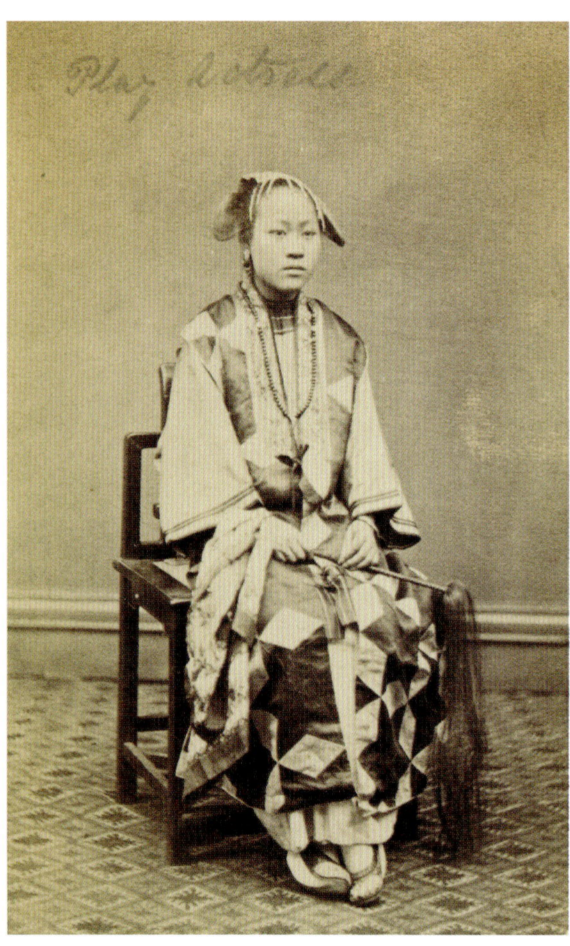

14 Pun-Lun studio, *'Play Actor'*, 1860s, albumen print *carte de visite*.

months (Yee Cheong) before moving on to Shanghai where the market was more established (illus. 15, 16, 17).[22] Among the earliest known photographers working in Shanghai were the Frenchman Louis Legrand (*c*. 1820–?), and the Kung Tai studio owned by Luo Yuanyou, both active in the 1850s.[23] Studios worked hard to distinguish themselves and find market niches. Kung Tai was well known for panoramas bound as fold-out souvenir albums; Pow Kee, established in 1889 by Ouyang Shizhi, catered to the tastes of the scholar-gentry and Sze Yuen Ming developed a reputation as the finest photographer of courtesans.

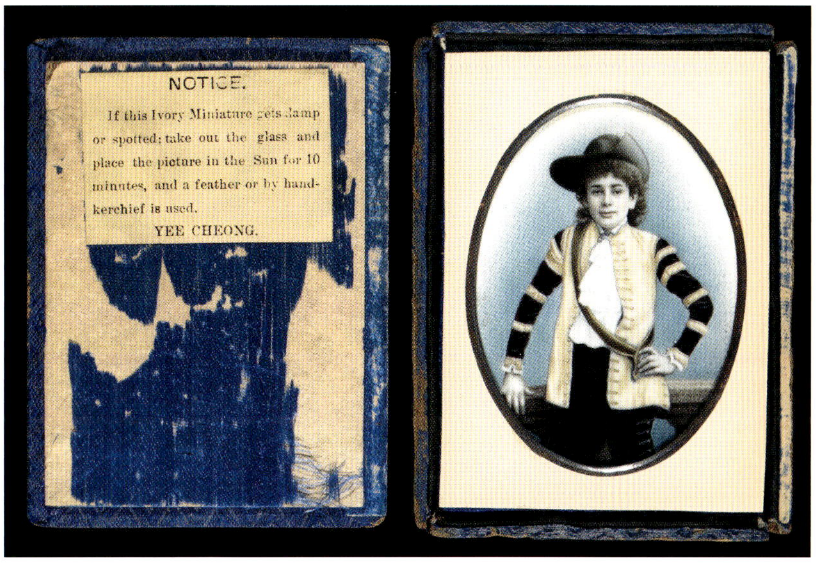

15 Yee Cheong studio, Fuzhou, *Portrait of a Boy in Cavalier Costume*, c. 1870, painting on ivory.

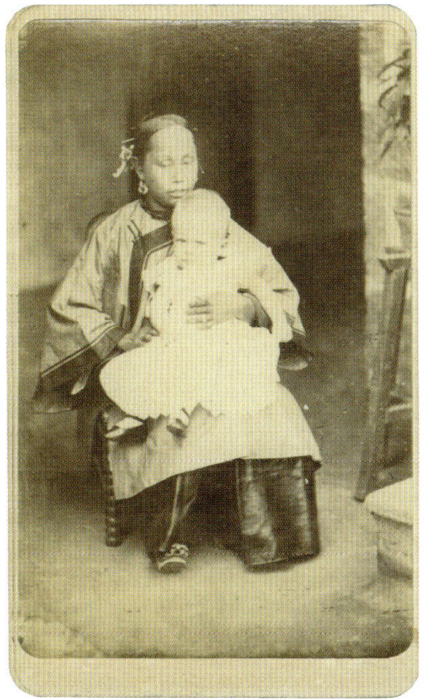

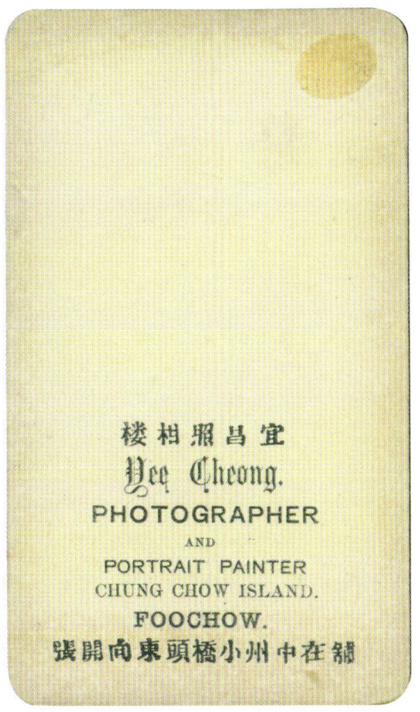

16 (front), 17 (back) Yee Cheong studio, *Portrait of an Amah and Child*, c. 1863, albumen print *carte de visite*.

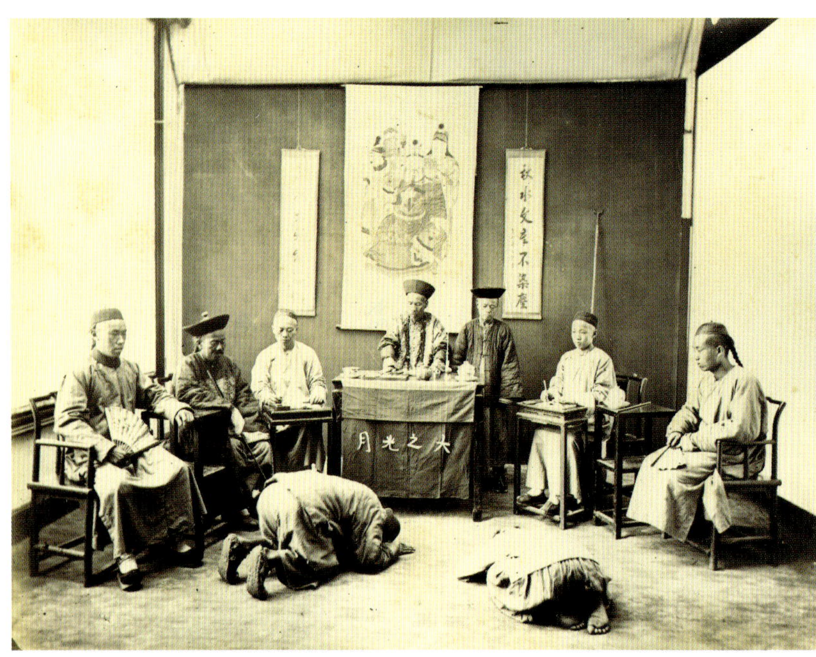

18 William Saunders, *Chinese Court Room*, c. 1870, albumen print.

Sze Yuen Ming & Co., which also traded under the name Yao Hua, meaning 'dazzling China', was one of the most successful photographic studios in Shanghai. The dual names suggest a different marketing strategy for foreign and Chinese clientele respectively. Shi Dezhi (1861–1935), whose father was a British sailor and his mother Chinese, moved from Hong Kong to Shanghai and established the Sze Yuen Ming & Co. studio in 1892. Images bearing the studio name in the emulsion or on the mount include views of churches and other buildings in the foreign concession areas, providing foreigners with evidence of progress in the city, as well as picturesque scenes of houseboats on the nearby Yangtze River.[24] The Yao Hua studio also took formal portrait photographs and tableaux of people engaged in what were perceived by foreigners as curious or exotic activities. Régine Thiriez has argued that a series of photographs illustrating 'Chinese life and character' created by the British photographer William Saunders (1832–1892, active in Shanghai 1862–87) was a source of inspiration.[25] Saunders' genre scenes include a court of justice, a public beheading, opium smokers, itinerant traders and pedlars, themes that had

19 Yao Hua studio, *Court Scene*, 1893, albumen print.

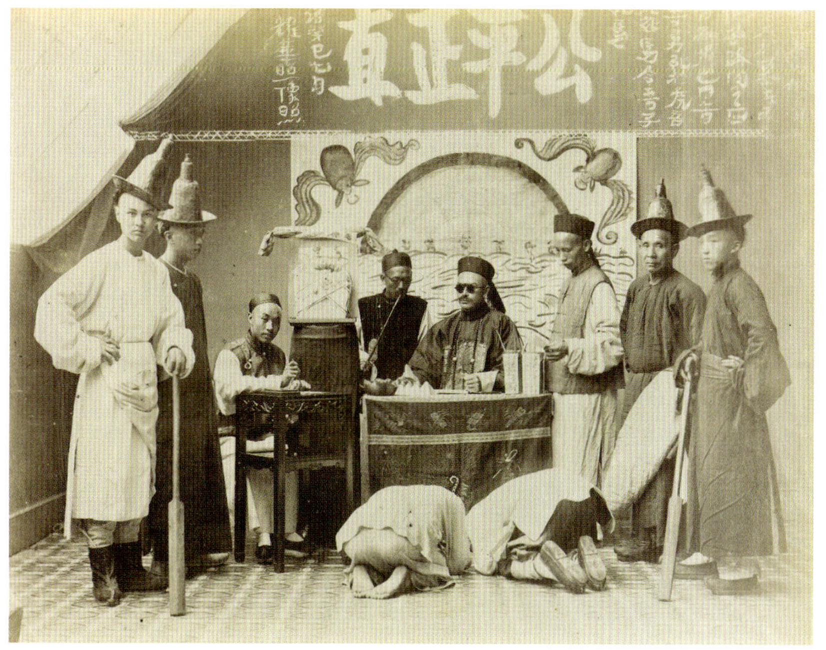

appealed to earlier visitors, such as William Alexander (1767–1816), the English artist who travelled to China as the draughtsman attached to Lord Macartney's embassy to China in 1792, and George Henry Mason, whose rendition of a courtroom scene appeared in his illustrated book *The Punishments of China* (1801). Despite their obvious lack of authenticity, such scenes were intended to provide information about Chinese life and character and were widely copied. In a photograph in a souvenir album titled 'Actual Photographs of China', a photograph by the Yao Hua studio gives us a crude re-enactment of a courtroom scene. An inscription in the emulsion reads 'Justice and honesty', giving the name of the photography studio and the date, 1893. Three of the court attendants stare straight at the camera, conscious of their role as actors on a stage, while the official wears sunglasses heightening the bizarre theatricality of the hastily prepared tableau. Yao Hua, like other photographic studios, was less concerned with cultural authenticity than creating potent images of Chinese life that reinforced Western stereotypes, many of them negative.

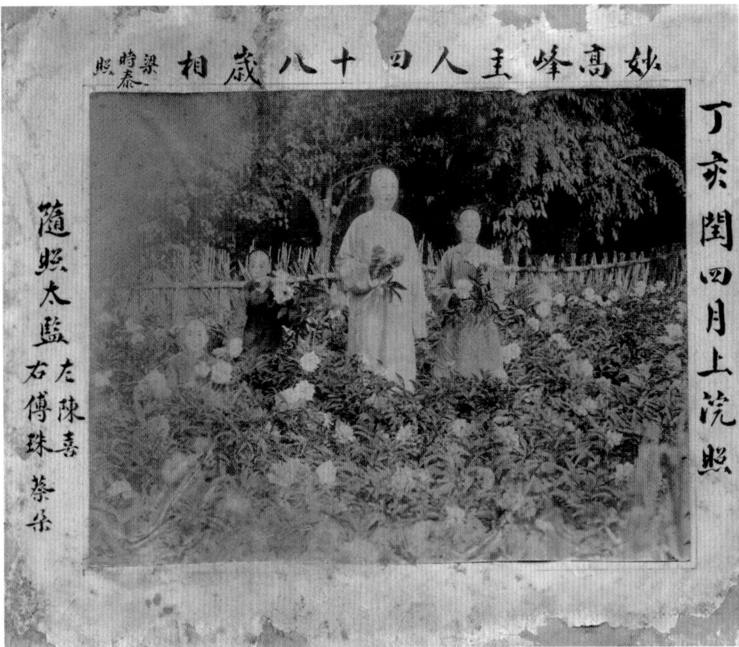

20 Liang Shitai, Prince Chun, Yihuan, in peony garden, 1887, albumen print on card.

In the second half of the nineteenth century portraiture was the most popular genre of photography among Chinese people. Early advertisements in Chinese newspapers refer to photography as a mysterious process (*shen fa*) learned from the West that could capture and keep an image of someone forever. Photographs could be printed onto slivers of stone, ivory, porcelain or silk – materials that were more permanent than paper and more robust than glass – and carry the spirit of the person into the future.[26] The Chinese term for this is *chuanshen*, meaning literally to 'transmit spirit'. The idea of creating a lifelike image of a living person was attractive, but even more powerful was the idea that a hauntingly real likeness of a loved one could be kept forever.

Various terms were used to translate the concept of photography into Chinese, including 'writing the truth' (*xiezhen*), 'small portrait' (*xiaozhao*), 'to take a likeness' (*zhaoxiang*), 'to capture a shadow image' (*sheying*) and 'shadow image' (*yingxiang*). *Xiaozhao* derives from the language of Chinese portrait painting, whereas the terms *yingxiang* and

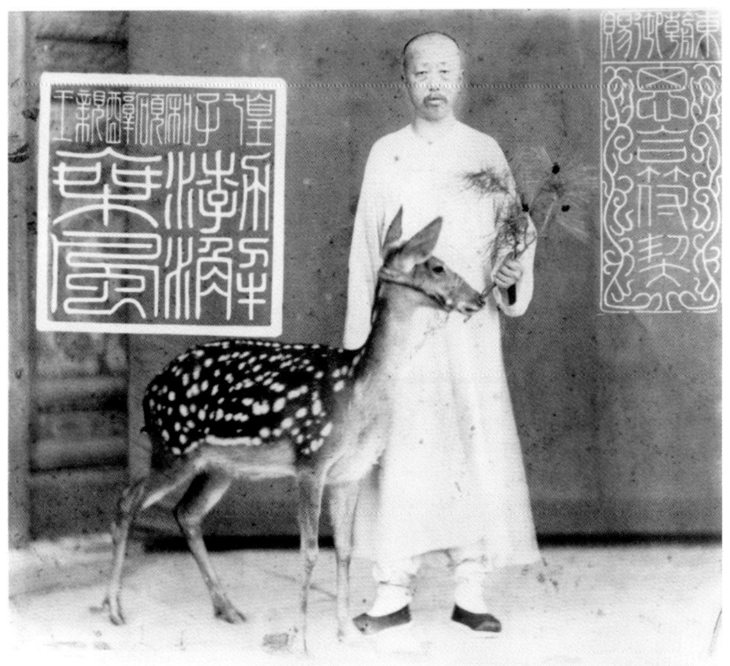

21 Liang Shitai, *Seventh Prince Feeding Deer, Stamped with His Seals*, 1887, albumen print.

sheying allude to shadows (*ying*) and reflections that lack true existence according to Buddhist belief. The language suggests some of the different ways the medium of photography was understood in the early decades after its introduction to China. Concepts drawn from traditional Chinese visual culture and philosophy were used to describe the new technique in an attempt to convey its unique qualities and special powers.

Liang Shitai (known to non-Chinese as See Tay), who started in Hong Kong, moved to Shanghai in search of new markets before travelling further north to Tianjin, not far from the imperial capital. In the 1860s Liang began taking portraits of Prince Chun, Yihuan, (1840–1891), father of the Guangxu Emperor, who was fascinated by the new technology. Liang's photographs of the prince in official dress, on horseback, with his wife and family members, and on duty at the Nanyuan Barracks, offer rare glimpses into imperial life. Many of the portraits are documentary in nature, recording events such as a tour of duty or a significant birthday. Others have a more poetic or scholarly dimension. A photograph dating from 1887 shows the prince posing in a peony garden with three young eunuchs, taken in an imperial pleasance in the Western Hills outside Peking to mark the prince's 48th year. Fine ink lines have been painted onto the photographic print to give definition to Yihuan's face, highlighting eyebrows and moustache. The eyes are dotted to give them life. The picture is improved to prevent it from looking too much like a 'shadow image' of a ghost or dead person. The mount is inscribed by Yihuan with details of the event, and the names of the three young eunuchs, in the manner of a Chinese commemorative painting. Using modern technology Liang Shitai and Yihuan have created a new hybrid form of visual representation that maintains strong conceptual links to traditional paintings of leisure and enjoyment. In another portrait, also from 1887, Yihuan faces the camera holding a branch from a pine tree, posing with a live deer at his side (you can make out a harness). Deer and pine are symbolic of longevity, auspicious attributes for a birthday image. Impressions of two of Yihuan's imperial seals have been added, creating a striking performance-based representation that simulates a traditional painting, but using live subjects in combination with the latest technology for image making.[27] The portrait was included in an album of photographs relating to the life of Prince Yihuan taken by Liang Shitai and presented as a special gift to the wife of an American financier in 1888.[28]

Eventually photography penetrated the inner chambers of the imperial court. In 1903 Xunling (*c.* 1874–*c.* 1943), son of a distinguished official who had just returned from diplomatic posts in France and Japan, received a summons from the empress dowager Cixi to take her photograph.[29] He had 'studied photography for some considerable time' while overseas. As her 70th birthday approached, Cixi was not only conscious of the tradition of imperial portraiture but also aware of the growing importance of photography in diplomacy. She had received photographs of Western monarchs and heads of state as gifts and would have been aware of the flattering regal portraits of Queen Victoria created by the Southwell Brothers Studio (active 1862–76) and later by the W. & D. Downey studio on the occasion of her diamond jubilee in 1897, that circulated widely as *cartes de visite*. The empress dowager needed to improve her image after a series of political disasters and challenges: China's humiliating defeat in the First Sino-Japanese War (1894–5); her quashing of the 1898 *coup d'état* mounted by the Guangxu Emperor and reform-minded supporters, notably Kang Youwei; growing resentment towards the 'foreign' Manchu–Qing Dynasty, widely regarded as corrupt and out of touch; and the xenophobic Boxer Rebellion of 1900 in which many foreigners and Chinese were killed. The photographs taken for her birthday celebration would also be given out as mementos.

Xunling created a series of carefully staged full-length portraits of the empress dowager in a variety of mock settings, many of them styled in

22 Xunling, *The Empress Dowager Cixi*, 1903, collodion print.

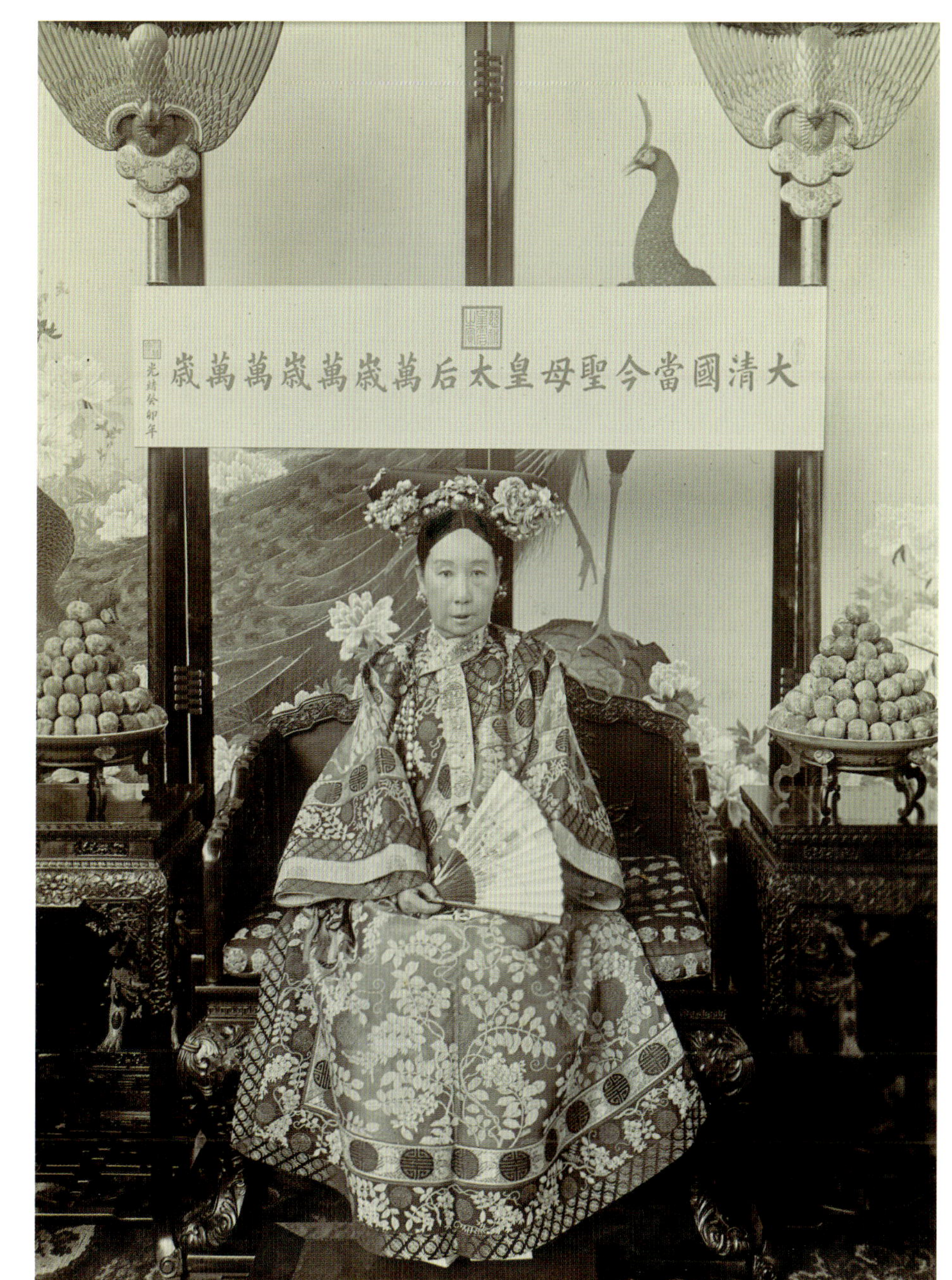
大清國當今聖母皇太后萬歲萬歲萬萬歲
光緒癸卯年

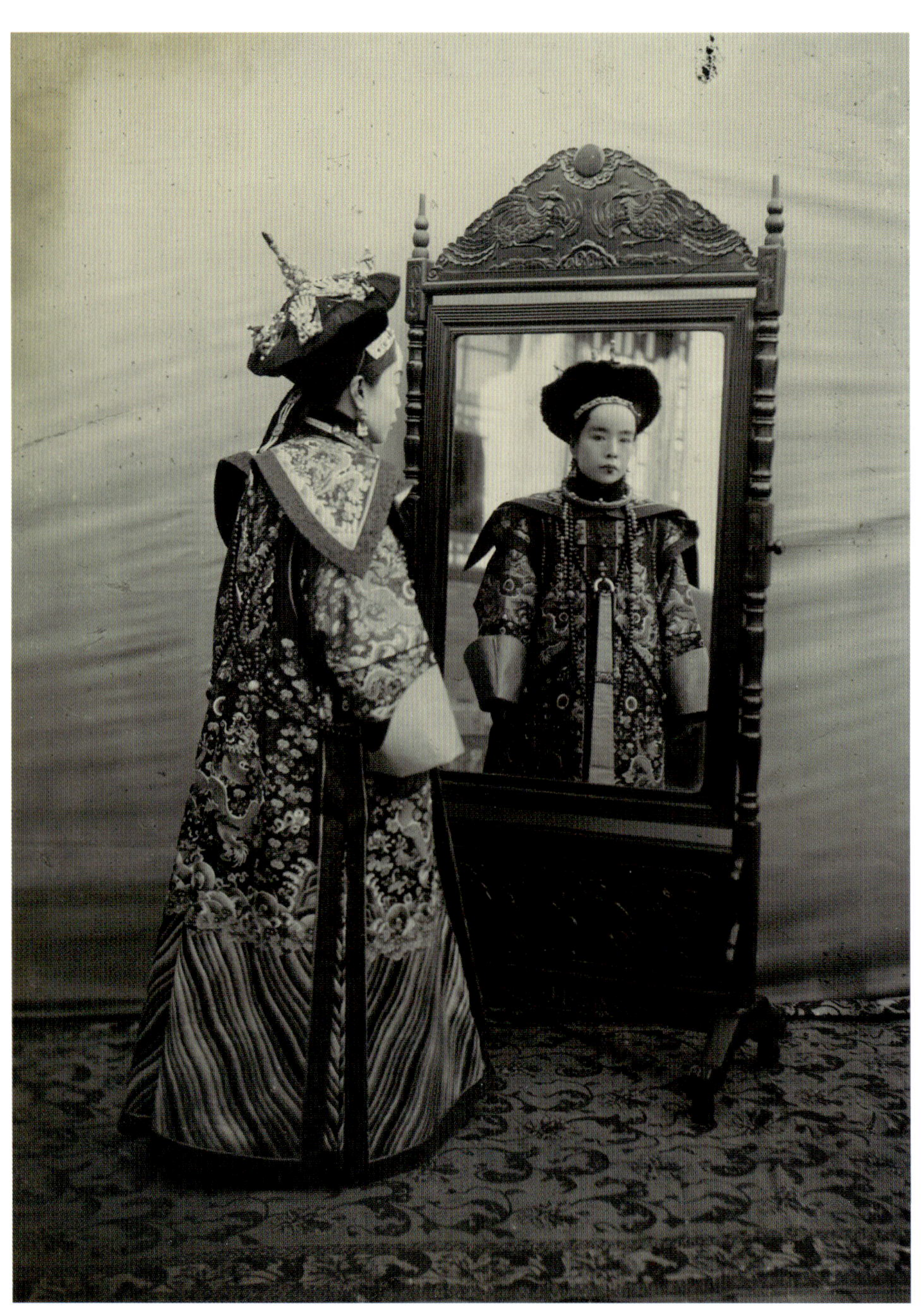

the courtyard of the Hall of Happiness and Longevity at the Summer Palace where there was plenty of natural light. In a number of images Cixi is seated with a sign suspended above her head on two peacock feather standards displaying her title and hope for a long life (illus. 22). The Empress Dowager stares straight at the camera. The symmetrical composition, borrowing props from nearby palace rooms, enhances the impression of power. According to court records 103 copies of a version of this photograph (holding a round fan) were made, suggesting that it was a favourite.[30] A different version was presented to Alice Roosevelt, daughter of the American president and a member of an American diplomatic mission to China in 1905. These images refer to earlier imperial commemorative portraits, but equally anticipate the carefully constructed mass media images of later leaders, such as Sun Yat-sen, Chiang Kai-shek and Mao Zedong, who used photography as propaganda to promote themselves as popular and powerful leaders.

Other photographs of the empress dowager taken by Xunling in the period 1903–5 are more ambitious in their theatricality and show Cixi on a barge in a lake surrounded by lotus flowers, and in the guise of Guanyin, the goddess of mercy. The two-dimensional, stage-like format of a photograph was a medium over which, as director and subject, the empress dowager could exert a high degree of artistic control. The manipulation of reality extended to the glass plate negatives, some of which have been touched up in order to lessen the extent of shadowing on Cixi's face, in accordance with Chinese taste and cultural mores.[31]

In the late 1800s and early 1900s a number of commercial photographers in Peking were engaged to take photographs of Qing officials and members of the court. They included the Japanese photographer Yamamoto Sanshichiro (1855–1943) who moved from Tokyo to Peking and was well known for his portraits and views of the city; the American C. E. LeMunyon (active in Peking *c.* 1903–27); and Ren Jingfeng, who learned his craft in Japan and, in 1892, established the Fung Tai studio, specializing in portraits and opera photographs.

Like Xunling's photographs of the Empress Dowager, the portrait of Princess Su in formal court dress taken by the Fung Tai studio and presented to Sarah Pike Conger, wife of the American ambassador to China, also

23 Fung Tai studio, *Princess Su in Robes of State*, early 1900s, gelatin silver print

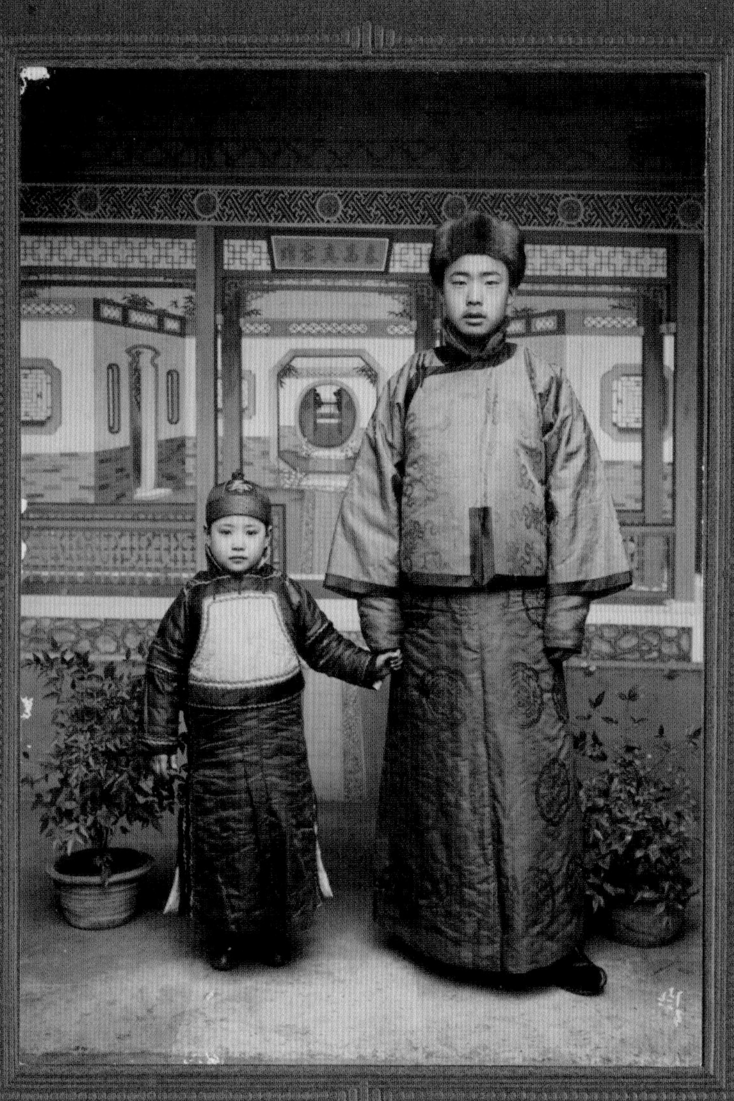
Remembrance

appears to have been taken in a palace courtyard, though the set up and styling is crude by comparison. The subject looks into a cheval mirror and also engages with the viewer. The novelty of showing the front and back of the princess simultaneously satisfied a traditional Chinese desire to represent the whole person, while conveying the modern, all-seeing power of photography. Variations of this clever and much copied compositional type can be found in both Chinese and Western painting, and in photographs of Shanghai courtesans. Many of the portraits in Conger's collection are inscribed and personally dedicated to her, showing how early Chinese portrait photography functioned as an upper-class activity. Images produced for individual pleasure or commemoration also served as personally and politically charged remembrances.

A marvellous example of commercial portrait photography from the early twentieth century is an image of a proud father and son taken in the 'Tai Kang True Face Photographic Studio'. The photograph situates the father and son in an idealized, illusionistic space. It has the word 'Remembrances' in English printed on the mount and was given to George Ernest Morrison (1862–1920), the long-term correspondent for the London *Times* newspaper in Peking. In a little more than half a century, the new visual medium has adapted creatively to a Chinese conceptual setting, demonstrating its power to mediate between past and present, in exchanges between individuals or across cultures.

24 Tai Kang True Face Photographic Studio, *Father and Son*, *c.* 1910s, gelatin silver print on card.

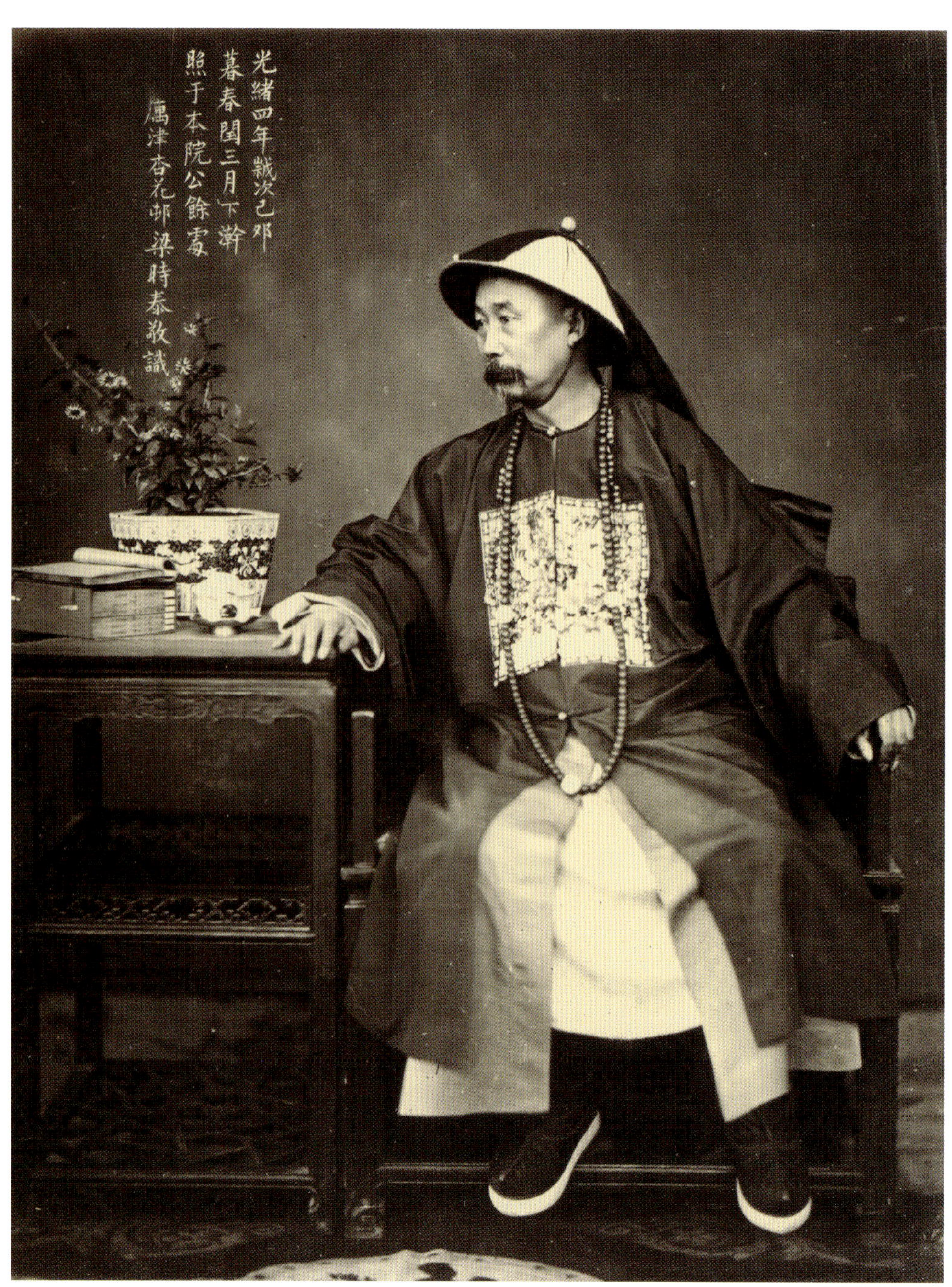

光緒四年嵗次己夘
暮春閏三月下澣
照于本院公餘霎
鷹津杏花邨梁時泰敬識

two

The True Record

Photography was part of a new wave of technological innovation that Chinese individuals and institutions embraced as they sought ways to respond to the humiliating burden of the 'unequal treaties' and the devastation caused by the Taiping Rebellion (1851–64). The imperial government adopted a policy of 'self-strengthening', reforming the country's internal organization, creating institutions and industrial and military capabilities designed to protect China and enable more effective interaction with the international world. Prince Gong, as counsellor and head of the newly established Zongli Yamen (which functioned as a ministry of foreign affairs), was effectively China's first 'foreign minister'.[1] The Imperial Maritime Customs Service, established in 1854 to regulate shipping in the wake of the Taiping wars, collected taxes that the Chinese government would use to finance military arsenals and shipbuilding industries. In 1862 the Imperial College, or Tongwen Guan, was established to promote the study of foreign languages to train future diplomats and translate science and technology texts into Chinese. Modern corporations came into existence using predominantly Chinese capital, such as the China Merchants Steam Navigation Company. Government-funded students were sent overseas to develop specific expertise and acquire first-hand experience of other cultures. Foreigners, some of whom were bilingual, played important roles in these institutions, acting as managers and conduits of knowledge. The Anglo-Irish civil servant Sir Robert Hart, for example, was Inspector General of Imperial Customs from 1863 until his departure from China in 1907. John Dudgeon, a Scottish physician who arrived in Beijing in 1863 to work for the London Missionary Society, helped popularize photography

25 Liang Shitai, *Li Hongzhang*, 1878, albumen print.

at this time. As Professor of Anatomy and Physiology at the Imperial College in Beijing, he translated many medical and scientific texts into Chinese. He also compiled *On the Principles and Practice of Photography* (1873), an illustrated manual that explained the scientific principles of photography and provided a practical do-it-yourself guide for Chinese readers. Another important figure was John Fryer, who taught English at the Imperial College in 1863 and from 1868 worked at the Jiangnan Arsenal in Shanghai as a translator, rendering many scientific texts into Chinese. In 1887 Fryer and his colleague Xu Shou published their introduction to photography.[2]

Photography played a role in the process of 'self-strengthening'. It was used to record important meetings and gatherings and to document new industrial facilities around the country, accompanying written reports prepared for the court as visual testimony. Portraits of the statesmen who championed China's reforms were widely circulated and displayed in photographic studios as a way of attracting business. Li Hongzhang, Viceroy of Zhili and Superintendent of Trade at the treaty port of Tianjin, was a key figure in the modernization of military, trade and foreign policy. Portraits of him taken in the Liang Shitai studio in Tianjin in official dress are found in many photographic albums and collections from the period (illus. 25).

Photographic records of newsworthy events created opportunities for sales. A fierce typhoon struck Hong Kong on 22–23 September 1874. William Pryor Floyd, who was then preparing to leave the colony, documented the devastation, as did Henry Everitt of the Hong Kong Photographic Company.[3] Views of the typhoon's destructive force, with English captions, could be purchased singly or assembled in thematic albums. After Floyd left Hong Kong in late 1874 and Everitt in 1877, Chinese studios dominated the market. A notice in an album produced by Afong refers to 'a collection of 35 views of the effects of the late typhoon', and in another album an unidentified advertisement describes 'the most numerous, the largest, the most complete and the most comprehensive' set of such photographs, suggesting that the Afong studio either took photographs of the typhoon too or recycled those of Floyd and Everitt.[4]

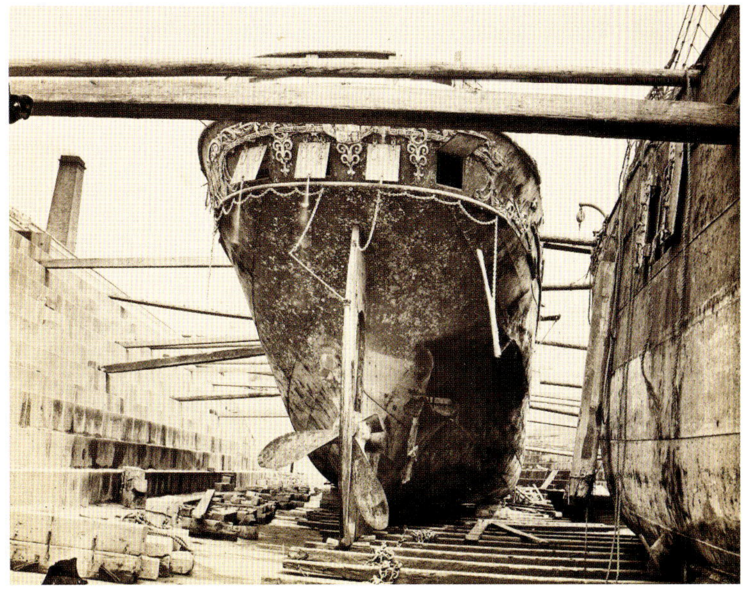

26 Hong Kong Photographic Company, or the Afong studio, *Albay after Typhoon*, 1875, albumen print.

The Afong studio was commissioned to photograph popular beauty spots. A photograph titled *The Bankers' Glen, Yuen-Foo River* records a party of British expatriates, including the British consul and his wife, enjoying a day trip in the mountains outside the treaty port of Fuzhou (illus. 27). This was one of John Thomson's subjects too. As suggested by the colonialist appellation, with its echo of places at home in Britain, the area was a popular leisure destination for expatriates. Thomson's photograph *The Banker's Glen*, published in *Foochow and the River Min* (1873), offers a majestic view from the top of the valley looking down to the river Min, devoid of people. Afong's photograph is very different. The figures are dwarfed by a dramatic mountain landscape that might almost be interpreted in terms of traditional Chinese aesthetics. In Chinese brush-and-ink painting such figures are enlivening elements in a rendition of the cosmos.

Another business active in the area was 'photographer and portrait painter' Tung Hing, who is listed as 'portrait painter' in Hong Kong in the 1874 *China Directory*. The best access to Mount Wuyi, famous for its black tea, was by boat along the Min River and its tributaries. Views sold by

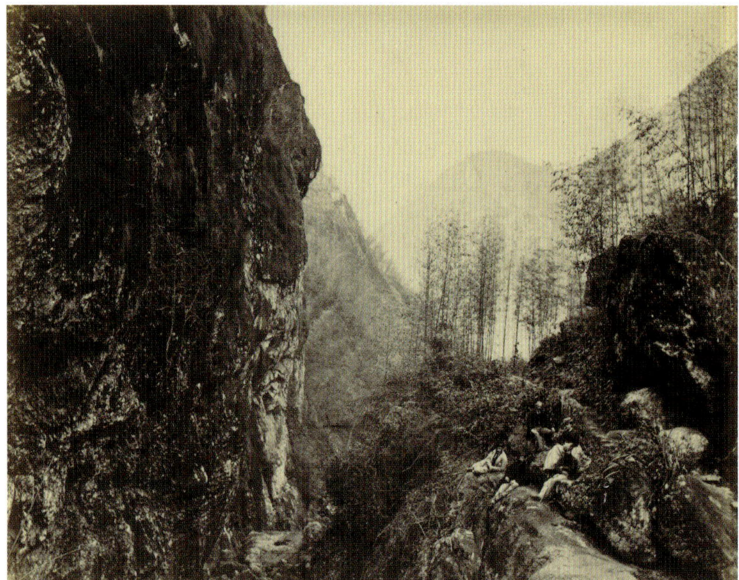

27 Afong studio, *The Bankers' Glen, Yuen-Foo River*, 1869–70, albumen print.

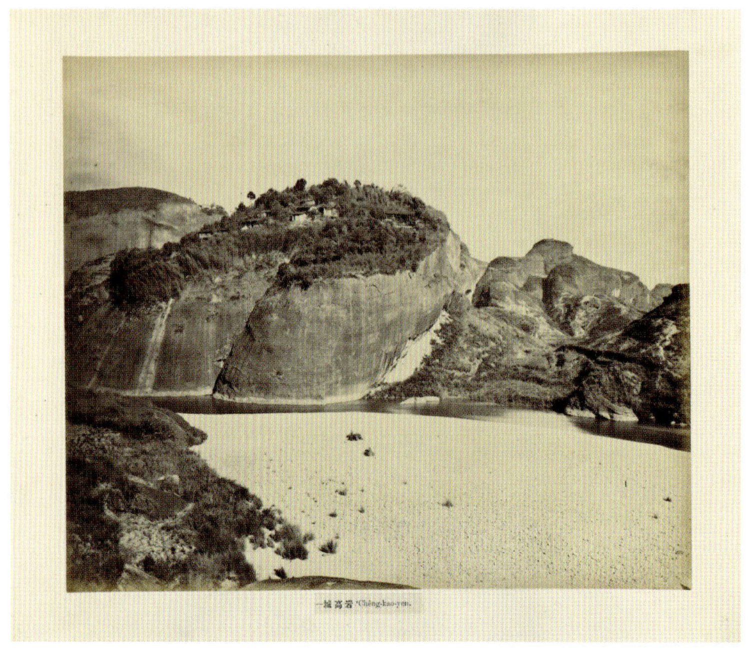

28 Tung Hing studio, *Ch'eng-kao-yen*, 1870s, albumen print.

the studio included bridges, temples and monasteries, hill and river scenery and the tea districts. Tung Hing advertised their location as 'opposite Messrs Russell & Co's Hong', suggesting that the studio's primary customers were foreign merchants engaged in the tea trade.

An album of such views, now in the Getty Museum, is captioned with place names in Chinese characters followed by a romanized version, sometimes with an English translation. While the views were most probably the result of an expatriate commission, the locations and captioning suggests an appreciation of the landscape from a Chinese cultural perspective. Cody and Terpak describe the photographs as 'historically significant natural settings' that 'would have resonated with the local literati'.[5] 'Clifftop Village' (Ch'eng-kao-yen), for example, is a historic Daoist site famous for its prayer altar and rare varieties of bamboo.

With the growth of expatriate communities in the treaty ports and the improvement of accommodation and facilities, international travellers were attracted to China in increasing numbers. The wealthy American art collector and patron of the arts Isabella Stewart Gardner (1840–1924) and her husband John arrived in Shanghai from Japan in September 1883. Gardner created a scrapbook of her travels, pasting in photographs and items of memorabilia to record her activities and experiences. The album contains a photograph of Beijing's Zhengyangmen, the southern entry to the inner city, taken by the English photographer Thomas Child (1841–1898) in 1875 (illus. 29), scenes of Shanghai by William Saunders (1832–1892) and a portrait of Li Hongzhang by Liang Shitai. Repeated entries in the diaries of Gardner and her husband indicate that acquiring photographs, mostly ordered and purchased at sales outlets in the major hotels, was an important tourist activity.[6]

Improvements in photographic technology and the growth of expatriate communities were important factors in the formation of amateur photographic societies. The Fuzhou Camera Club was established by foreigners in 1892 and became part of a worldwide network of amateur associations. Among the members was Juan Mencarini, who worked for the Imperial China Maritime Customs Service. His photographs, taken around 1895 at the request of the French consul, include views of Fuzhou, evidence of agricultural and cultural activity, as well as portraits of

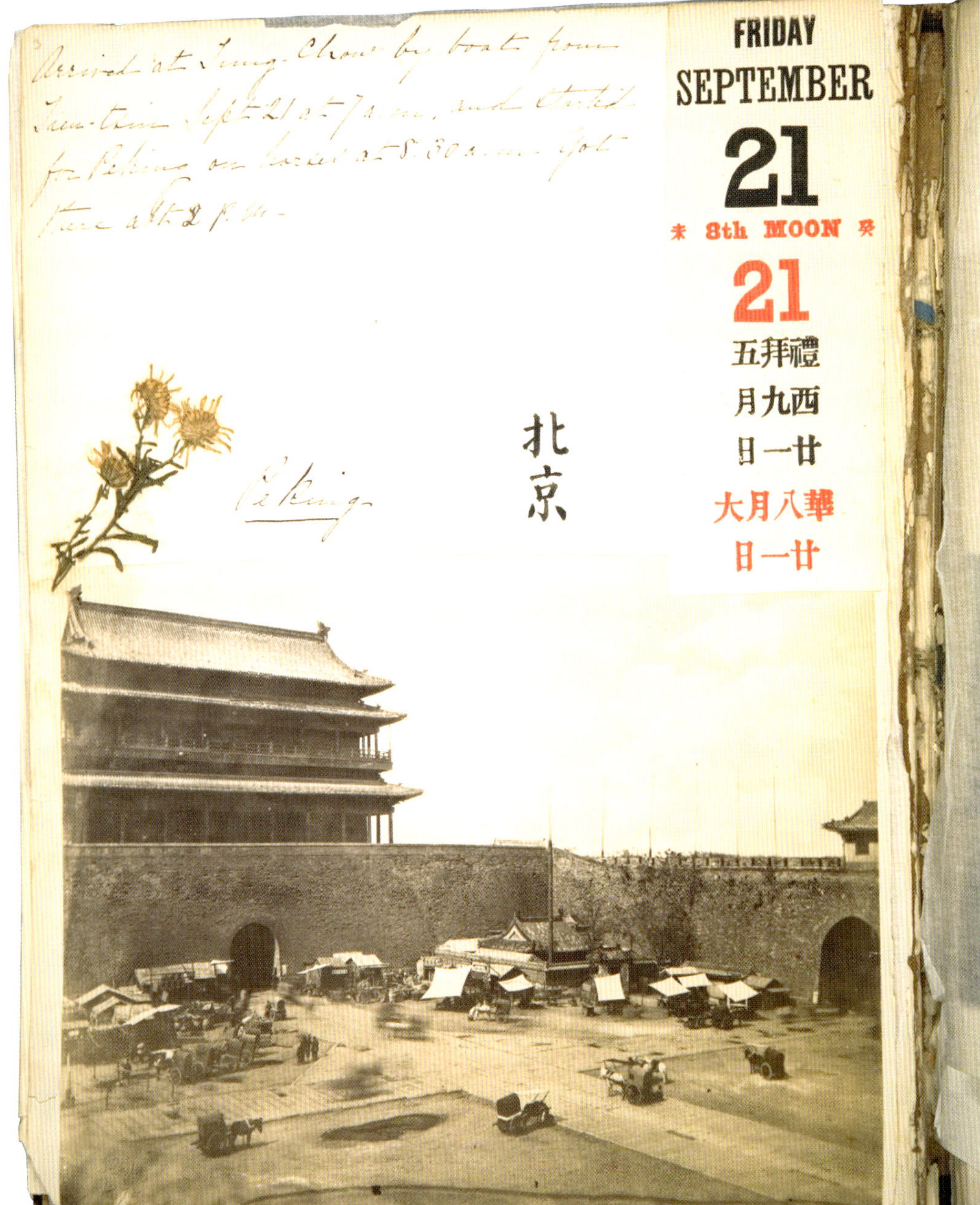

Arrived at Tung-Chow by boat from Tien-tsin Sept 21 at 7 a.m. and started for Peking on horses at 8.30 a.m. got there at 2 P.M.
Peking
北京
FRIDAY
SEPTEMBER
21
8th MOON
21
五拜禮
月九西
日一廿
大月八華
日一廿

‘Gentleman of leisure with long finger nails’ and ‘Cangue worn by criminals’, offering evidence of ‘curious’ and ‘grotesque’ scenes that he witnessed.[7] With the subjects cast in passive roles, Mencarini’s photographs reflect his personal experience as a foreign observer of China.

In different hands the camera could equally be used to furnish proof of abuses. Yung Wing (Rong Hong, 1828–1912) was a Chinese American who played an important role in China’s reform and regeneration. Macao-born and Yale educated – he was the first Chinese student to graduate from an American university – Yung Wing was asked by Li Hongzhang to deal with the Peruvian government’s request for a treaty to continue the coolie trade. His written report to the Chinese government in 1873 included ‘two dozen photographs of Chinese coolies, showing how their backs had been lacerated and torn, scarred and disfigured by the lash’. In his memoir Yung Wing explains: ‘I had these photographs taken in the night, unknown to anyone except the victims themselves, who were, at my request, collected and assembled together for the purpose. I knew that these photographs would tell a tale of cruelty and inhumanity perpetrated by the owners of haciendas, which would be beyond cavil and dispute.’[8] When the Peruvian commissioner denied the accusations made in the report, the photographs were tabled as ‘incontrovertible evidence’, bringing an end to the coolie trade to Peru and Cuba.

Some years later photography was used to record the discovery of 41 boys and girls found hidden in a boat off the coast of Fuzhou. An inscription on the mount of a photograph tells us that the children had been kidnapped, rescued by the Lam Hing Lan Company and placed in temporary foster care; 23 kidnappers were arrested in the process. The photograph, taken by the Chang Yee Lau Studio in Nantai, Fuzhou, shows children posing for the camera, each holding a piece of white card. The children’s names have been inscribed onto the photographic print in the hope that they might be identified (illus. 30). Poverty forced families to give up their children. Some were sold as labourers or child brides, and others were stolen. The photograph is from the collection of Edwin Bangs Drew (1843–1924), an American who joined the Imperial Maritime Customs Service in 1864 and was commissioner of customs in Fuzhou from 1875 to 1877 and again from 1902 to 1905. Photography with its

29 Thomas Child, *Zhengyangmen*, Beijing, 1875, albumen print; page from Isabella Stewart Gardner’s travel album, China, 1883.

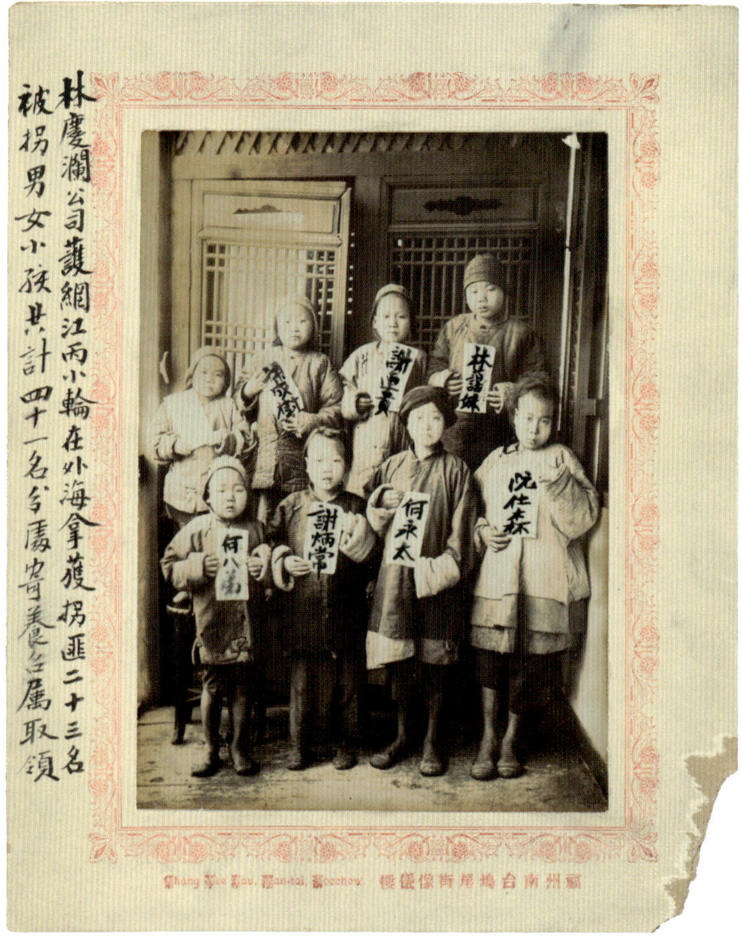

30 Chang Yee Lau studio, *Kidnapped Children*, Fuzhou, early 1900s, gelatin silver print on card.

multiple prints was the best possible medium to disseminate likenesses of the children in an attempt to resolve their fates. It was readily adapted by Chinese practitioners for its usefulness in such cases.

Foreign missionary organizations offered food, lodging and education to poor, abandoned or disadvantaged children. A photograph of Amy Wilkinson's School of Spiritual Light, a school for the blind in Fuzhou, taken in 1905, for example, presents the headmistress surrounded by a flock of blind children engaged in craft activities including basket-making, weaving and printing. An English sign hangs over the

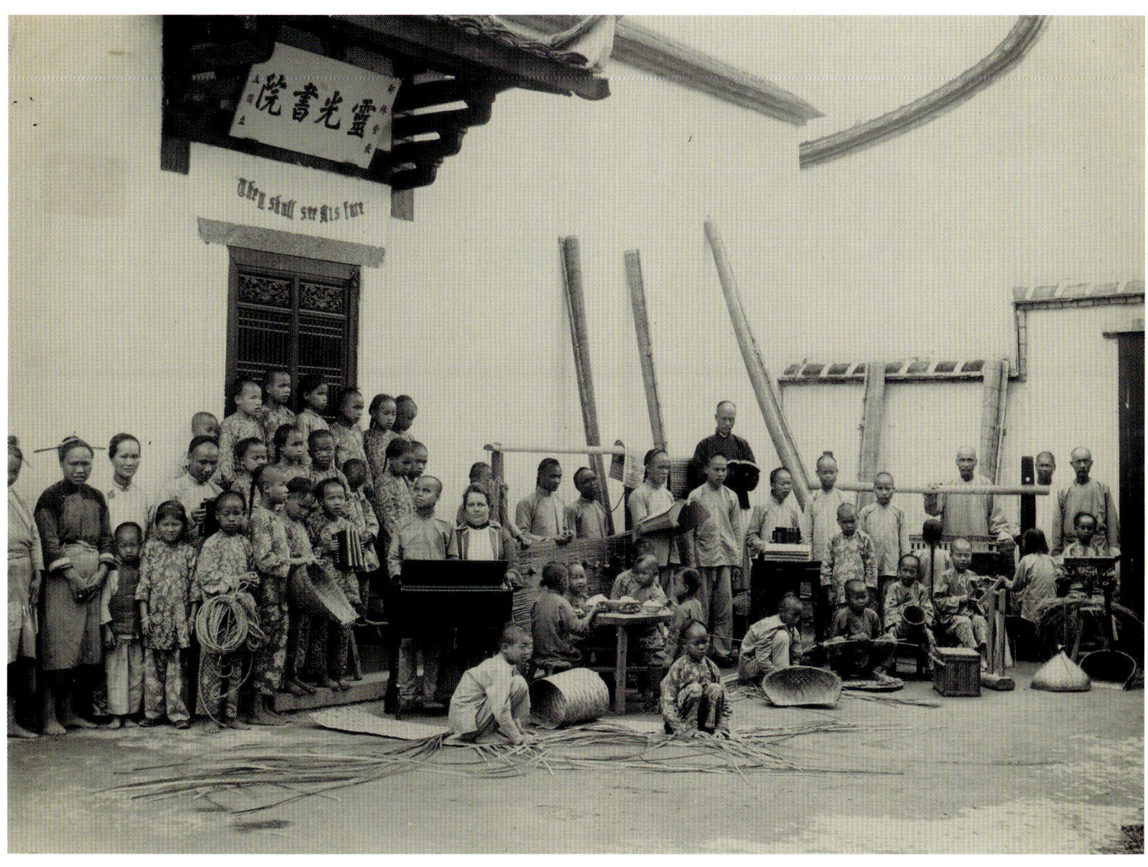

31 *Mrs Wilkinson's School of Spiritual Light*, 1905, gelatin silver print, photographer unknown.

doorway: 'They shall see his face', a quote from the Bible (Revelation 22:4) which continues 'and his name shall be in their foreheads', underlining the missionary intention of the school. The spiritual light was to act as a substitute for real light. The image that the children themselves could never see serves as a reminder of the transfer of meaning that photography performed between real and symbolic domains, between subjection and empowerment.

Items produced by the children could be sold to raise funds for the school. In a letter to a friend Wilkinson writes 'A NangKing Mandarin has asked that five Blind Boys may go to the Exhibition and work there so that the Chinese may see that the blind can work. I hope it will be the means of opening up work among the Blind all over China.'[9] The exhibition was China's first trade fair, the Nanyang Industrial Exposition held in Nanjing in 1910, where the work of a number of the students won prizes.

Tensions over the activities of foreign missionaries amidst an increasing Western presence in China had been simmering for decades when violence erupted in northern China in 1900. Anti-Christian activists, rampaging with the tacit approval of the court, targeted foreign interests and mission stations, attacking and killing missionaries, Chinese converts and those in foreign employment. In June 1900 foreign interests in Tianjin and Beijing came under threat, causing European powers led by Britain, Germany and France, together with the United States and Japan, to send military forces to China. The assassination of missionaries and high-profile foreign diplomats – Germany's Baron von Ketteler and Japan's Sugiyama Akira – and the siege of the foreign legations created headline news around the world. James Ricalton, working for the American stereoscope firm Underwood and Underwood, had come to China from the Philippines where he had photographed the Spanish–American War of 1898–9. A set of 100 stereographs taken by Ricalton and titled *China*

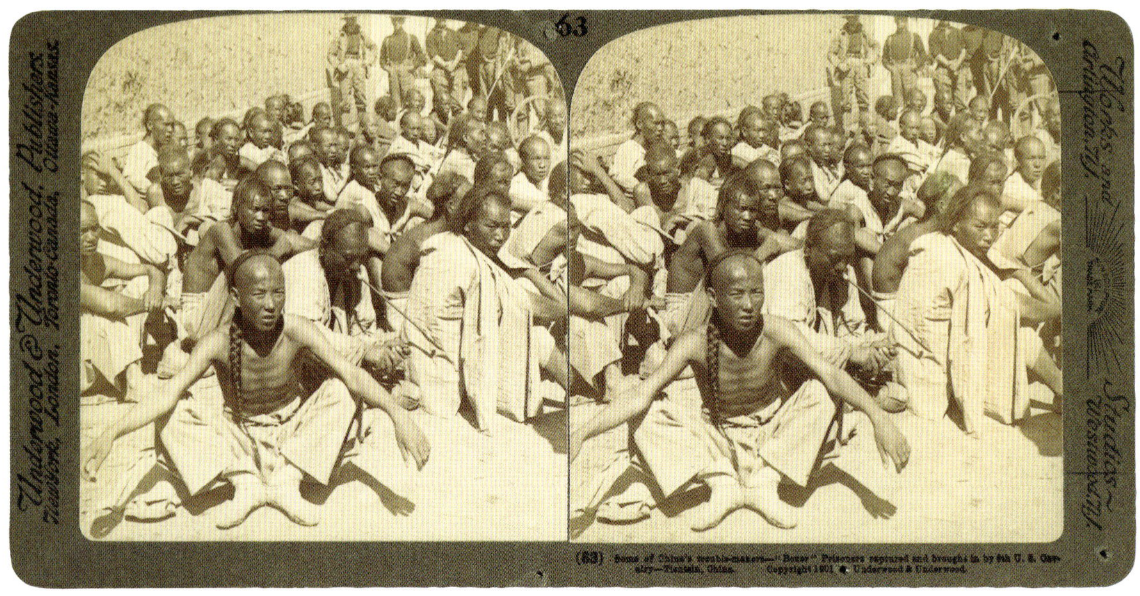

32 James Ricalton, '*Some of China's Trouble-Makers – 'Boxer' Prisoners Captured and Brought in by the 6th U.S. Cavalry – Tientsin, China. No. 63*', 1900, albumen print stereograph.

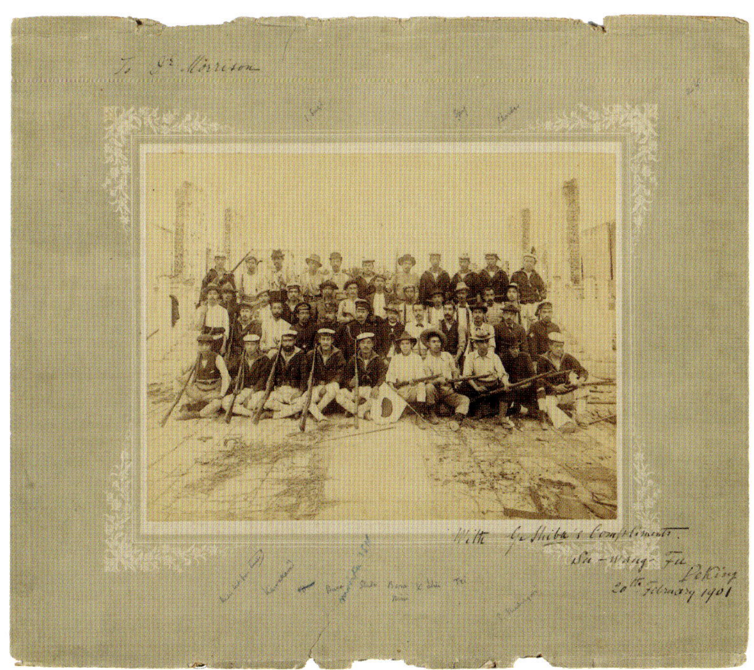

33 Yamamoto Sanshichiro, *Japanese Defenders of the Beijing Legations*, 1900–1901, albumen print on card.

through the Stereoscope was published in 1901. The accompanying book was given the subtitle 'A Journey Through the Dragon Empire at the Time of the Boxer Uprising' 'personally conducted by James Ricalton', and came with extended text and maps so that viewers could feel as if they were part of the tour. Ricalton chose subjects that were well suited to 3D stereoscopic rendering – layered compositions with deep perspectival space, figures to provide a sense of scale, human drama for emotional affect, and scenes of death and destruction to contribute to the experience of spectacle. The powerful combination of ideologically driven interpretive text and binocular images, part of what James Hevia describes as the 'photography complex', exemplifies the role of photography as a technology of rule.[10]

Photographic studios, regarded as foreign businesses, were also attacked and torched. A souvenir photograph taken by Yamamoto Sanshichiro (1855–1943) documents the contingent of Japanese military and civilians who defended Chinese Christians barricaded inside Prince Su's palace, adjacent to the Legation Quarter. The photograph, signed 'With G. Shiba's compliments. Su-Wang-Fu. Peking, 20 February 1901', was presented to George Ernest Morrison, who had been actively involved in the siege. Among the contingent of men posing with rifles, successfully led by Goro Shiba, are photographers from the Yamamoto studio.[11]

The Boxer Rebellion was settled with the signing of the Peking Protocol on 7 September 1901. Prince Qing, Li Hongzhang and representatives of the allied nations were signatories. A two-plate photograph

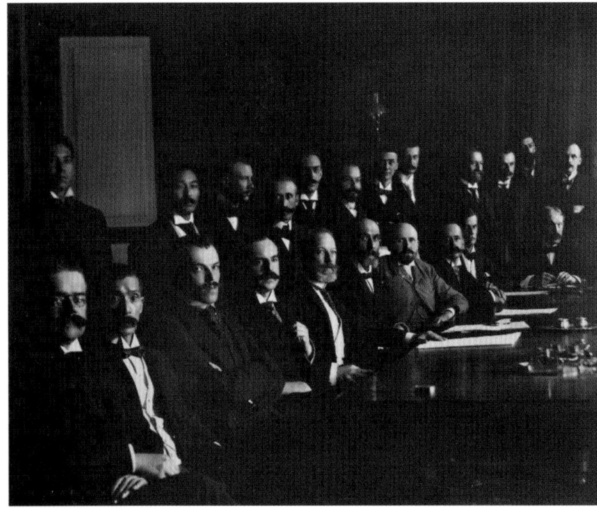

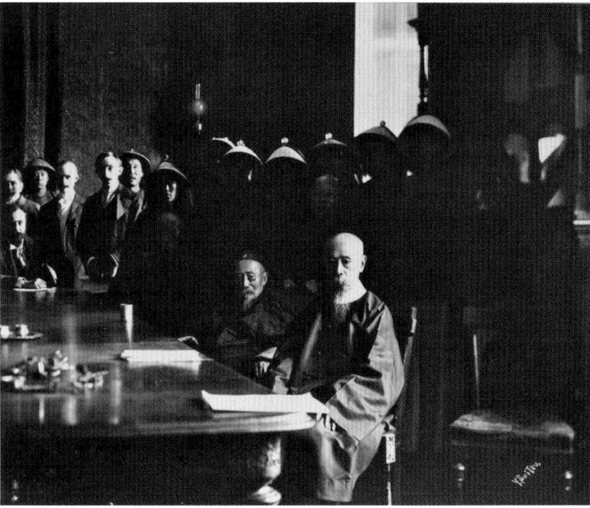

34 and 35 Y Sui Tsu, *Signing of Protocol at Peking*, 1901, albumen print.

records the occasion (note the signature 'Y Sui Tsu', lower right) showing Chinese and foreign officials facing each other across a huge table, symbolic of the political divide separating the two parties. The protocol required China to pay massive indemnities to the allied nations, much of it to be raised through taxes. The national burden caused by such 'unequal treaties' and protocols only increased the need for political and social reform.

The first railway to be designed, constructed and funded by the Chinese was officially opened in 1909. The 200-kilometre (125-mile) Jing-Zhang railway from Beijing to Zhangjiakou, en route to Mongolia, was an important corridor for trade and security, connecting with other railroads emanating from a new transport hub in the capital. Back in 1876 the Hing-Qua Studio was commissioned to take photographs of the first (British-built) railway in Shanghai and placed an advertisement in the newspaper inviting locals to come to the track and create a crowd for the camera.[12]

China was catching up not only by building railways but by documenting them in the formats used for such enterprises around the world. For image makers the train marked the advent of industrialization and modernity, and photo documentation came with it. To commemorate the completion of the historic four-year project, the Qing government commissioned Tan Jingtang of the Shanghai-based Tong Sheng Photography Studio to produce a series of photographs to document the project in its entirety. The deluxe two-volume presentation book features portraits of project leader Zhan Tianyou (who had trained in railway engineering at Yale University), the opening ceremony, tunnels, bridges, stations, rolling stock and engineering workshops. One of Zhan Tianyou's proudest achievements was a section of zigzag track that used engines to push and pull trains up and over the mountains. In one image, captioned 'West of Qinglongqiao station. Two trains travelling at the same time. Looking south', the trains are stationary (people are standing on top of loaded carriages) and blow smoke to simulate movement.

By the late nineteenth century Shanghai had become the publishing centre of modern China. Modern printing presses were first imported by missionary organizations in the 1870s and, with continuing innovation in print technology and the need to disseminate ideas and information in ever-changing times, magazines and newspapers proliferated. Reformers advocated an educational system that would prepare Chinese citizens for modern life and in 1905 the antiquated imperial examination system for

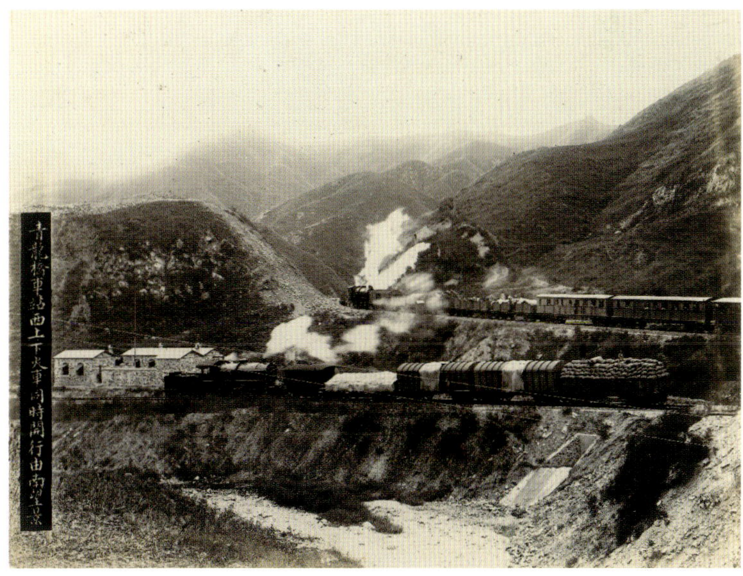

36 Tong Sheng studio, *'West of Qinglongqiao station. Two trains travelling at the same time. Looking south'*, 1909, gelatin silver print.

educating officials for civil service was finally abolished. Scholars and intellectuals who would otherwise have been drawn into government service were forced to seek other paths of employment. Many gravitated towards the emerging publishing industry that had its base in the foreign concessions in Shanghai. They found jobs as writers and editors, illustrators and later photographers, using their considerable intellectual skills to mediate the cultural changes that were taking place.

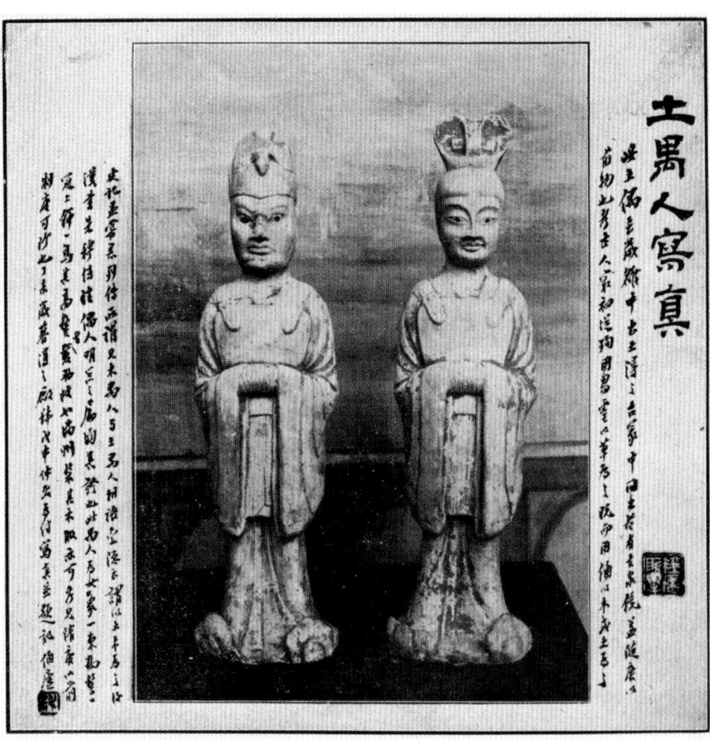

37 Photograph of two recently excavated tomb figures, from the collection of Luo Zhenyu with details inscribed on mount by Luo, published in *National Glories of Cathay* (*Shenzhou guoguang ji*), v (October 1908).

In 1908 the Cathay Art Union began to publish *National Glories of Cathay*, a large folio magazine using glass-plate collotype printing introduced from Japan to reproduce artworks from private collections. Works of art appeared with details of medium, dimensions and the collector, 'so that when readers open the magazine they feel as though they are looking at a real object'.[13] An annotated photograph of tomb figures from the collection of the scholar Luo Zhenyu (1866–1940), for example, gives details of what the objects are and where they were excavated. The Art Union also printed large-scale reproductions of artworks which could be mounted as a scroll, framed and hung on the wall, or placed under a glass table-top, catering to a market of 'impoverished scholars' by providing access to masterpieces for a fraction of the cost of an original.[14] The publishers Deng Shi and Huang Jie, who were from Guangdong, had established the Association for Preservation of the National Essence and the Cathay Art Union in 1904. At a time of widespread modernization and waning interest in the classical arts entrepreneurial scholars utilized new reprographic technology to re-engage readers with Chinese culture.

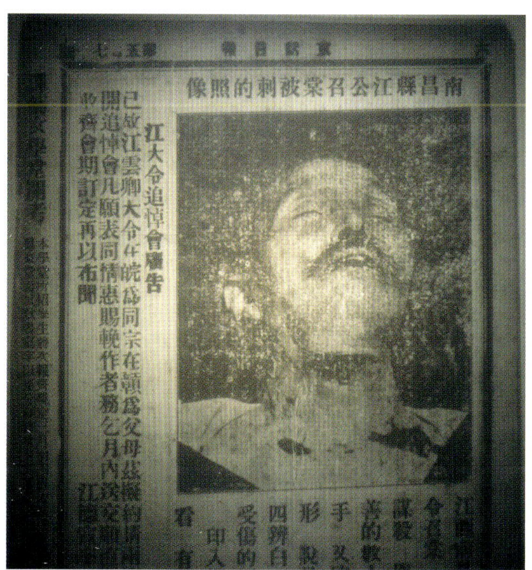

南昌縣江公召棠被刺的照像

江大令追悼會廣告

38 Photograph of a dead Chinese man, published in *Jinghua Daily* (29 March 1906).

One of the most influential modern journals was *Eastern Miscellany* (1904–48), published by Shanghai's Commercial Press as a forum for discussion of foreign affairs and subjects of public interest. Xia Ruifang and others who were trained in English typesetting at missionary schools established the press in 1897. The first issues of the magazine were devoted to the Russo-Japanese War (1904–5), which was being fought on China's doorstep. In addition to lengthy articles on the conflict, the journal published numerous portrait photographs of Russian and Japanese political and military figures, and images of the conflict. Advertisements offered readers the opportunity to purchase albums of war photographs produced by an 'artist' who had trained in Tokyo using 'the latest photographic techniques'.

Valued for their depiction of 'truth', photographs also began to appear in Chinese newspapers. In March 1906 a gruesome picture of the head of an 'assassinated' Chinese was published in the *Jinghua Daily*. According to the accompanying report, the magistrate of Nanchang had been tricked into having a meal with a French missionary – Father Lacruche, head of the Catholic mission in Nanchang – and killed. Though the death was claimed to have been suicide, the photograph was presented as evidence of murder:

> Today we have specifically taken a photograph of the wounded Jiang Zhaotang, created a photogravure from a copper plate and printed it in the newspaper. We invite everyone to look at it. Does suicide look like this?[15]

The photograph of Jiang's head, his eyes closed and a gaping wound to his neck, appeared to corroborate a story of his death at the hands of a European. In retaliation for Jiang's death, nationalists went on a rampage, killing foreign missionaries including Father Lacruche and burning down buildings, highlighting the hostility between local populations and foreign sodalities in Nanchang and many other parts of China.[16]

Celebrity, death and war, and events that had a dramatic impact on the lives of individuals and communities, were attractive to Chinese publishers. In 1904 the Youzheng Publishing House published previously forbidden images of the empress dowager, Longyu and other imperial family members, circulating them in large numbers. In an advertisement highlighting the reformist attitudes that were increasingly prevalent in the early 1900s, the Japanese publishers stated that their aim was to 'allow people of the Qing nation to look upon imperial countenances in the same way that Western people hang portraits of their kings and queens at home'.[17] Commercial photography studios quickly took advantage of the changing climate. In 1904 the Yao Hua studio advertised portraits of the emperor and empress dowager for sale in *Shenbao*, one of Shanghai's most popular newspapers.[18]

The deaths of the Guangxu Emperor and the Empress Dowager in November 1908 (Cixi is thought to have been involved in Guangxu's demise) were big news stories. Court-approved photographs of the procession of the Guangxu Emperor's coffin to the Western Imperial Tombs were sold as commemorative postcards, highlighting the desire to control the circulation of sensitive imagery. At the time newspapers and magazines generally relied on photographs supplied by commercial studios. The American C. E. LeMunyon photographed Cixi's funeral procession, and Fu Sheng studio photographers, sensing a commercial opportunity, attempted to photograph the interment ceremony but they were arrested for violating imperial protocol. In the space of a few short years it had become possible for members of the general public to view images of members of the imperial family, and commercial studios took risks to capture rare views that would be published and viewed in large numbers.

Dramatic change came to China following the October 1911 Wuchang Uprising that heralded the fall of the Qing Dynasty (1644–1911). In 1910 Li Bozhen had established the Rongchang Photography studio in Hankou and the following year he became a member of the Kung-Chin Hui, the Society for Mutual Progress, a secret organization that played a key role in the revolution. The studio was used as a base for the group's operations. Li is said to have accompanied troops to the front line and

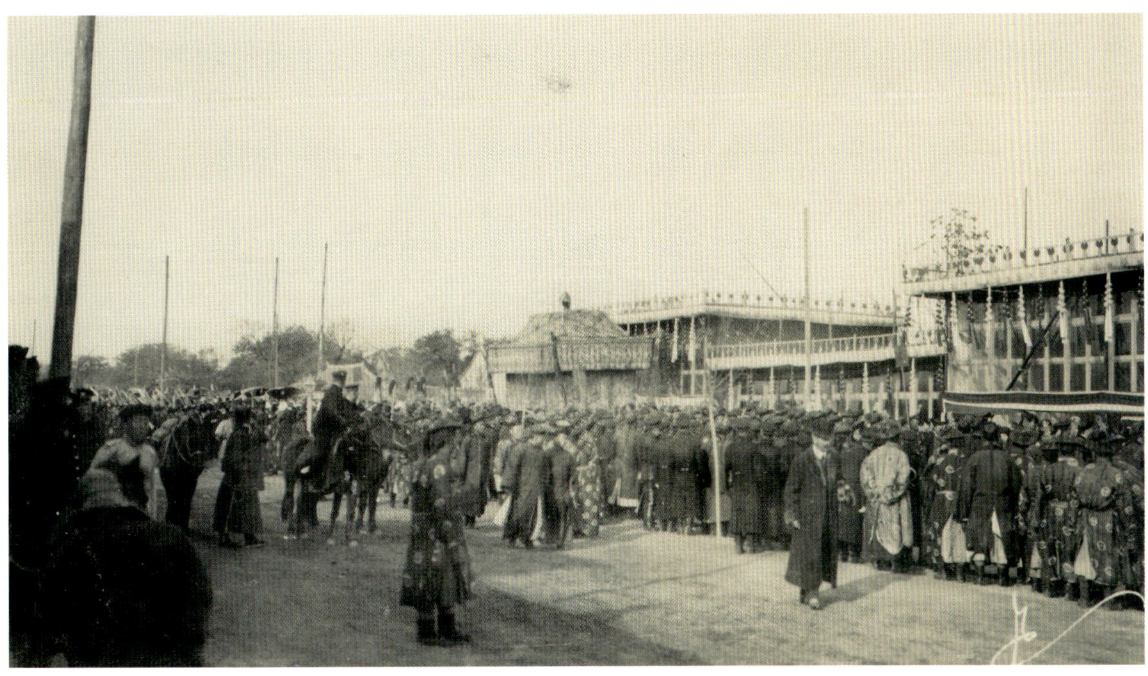

39 C. E. LeMunyon, *Funeral of the Empress Dowager*, 9 November 1909, gelatin silver print.

photographed battles associated with the 1911 uprising. His studio was destroyed, however, and none of his work is thought to have survived.[19]

The most comprehensive record of the 1911 revolution is a series of fourteen volumes of photographs titled *War Scenes of the Chinese Revolution* published by Shanghai's Commercial Press. Each volume is designed to function as an educational souvenir and contains 40 photographs with Chinese and English captions. Drawn from a wide variety of sources, the images focus on people and events (illus. 40). The American Francis Stafford (1884–1938) arrived in Shanghai in 1909 to work as the senior photographer at the Commercial Press. He recorded the revolution as it unfolded, including the burning of Hankou, and many of his photographs appear in *War Scenes*.[20] In 1912 Sun Yat-sen, having returned after sixteen years' exile, was proclaimed provisional president of the new Chinese Republic. Stafford photographed the historic moment of Sun leaving Shanghai for Nanjing to assume his new role.

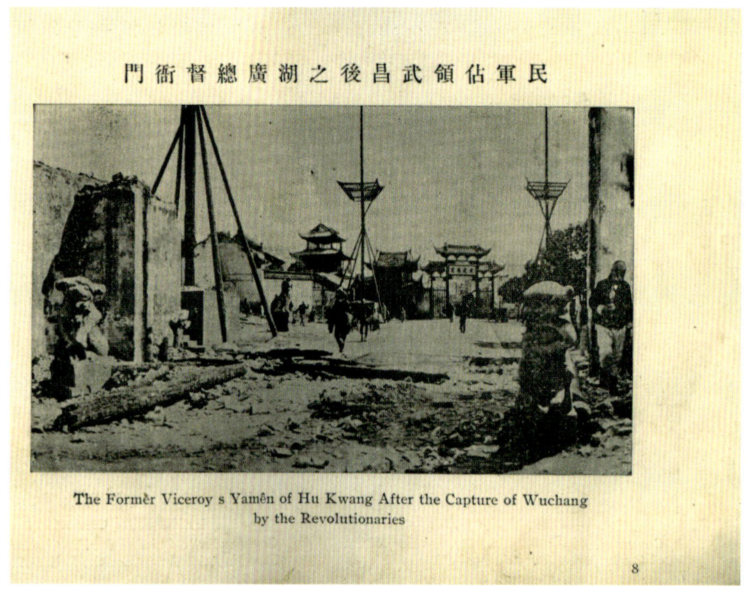

40 Francis Stafford, 'The Former Viceroy's Yamen of Hu Kwang After the Capture of Wu Chang by the Revolutionaries', reproduced in The Commercial Press, ed., *War Scenes of the Chinese Revolution*, I (1911).

One of the most important illustrated magazines in the early years of the Republic was the *True Record* (1912–13) established by the artist brothers Gao Jianfu (1879–1951) and Gao Qifeng (1889–1933), who had studied in Japan where they met Sun Yat-sen. Like him they were originally from Guangdong. New ideas continued to come from the south with its comparative openness to the outside world. The Gao brothers formed the China Photography Brigade with the aim of documenting Sun Yat-sen's activities through photographs published in the *True Record*.

The covers of the magazines, many of them illustrated by Gao Qifeng, reveal the intelligent playfulness that lies at the heart of the *True Record*'s conception of news and communication. On one cover a man in Western dress pulls back a curtain to reveal the Chinese expression *zhenxiang*, meaning 'true record' (derived from the Japanese *shashin*), lighting up the darkness like a ghostly apparition (illus. 42). Produced in Shanghai, the magazine featured a unique combination of text and imagery that reflected the spirit of the new republic and a society in process of change. Layouts combine customized illustrations, paintings, photographs and some bilingual text. In most issues there were souvenir

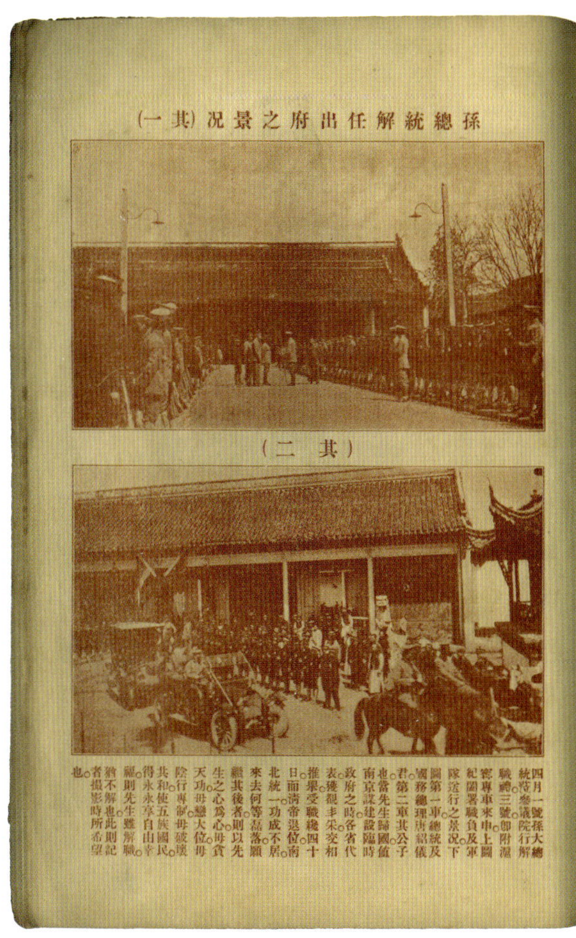

孫總統解任出府之景況（其一）

（其二）

四月一號孫大總統於參議院行解職禮。三號卽附滬寗專車來申。上圖紀國署職員及軍隊送行之景況。下圖第一車。總統及國務總理唐紹儀君。第二車其公子也。當先生歸國值南京謀建設臨時政府之時。各省代表。獲觀丰采。交相推舉。受職纔四十日。而淸帝退位。南北統一。功成不居。來去何等磊落。願繼其後者。則以先生之心爲心。毋貪天功。毋戀大位。毋陰行專制。毋破壞共和。使五族國民。得永永享自由幸福。則先生雖解職。猶不解也。此則記者攝影時所希望也。

41 Sun Yat-sen en route to Nanjing as provisional president, photograph published in *True Record*, I (1912).

visual fold-outs that could be clipped out, framed and hung on the wall. The inaugural issue featured three linked photographic panoramas of Wuhan: Hangyang and Hankou, the Han and Yangzi rivers, and Wuchang, where the historic 1911 revolution began. The magazine was closed down in 1913 following Yuan Shikai's suppression of activities linked to the Nationalist Party. Yuan, chief of the powerful Beiyang army in the north, forced Sun Yat-sen to flee to Japan and installed himself as emperor of China for a brief period before his death in 1916.

With all the instability of late dynastic and early modern China, photographic studios sought timeless subjects to offer for sale. The Me and Myself studio (Erwo Xuan) in Hangzhou was established during the Guangxu period (1875–1908) and managed by Yu Yinchu. Erwo Xuan was the first studio in Hangzhou to use electric lighting and came to public attention when Sun Yat-sen had his photograph taken there. It also known for the award-winning book of scenic views of Hangzhou published as *West Lake Landscape*.[21] Each of the 48 photographs is accompanied by a facing page of Chinese text and the book is bound in the traditional style, combining Chinese taste with cultural tourism. The views are of historic sites and beauty spots around the West Lake that have been depicted in paintings and poems since the twelfth century when Hangzhou was capital of the Southern Song Dynasty (1127–1279). But the album adds views of the grave sites of the revolutionary martyrs Xu Xilin (1873–1907) and Qiu Jin (1875–1907), who were executed following a failed uprising against the Manchu–Qing in 1907 (illus. 43).

It is interesting to compare the Erwo Xuan photograph of Qiu Jin's grave site, taken from a boat on the lake, with a photograph of a Chinese painting of the same subject (illus. 43, 44) and a close-up commemorative photograph (illus. 45) both produced by Shanghai's Kwang Wa studio.

The painter employs a bird's eye perspective, giving the viewer a greater sense of West Lake topography and the location of the grave within the landscape setting. The painting, created for Qiu Jin's friend Wu Ziying (1868–1934) who risked her life to arrange for Qiu's burial, was photographed soon after Qiu's death, suggesting that there was a market for painted commemorative images as well as modern photographic views.

Erwo Xuan studio's album of contemporary views of the West Lake was submitted to the 1910 Nanyang Industrial Exposition and awarded a medal. The exposition included photographic entries from around the country. Medals were also bestowed on the Ying Cheong Studio, Shanghai, for a large-scale group photograph, Liu Zhiping for his portrait of Li Hongzhang, and Chen Yiyi for 'Postcard photographs taken in moonlight, and six photographs taken with a blue light'. Photography featured in the Expo advertising and within displays, and there was a dedicated photographic studio for members of the public to have souvenir portraits taken on site. The prominence of photography at China's first trade fair indicates familiarity with the medium and an awareness of its widespread application for commemorative, creative and educational purposes.

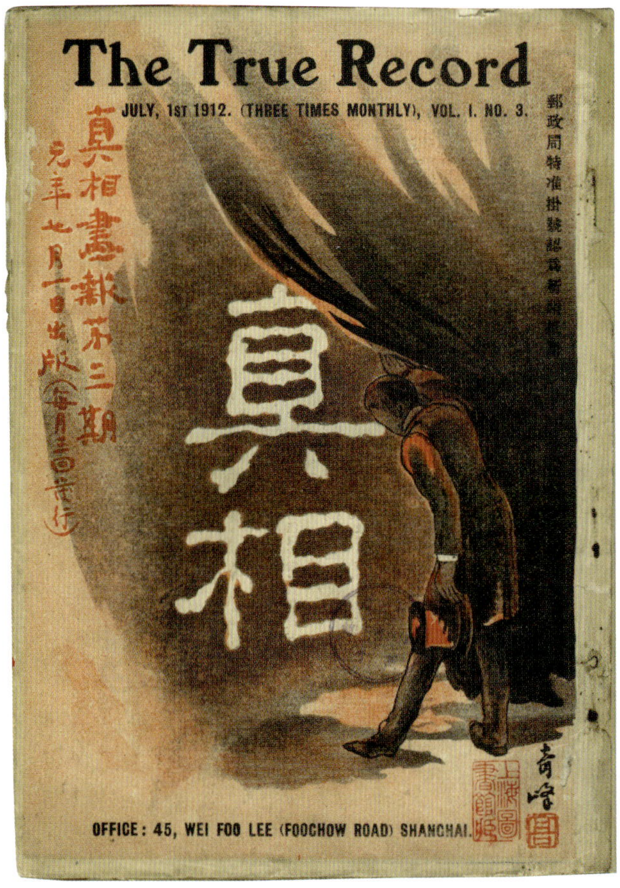

42 Gao Qifeng, cover of *True Record*, III (1912).

In 1914 the Chinese scholar and progressive educationalist Huang Yanpei (1878–1965) was employed by the Shanghai newspaper *Shenbao* as an itinerant journalist to report on the state of education in China. Huang had been director of the Department of Education in Jiangsu, but had resigned over growing political differences. Accompanied by the photographer Lü Tianzhou and the writer Gu Zhilian, he visited schools over an initial three-month period, interviewing local officials and recording

43 Erwo Xuan studio, Qiu Jin's grave, *West Lake Landscape*, 1908–10, gelatin silver print in book.

44 Kwang Wa studio, photograph of a painting of Qiu Jin's grave, 1908–10, gelatin silver print on card.

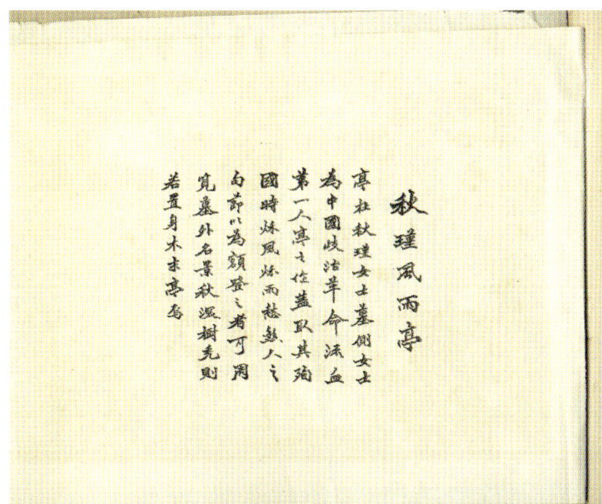

秋瑾風雨亭

亭在秋瑾女士墓側女士為中國政治革命流血第一人亭之位蓋取其殉國時秋風秋雨愁煞人之句節以為額登之者可周覽墓外名景秋澀樹光則若置身木末亭焉

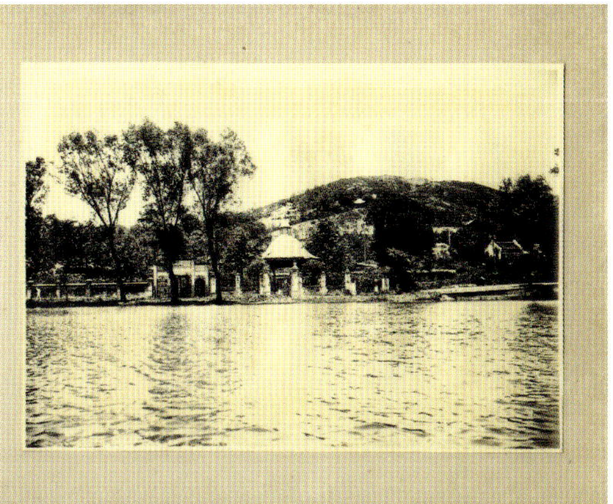

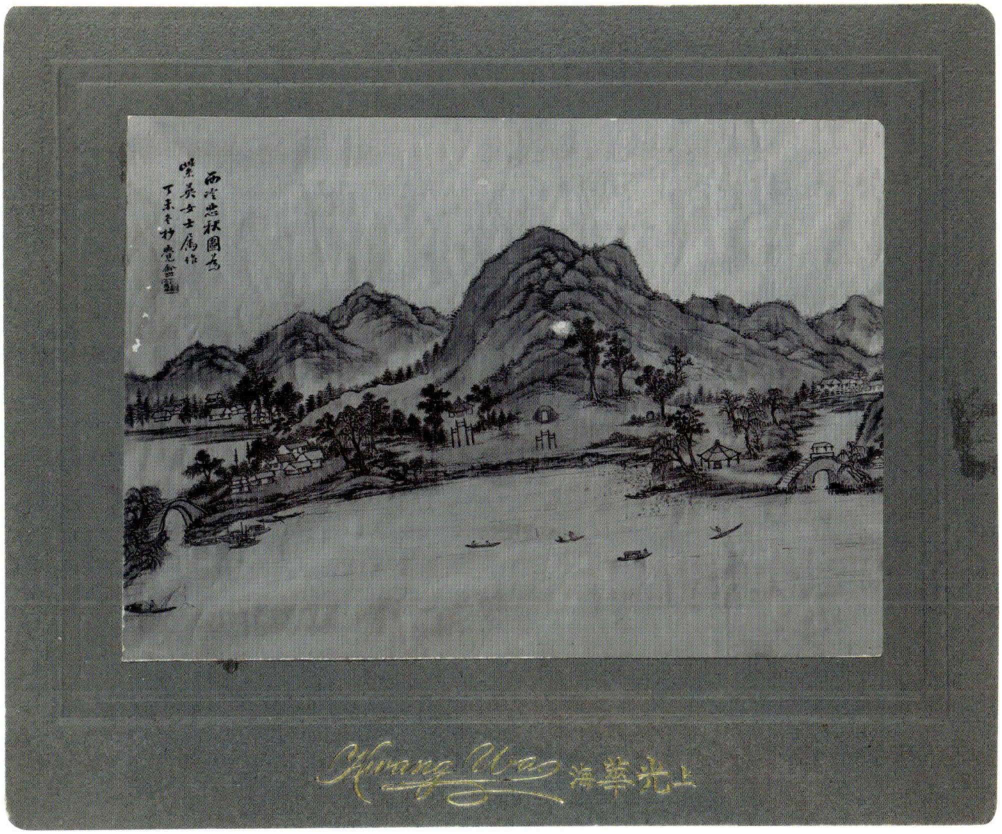

Kwang Wah 上海光華

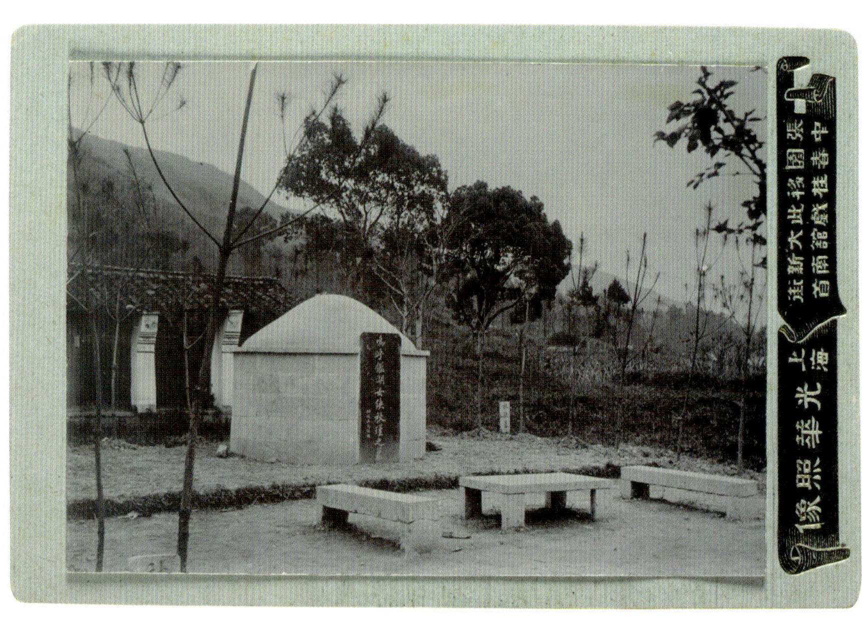
上海
光華照像
張園移此大新街
中春桂戲舘南首

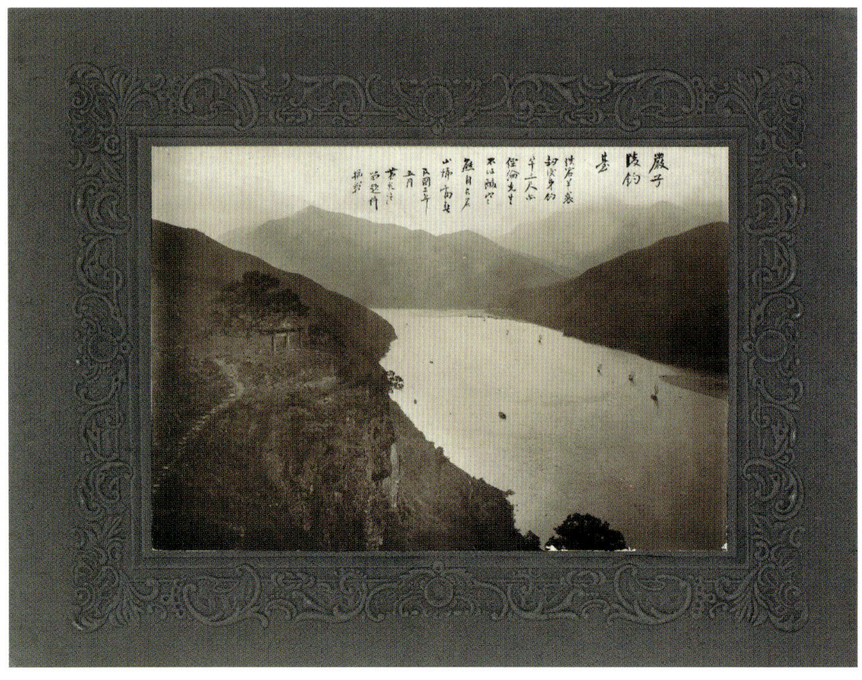

his experiences. Huang would publish a diary of the journey incorporating photographs, including some of his own.[22] A series of bilingual books called *Scenic China* was also published following the trips (the first two volumes edited by Huang with photographs by Lü).[23]

A group of prints from the trip in the Shanghai Library is inscribed by Huang. One of them shows a rustic pavilion as a vantage point for gazing down at the Fuchun River in Zhejiang and is captioned 'Yan Ziling Fishing Platform'.[24] Yan Ziling was a scholar during the Eastern Han Dynasty (25–220) who refused to serve a corrupt ruler and returned to the countryside to live a simple life. By invoking the historic figure, Huang is drawing a parallel with his own life experience. Like many reform-minded scholar-officials of his generation, Huang not only used photography as a modern medium to create a true record, but also to connect him in specific and personal ways to the past. His photograph, with its calligraphic inscription, has a detached scholarly air, not unlike a Chinese brush-and-ink painting, and records memories and feelings associated with place. While photography was the obvious medium for Huang's reportage, his photograph of the Yan Ziling fishing platform is a fascinating syncretic cultural product of early Republican China, reflecting the tensions between past and present in a society undergoing dramatic political and technological change.

45 Kwang Wa studio, Qiu Jin's grave, 1908–10, gelatin silver print cabinet card.

46 Huang Yanpei, Yan Ziling fishing platform, Fuchun River Zhejiang, 1914, gelatin silver print on card.

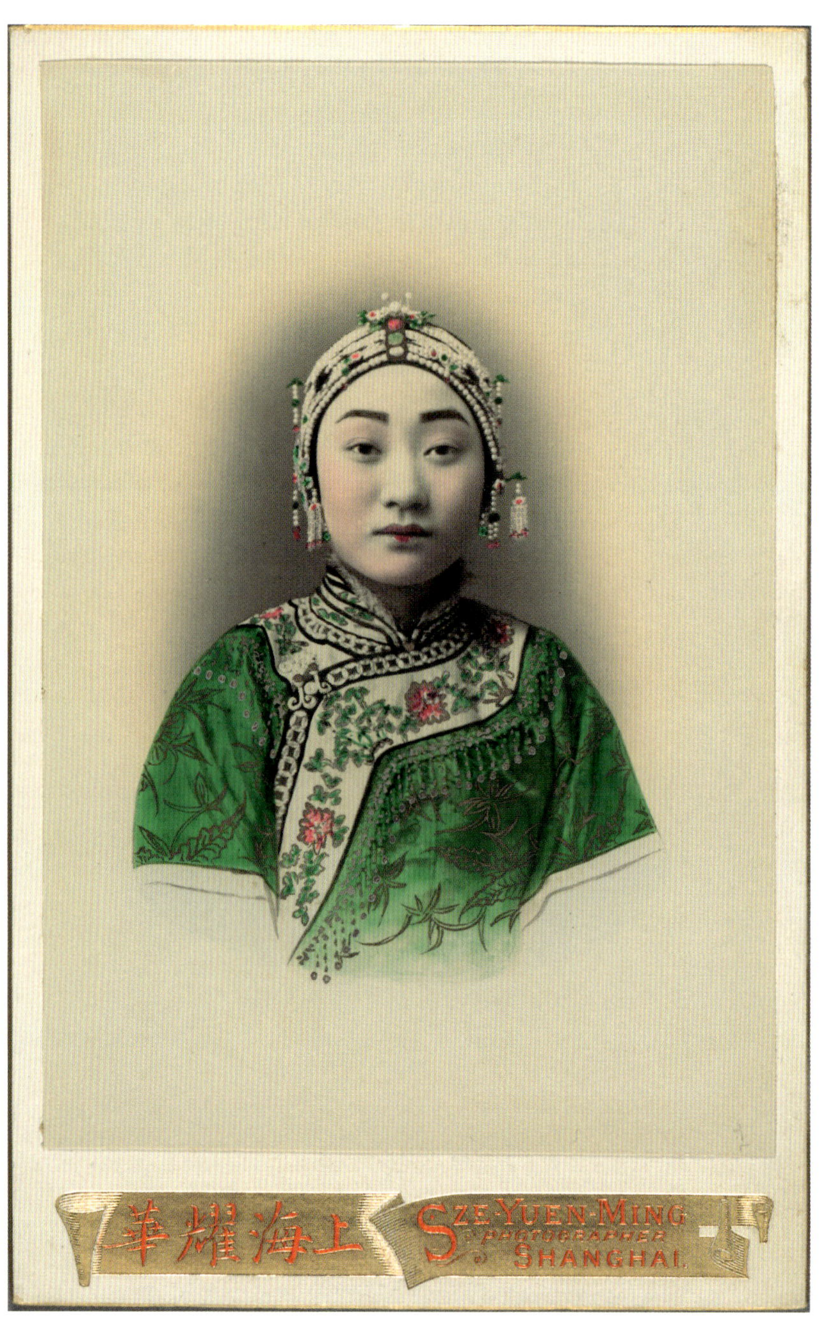
上海耀華
SZE-YUEN-MING
PHOTOGRAPHER
SHANGHAI

three

China Modern

During the Republican era (1912–49) Shanghai was the centre of cosmopolitanism in China and photographic studios were well positioned to capitalize on a growing interest in novelty and visual culture. Portrait photographs, recording important personages, commemorations and rites of passage, were shared with family, friends and associates, and published in the growing number of illustrated magazines and newspapers reporting on social and political change. As photography became more familiar, cheaper and less challenging, it was taken up by a growing number of enthusiasts who used the new medium to explore personal and artistic expression. As Wen-hsin Yeh has observed: 'Much of Shanghai's urban history in modern times concerns the efforts made by a Westernizing economic elite, in collaboration with the state, to bring about the indigenization of the foreign and the domestication of novelty.'[1] Photography was a global phenomenon and the first decades of the twentieth century were a time when Shanghainese practitioners took pride in keeping abreast of world trends.

One of the earliest and most successful illustrated magazines was *Dianshizhai Pictorial* (1884–98), distributed free with the *Shenbao* newspaper. Lithograph-printed ink-line images that acknowledged Chinese traditions of woodblock printing presented vignettes of contemporary life in the fast-changing foreign settlements. They were often accompanied by captions that conveyed a degree of ambivalence towards cultural change. Some of the most memorable images show modern women playing billiards, using sewing machines, eating with knives and forks, and looking through binoculars at a church spire. These women

47 Yao Hua, Sze Yuen Ming studio, *Shanghai Courtesan*, c. 1901, hand-coloured gelatin silver print cabinet card.

chose to be seen in public. They took risks and set fashion trends. They did not stay at home leading sheltered Confucian lives. The pictorial found an avid readership among an expanding class of image-conscious Shanghai urbanites and was a precursor to later stand-alone photographic pictorials such as the *Young Companion* (1926–45).[2]

To meet the needs and cultural mores of a growing Chinese clientele, photographic studios accommodated the formality associated with traditional Chinese portraiture by placing sitters in fantasy settings, accompanied by symbolic attributes that projected an idealized image.

The courtesan became one of the most popular subjects of portrait photography in turn-of-the-century Shanghai. Female entertainers were happy to perform for the camera, knowing that business would follow from such publicity. Photographic studios vied for their custom, aware that images of bold and beautiful women were in turn a powerful means of promoting their own skills in turn.

The Yao Hua studio, Shanghai's most famous creator of courtesan photographs, produced dazzling portraits of upper-class courtesans, hand painted in brilliant jewel-like colours (illus. 47). The cabinet cards printed with gold or silver lettering appealed to Shanghai's growing merchant class, functioning as calling cards and advertisements. The brightly coloured images present the women as beautiful flowers, continuing the penchant of literati for 'flower appreciation' through refined cultural allusion.[3] Courtesans engaged in play-acting, riding bicycles, dressing up and carrying flower baskets or flywhisks, attributes associated with literary or mythical beauties. They were given names such as Jade Phoenix and Lin Daiyu, the heroine of the classic novel *Dream of the Red Chamber*. The illusory verisimilitude of photography appealed to courtesans and their customers alike. A photograph was a unique representation of an individual, yet it could be printed in various sizes and formats and in great numbers.

An image taken by the Yao Hua studio and produced as a postcard shows the studio interior, made to appear like a teahouse, hung with large, framed photographs of courtesans. The scale of the images suggests the technical sophistication of a studio renowned for its innovation and its ability to lure high-class customers. Notices placed in Shanghai's *Shenbao*

48 Printed postcard from a photograph by the Yao Hua studio, early 1900s.

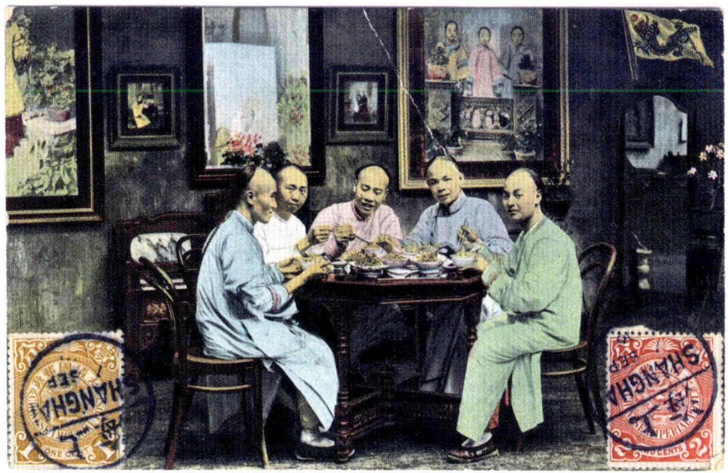

newspaper during the 1890s advertise printing on a wide variety of materials, in dimensions that were larger than life-size. Photographs could be taken for any occasion, in the studio (with props including lions, tigers, deer and exotic dogs), at home or outdoors. The Yao Hua studio was particularly proud of its lighting effects, using the latest German technology to create what it described as truly three-dimensional looking portraits. The studio emphasized the importance of contrast in order to achieve a modern, life-like effect. This departed from an earlier preference for flattened images that were evenly lit with a minimum of shadow, which was regarded as disturbing and inauspicious.

Yao Hua's owner, Shi Dezhi, was also known as Star Talbot, a Eurasian entrepreneur who established the first medicine factory in Shanghai and went on to develop a method of porcelain manufacture to reproduce the finest Qing-style enamel wares.[4] In his photographic business he saw a business opportunity in making women feel at ease in a photographic studio, as gradually it became acceptable for a woman to have her photograph taken either in commercial rooms, or outdoors. In 1905 Shi opened a branch of his operation near the racetrack, operated by his eldest daughter Mae Linda Talbot (1886–1964) until her marriage in 1908, making her one of the earliest documented female photographers in China.

Performing for the camera took many forms, including double exposure portraits known as 'images of me and myself' (*erwo tu*), which explore the idea of the 'me' in the photograph and the 'me' in the real world, playfully suggesting representations of spirit and body, or the generation of another self. A photograph of Aisin-Gioro Puyi (1906–1967) seated on a couch in front of a screen or 'shadow wall' in the Forbidden City – one self looking at the camera, and the other to the side – is conceived to trick the eye. The photograph probably dates from the late 1910s or early 1920s and is a technical tour de force created for the delight and amusement of the young dethroned emperor. An extant print is mounted on a card of the Tung Hua studio in Peking, though it is unclear if that studio created the image. Other related photographs taken at a similar time show Puyi and his younger brother Pujie (1907–1994), who look very much alike, sitting together on a couch. While their close physical resemblance may have been a factor in the creation of the photograph – Liang Shitai took a photograph of the brothers Yixin and Yihuan in 1889 – 'me and myself' painted portraits of scholars and emperors can be traced

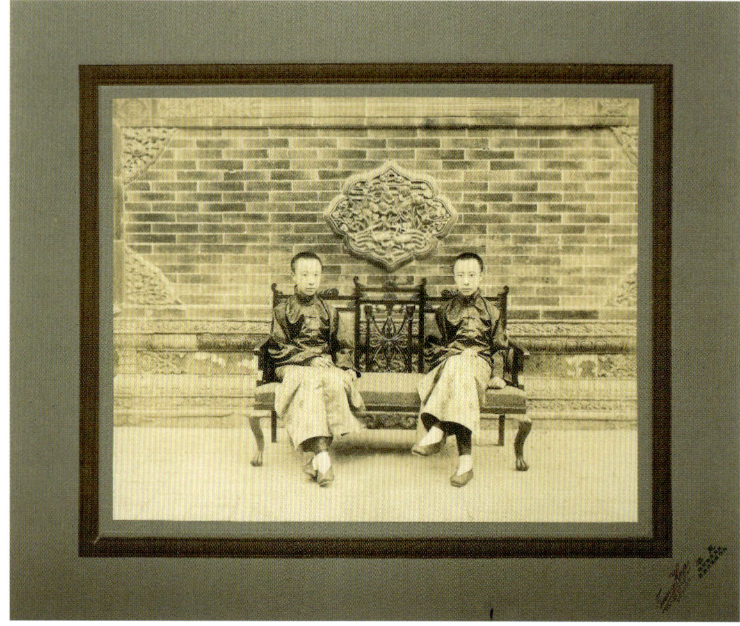

49 Double-exposure portrait of *Puyi*, early 1900s, gelatin silver print on card, photographer unknown.

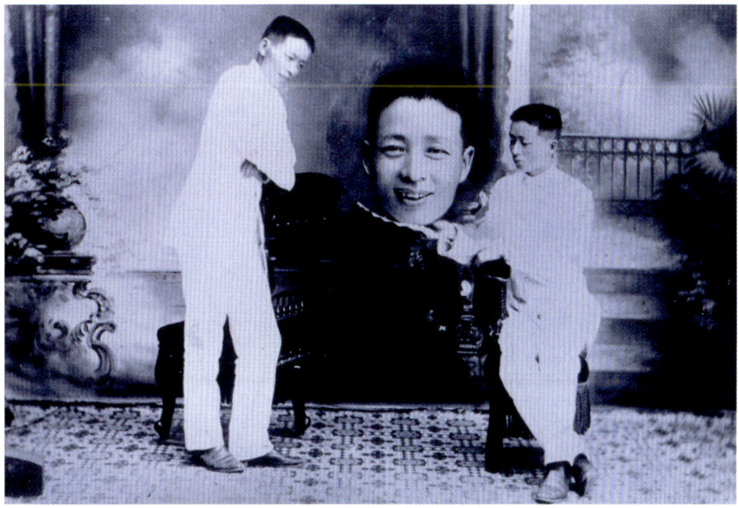

50 Lin Photographic studio, *Lin Cao around 35 Years*, 1916, gelatin silver print.

back to the Song Dynasty.[5] The photographic portrait of Puyi makes a modern contribution to a scholarly tradition of self-reflexivity.

Erwo Xuan was the name of the photography studio in Hangzhou discussed in chapter Two. A studio with a similar name was established by Shi Qiang (1876–1943) in Lukang, Taiwan by 1901, suggesting the popularity of such novelty images.[6] A striking portrait taken around 1916 in the studio of Taiwan photographer Lin Cao (1881–1953) uses photomontage to add yet another image of himself to his double exposure self-portrait. Lin learned his craft from Japanese photographers in Taichung (Japan occupied Taiwan in 1895), suggesting a likely Japanese influence. The double portrait of Puyi and the triple portrait of Lin Cao indicate the widespread interest in the genre and highlight the enduring fascination of photographic self-portraits.

Other well-known images that hint at the significance of role-play or play-acting within Chinese social and political life are photographs of the empress dowager dressed as Guanyin, the Daoist goddess of mercy, taken by Xunling in 1903–5, and those of Yuan Shikai (1859–1916). After the death of the Guangxu Emperor and Empress Dowager in 1908, Yuan, who had been Viceroy of Zhili and Minister of Beiyang and played an important role in government reforms, was removed from office and went into

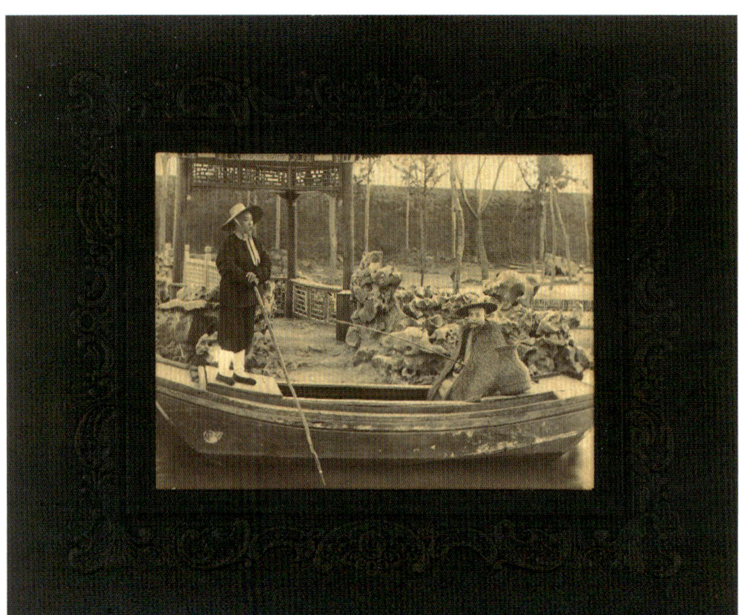

51 Yuan Kewen, *Yuan Shikai and Yuan Shilian*, 1911, gelatin silver print on card.

exile. A carefully staged photograph, standing with his elder brother Yuan Shilian (who had resigned from office due to illness) was taken by his son, Yuan Kewen, in 1911. The two men, dressed as Daoist rustics, pose for the camera in a boat on a man-made lake in the Garden for Cultivating Longevity, the family's Henan estate. The image, distributed to family and friends, and also published in *Eastern Miscellany*, gave the impression that Yuan had renounced his interest in fame and politics and retired to live a life of detached simplicity.[7] But after the insurrection in Wuchang on 10 October 1911, Yuan headed for the front line and then Peking, becoming prime minister, then president of the new Republic of China, and for a brief period the self-proclaimed Emperor of China. Like the Empress Dowager, Yuan Shikai exploited the modern medium of photography to communicate his version of the truth to a wide audience.

Images of actual theatrical entertainers were also popular and collectible. Photographs of famous Peking opera performers created a steady income for studios and were a means to advertise stars and shows.

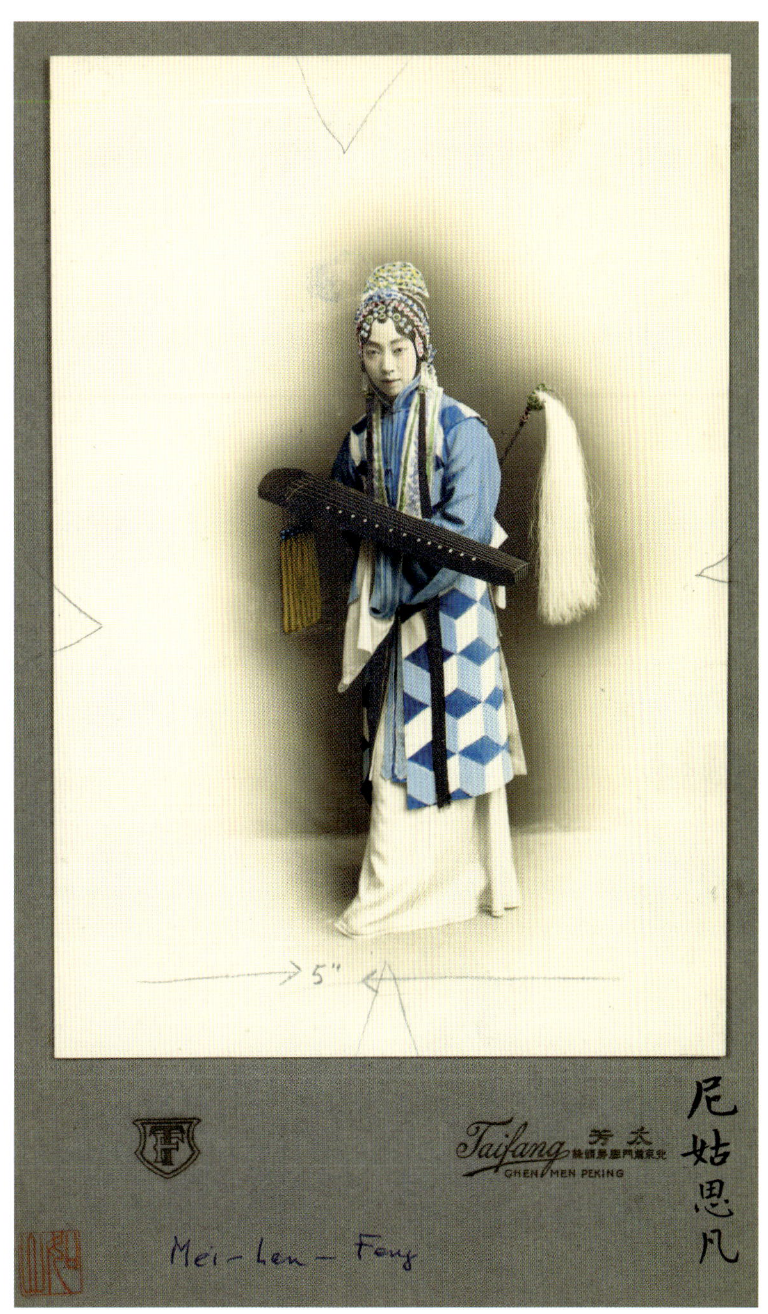

52 Taifang studio, *Mei Lanfang*, late 1920s, hand-coloured gelatin silver print on card.

One of the most famous Peking opera performers was Mei Lanfang (1894–1961), renowned for his female roles. He first performed Beauty Yu in the opera *Farewell to My Concubine* in Peking in 1922; it became one of his signature roles, photographed by many studios in Peking. In 1930 Mei Lanfang travelled to America at the invitation of the China Institute in America and performed on Broadway, where he was billed as China's greatest actor. Among the photographs prepared for the tour, now in the collection of the New York Public Library, are exquisite hand-tinted in-character stills from the operas *Rainbow Pass* and *A Nun Seeks Love* produced by the Taifang studio in Beijing (illus. 52). The photographs have pencil markings on the mounts indicating that they were used for publication. In a black-and-white photograph taken by the Yih Shenge studio from the same collection, out-of-frame assistants (holding trailing silk ribbons with tensile inner supports) and darkroom manipulation were used to create the impression of Mei Lanfang flying through the air, hands folded in prayer position, much like an *apsara* or celestial maiden. The photograph, a still from *Farewell to Princess Yu*, was used to create a graphic for 'Mei Lan Fong' brand cigarettes, produced by the Nanyang Brothers Tobacco Company, attesting to Mei Lanfang's star status.

In 1935 Mei Lanfang and Hu Ruihua (1908–1989) were part of a delegation of high-profile Chinese performing artists who toured Russia and Europe. Shanghainese movie star Hu Ruihua, better known as Hu Die or Butterfly Hu, had trained at the China National Movie School and achieved acclaim in silent movies following her debut in 1925. The actress was chosen for the cover of the inaugural issue of *Young Companion* in 1926. The magazine featured photographs of celebrities, fashionably dressed women and new female role models and became one of the most popular illustrated magazines.

By the time Hu Die played the lead female role in China's first sound movie *The Songstress Red Peony*, screened in Shanghai in 1931, she was China's most famous actress. In 1933 she was voted Movie Queen by the *Star Daily* newspaper, a broadsheet published by the Mingxing Film Company, the studio to which she was under contract and one of the largest film production companies operating in Shanghai and Hong Kong. Following the triumph of Hu Die's travels in Russia and Europe, on her return fans gathered at the dock in Shanghai, holding placards inscribed 'Long Live Miss Hu' and 'Long Live Chinese Film'. In 1935 *Young Companion* celebrated her success by publishing a diary-like chronicle of her European tour.

Another event of great public interest was the wedding of Chiang Kai-shek, president of the Republic of China, to Soong May-ling (1898–2003), who was from one of China's best-connected and influential families. May-ling was the youngest daughter of Charles Soong, a Methodist minister and businessman who had worked closely with Sun Yat-sen funding campaigns that contributed to the 1911 revolution. His other daughters Qing-ling and Ai-ling were married to Sun Yat-sen and H. H. Kung, banker and politician, respectively, and his son T. V. Soong would become governor of the central bank and minister of finance.

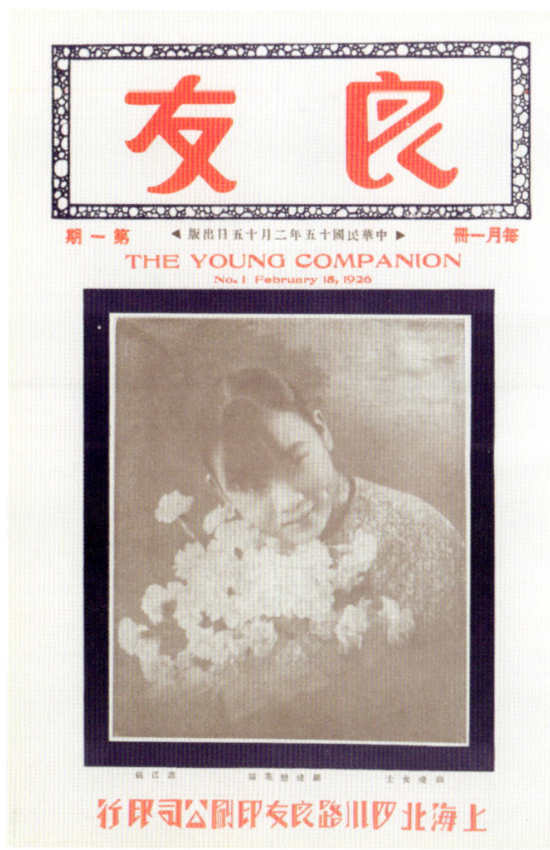

53 Photograph of Hu Die, published on the cover of *Young Companion*, 1 (1926).

The Chiang–Soong wedding took place in Shanghai on 1 December 1927. In April of that year Chiang had ordered the purge of Communists known as the Shanghai massacre or the April 12 Incident and went on to defeat various warlord factions and form a new Nationalist government in Nanjing. Formal wedding photographs of Soong wearing a chic Western-style white wedding dress and lace headpiece-cum-train, and Chiang in a three-piece suit with gloves and sporting a wedding ring, were taken by Chung Hwa, one of Shanghai's leading photographic studios (illus. 54). Portrait photographs of the couple in presentation mounts were given to friends and significant acquaintances. The mount was signed by the photographer, impressed with the studio's bilingual gold wax seal, and bore a personalized dedication. One was given to Arthur Holocombe, chair of Harvard University's Department of Government, who was invited to China in 1927 to advise on drafting a new constitution for Chiang's Nationalist Government. May-ling had studied at Wellesley College, graduating in

何爾康先生
夫人惠存

蔣中正
宋美齡贈

English literature and philosophy in 1917, and her brother T. V. was educated at Harvard. The gifting of photographic portraits, a custom first introduced to China in the treaty ports soon after the introduction of photography to China, remained an important aspect of diplomatic and business activity, highlighting the significance that was placed on personal connection and remembrance.

The Chung Hwa studio photographs of Chiang and Soong helped promote a trend for Western-style wedding photographs and the public display of carefully staged private moments. Illustrated magazines and newspapers featured portraits of famous couples, mothers and children, many of them sent in by individuals who wished to share nuptial and other personal news, using the new medium for social networking.

The Chung Hwa studio in Shanghai and the Kwong Hwa studio in Nanjing were named in celebration of the Republican era, inaugurated after the collapse of the Qing Dynasty in 1911. The word 'hwa' (*hua*), meaning splendid or flourishing, is one of the characters in the compound Chung Hwa (*Zhonghua*) used in the phrase for 'Chinese'. Most commercial studios had auspicious sounding names to lure customers to use their services to mark significant occasions, such as weddings, birthdays and life achievements. Attracting celebrity customers was the most powerful form of marketing.

In 1934 Chiang and Soong jointly launched a 'New Life Movement' aimed at improving education, strengthening the national character and ridding Chinese society of Communist influence. The movement drew on Confucian, Christian and militaristic values, and championed positive role models, especially for women and children. One such paragon was the female pilot and aerial stunt performer Li Xiaqing (1911–1998) who came from a wealthy revolutionary family in Guangdong. Li Xiaqing had starred in numerous action films produced by her father's Shanghai-based People's New Film Company. In 1929 she left acting behind and travelled with her diplomat husband to Geneva and later on to San Francisco, where she trained as a pilot, receiving her flying licence at the Boeing School of Aeronautics. In 1935, while practising a manoeuvre, she was unexpectedly ejected from the aircraft, but nonetheless managed to activate her parachute and land in the ocean off San Francisco, where she was rescued

54 Chung Hwa studio, Shanghai, *Wedding Portrait of Chiang Kai-shek and Soong May-ling*, 1927, gelatin silver print on card.

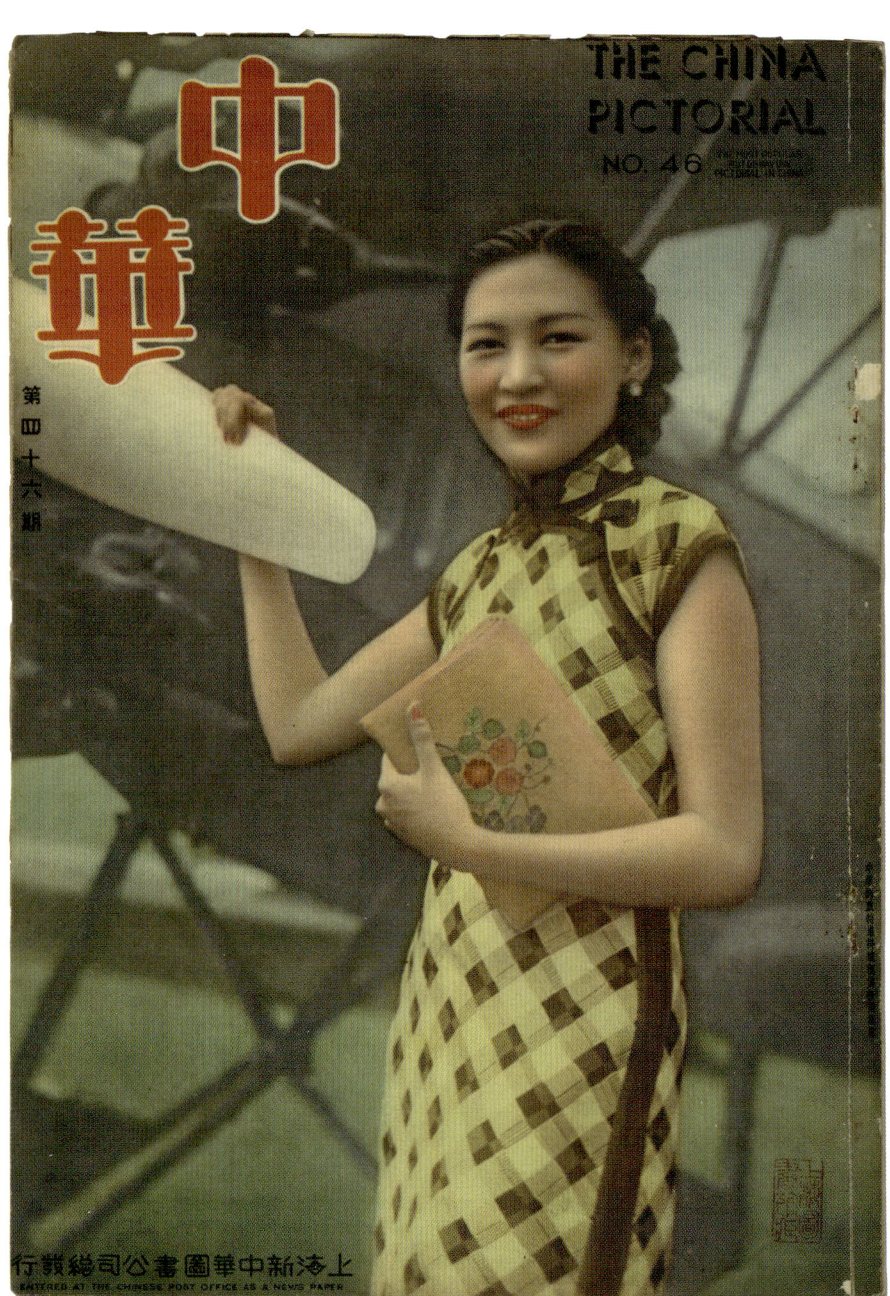
中華
THE CHINA PICTORIAL
NO. 46
第四十六期
上海新中華圖書公司總發行
ENTERED AT THE CHINESE POST OFFICE AS A NEWS PAPER

by American naval officers. She returned to Shanghai later that year, one of China's first female pilots, and in 1936 captivated local audiences with her long solo flights and aviatrix performances. On the occasion of Chiang Kai-shek's 50th birthday in 1936, Li was asked to perform an aerobatic display, part of a strategy to promote the purchase of fighter aeroplanes from the United States in order to combat Japanese military expansion in northern China. A striking image of Li Xiaqing, posing in a *qipao* (also known as a cheongsam) with her hand resting on the propeller of an aeroplane, was chosen for the cover of the September 1936 edition of *The China Pictorial* magazine. The photograph captioned 'Pilot Ms Li Xiaqing', which was taken by Zhu Jiaqing and printed with seven colours, is a powerful image of a modern Chinese woman.

With the increasing visibility of photographs of ordinary people in the media and simpler, cheaper photographic processes, individuals began to engage more directly with the medium (portable cameras were introduced in the 1890s and the Kodak Box Brownie in the early 1900s). In 1888 the Guang Ji Xuan studio opened in Zhang Garden and made use of the parklands as a backdrop. The Wuxi businessman Zhang Shuhe (1850–1919) had acquired the English-built, Western-style residence and garden some years earlier and opened the site to the public. It was the largest public garden in Shanghai and an important entertainment and meeting place. There was no entrance fee, but visitors were charged for a cup of tea, or wine or food and for movie screenings, performances and exhibitions. You could have your photograph taken: six *jiao* for a 4 *cun* print (about 13 cm; 5 in) and four *yuan* for one that was 12 *cun* (about 40 cm; 16 in).[8] An image from around 1907 of a Western photographer working in the garden advertised 'while you wait' photographs, indicating the attraction of being able to produce a take-home souvenir.[9]

During this period studio photography developed an increasingly broad appeal. In 1907 the Fuzhou-born Ye Jinglü (1881–1968) had the first of his annual portraits taken. It was the year after his marriage. He maintained the practice until his death in 1968.[10] Ye's first studio portrait was taken in London in 1901 where his relative Luo Fenglu was Chinese ambassador. With the exception of photographs taken with his wife Shuyu to mark their 40th, 50th and 60th wedding anniversaries, the

55 Zhu Jiaqing, 'Pilot Ms Li Xiaqing', published on the cover of *Zhonghua* magazine, 46 (September 1936).

portraits are solo shots. The focus is on the individual, with formats alternating between full-length standing, seated and close-up head and shoulders views, a number of them taken in the Shih Dai and Kuang Hwa studios in Fuzhou. It is not known what motivated Ye to make a photographic record of his life, but he was conscious of being a descendant of Zhu Yuanzhang, the first emperor of the Ming Dynasty (the family had changed their name). In the early 1900s Ye managed the family tea business and pawn shop. He was a collector and kept detailed records of his possessions as well as local news and events.

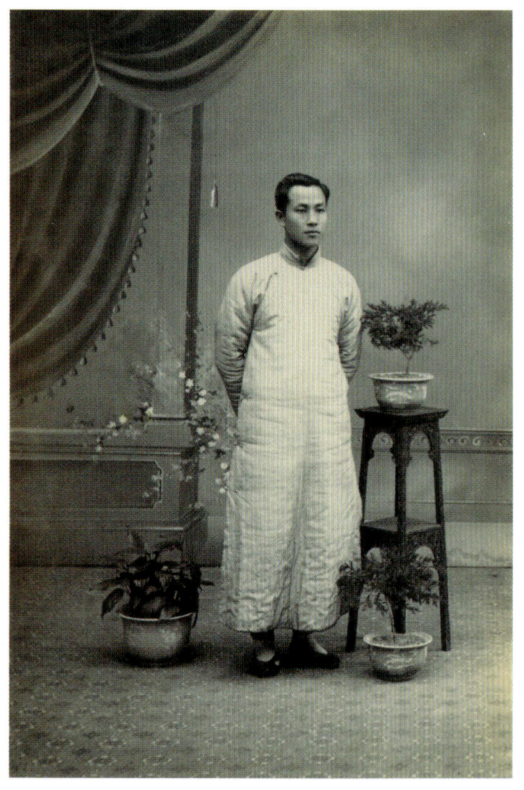

56, 57, 58 Studio portraits of Ye Jinglü taken in 1912, 1950 and 1967, gelatin silver prints, photographers unknown.

The studio portraits of Ye are abstracted from life (a few were taken outdoors), but with their brief captions they also reveal the impact of social and political change over the years: the short Western haircut that he sports in 1912 following the fall of the Qing Dynasty when he cut off his queue; the 'short clothing' and Lenin cap worn with a smile marking New Year's Day in 1950, and the rather sombre mugshot from 1967 with a comment about his hope to see the reunification of mainland China and Taiwan. The one gap in Ye's photographic chronicle is 1952. A paper cut silhouette ('paper shadow' in Chinese) replaces the photographic portrait. The likeness is surrounded by a long calligraphic inscription in which Ye, aged 72, describes a 'sullied year' of family difficulties in the changed political environment. The 'paper shadow' profile, which avoids the camera and the viewer's gaze, was chosen so that he would never forget what happened. In the context of an album that could only be completed by his death, the parts indivisible from the whole, the portrait photographs are conceived to bear witness to a life lived against the backdrop of extraordinary political change and social transformation.

As the 1911 revolution brought centuries of dynastic rule to a close, individuals were faced with radical change on the one hand and continuities of various kinds on the other. The portrait of Ye taken in 1908 at the age of 28 shows him wearing a singlet and shorts, holding an

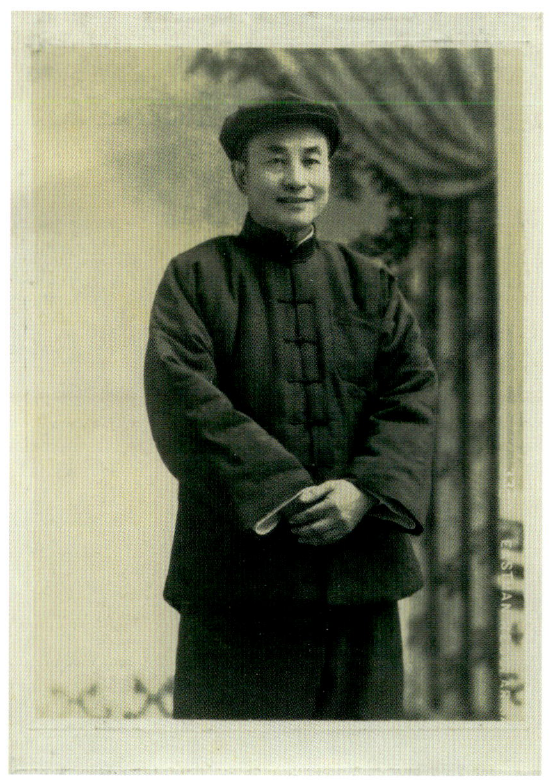

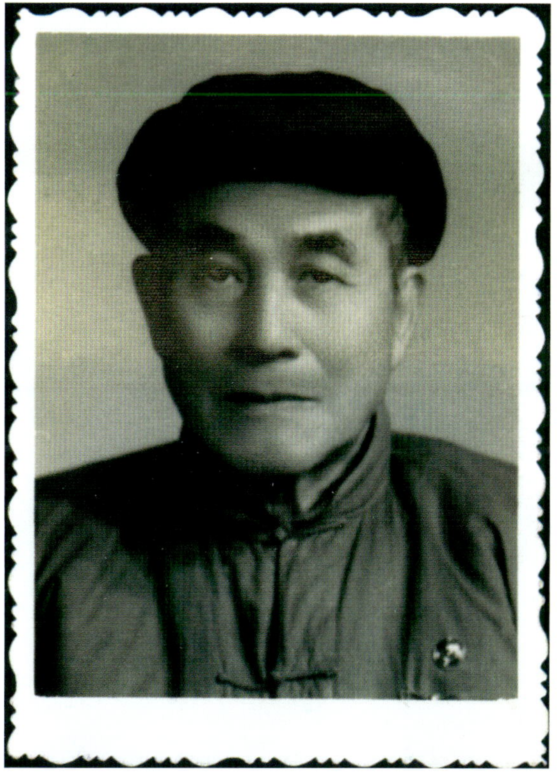

iron dumbbell in each hand. In the early 1900s there was widespread interest among young men in physical activity and self-defence, part of a conscious effort to restore balance to the national psyche and counteract feelings of cultural and political inadequacy. China's ancient martial arts of *wushu* in all their regional forms were revived, readying men for action, to exert control over the nation's destiny. It was against this historical backdrop that this phenomenon, further fuelled by the antics of strongman Hercules O'Brien who performed at the Apollo Theatre in Shanghai 1909 and is said to have challenged any Chinese to take him on, that the Chin Woo Athletic Association was formed. Soon after its foundation, a photography group was established to produce materials relating to martial arts. Photographs of martial arts postures were laid out in sequence and printed as do-it-yourself manuals. One of the key members of the group was Chen Gongzhe (1890–1961), who developed an interest in photography from an early age. A Tarzan-like portrait of Chen wearing nothing more than a leopard skin costume was reproduced in the club's tenth anniversary publication with the caption 'Intrepid and skilled'.[11] The photograph, which was probably taken by editor and member Chen Tiesheng, is a striking portrait reflecting the practical values and ideals of the group.

The association included women – women's physical activity was also promoted – and Chen's sister Chen Shichao was an active member. The camera club organized outdoor photographic excursions to nearby scenic locations. Chen Shichao's Pictorialist photograph of the West Lake in Hangzhou, which was commended by her peers, was included in the group's tenth anniversary publication. Chen Gongzhe's own artistic aspirations are apparent in his low shot from a boat on the West Lake taken in autumn 1917.[12] The setting sun creates silhouettes of the birds and a decorative marker in the lake heightening contrast within the image and a sense of the picturesque.

During the early twentieth century photography became a medium for artistic expression. Chinese photographers were influenced by the work of European and North American photographers and a modernist interest in the abstract beauty of forms and shadows. What came to be known as a photographic way of seeing was melded with Chinese aesthetics to create contemporary images that resonated with the past. Professional and amateur photographers established groups, held exhibitions and published photographs in magazines and books, sometimes combining commerce with personal enthusiasm.

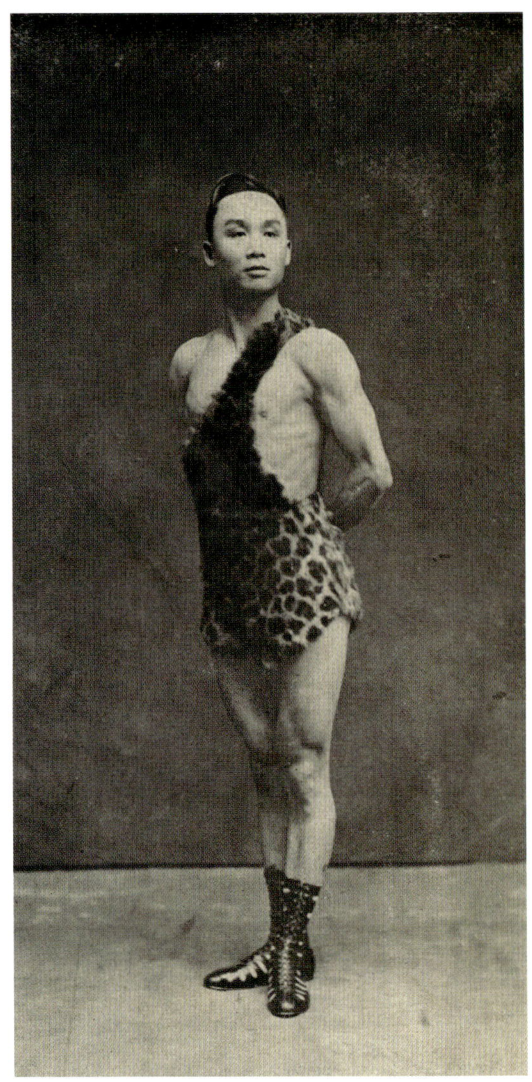

59 Chin Woo Photography Unit, 'Chen Gongzhe', published in *Jingwu benji* (1919).

The earliest amateur photographic group with a primary interest in artistic expression was the Light Society, which developed out of the friendship between Chen Wanli (1892–1969) and Huang Zhenyu (1895–1978), two young academics at Peking University.[13] On weekends

60 Chen Shichao, 'Su Causeway in the Mist', published in *Jingwu benji* (1919).

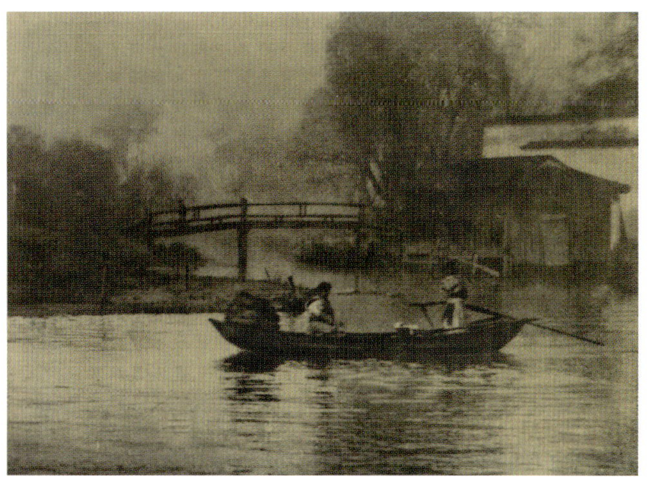

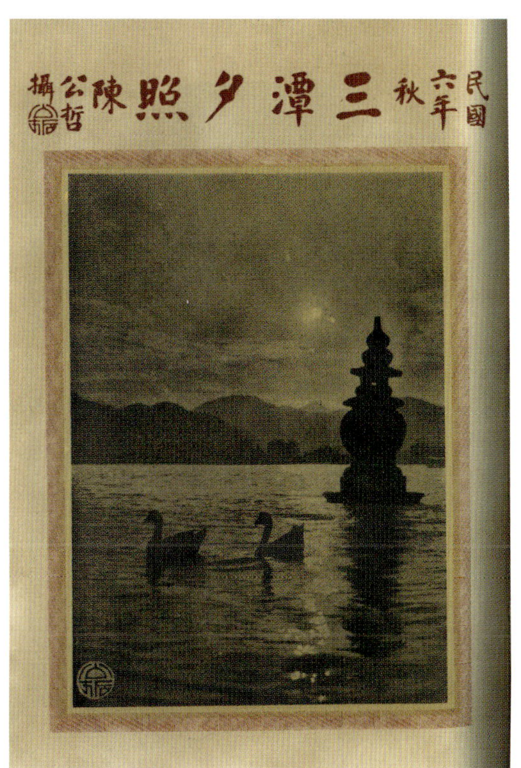

61 Chen Gongzhe, 'Sunset over West Lake', 1917, published in *Jingwu benji* (1919).

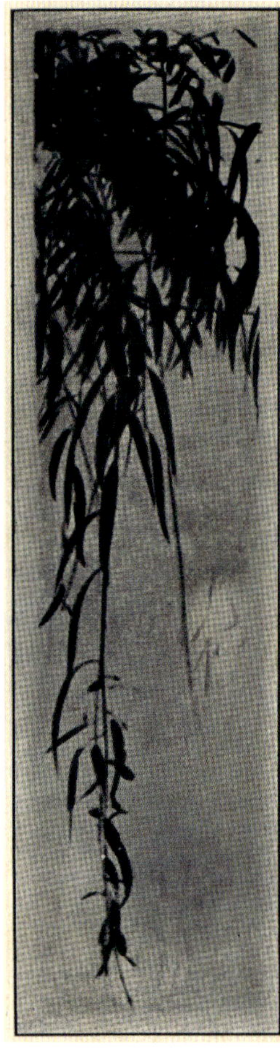

62 Liu Bannong, 'Hanging Willow', *c.* 1927, published in *Beijing Guangshe nianjian*, I (1927).

they took their cameras and tripods to the Forbidden City and other historic sites. Their enjoyment of photography as a leisure activity led them in 1919 to establish the Light Society.[14] For its members, photography was a hobby they took seriously, an attitude that distanced them from the commercial imperatives of professionals. Their philosophy of creative expression was encouraged by figures such as Cai Yuanpei (1868–1940), then president of Peking University, who advocated an 'aesthetic education' that encompassed literature, music and the arts as a way of cultivating a well-rounded individual. Between 1924 and 1928 members of the Light Society held exhibitions in Central Park (renamed Zhongshan Park), originally part of the grounds of the imperial palace.

Liu Bannong (Liu Fu, 1891–1934) edited the society's photographic annual produced in 1927 and wrote an important treatise titled *Bannong on Photography* (1927). He had studied literature at the Sorbonne in France (1921–5) and during his years in Paris had purchased a small box camera (his first encounter with photography was in China as a teenager). He taught himself photography by reading books and magazines and visiting exhibitions. Liu's *Hanging Willow* was included in the first annual publication and reflects his interest in closely observed details of the natural environment. The long vertical format, together with the contrast between the soft-focus dark leaves and the pale ground, evokes the aesthetic of Chinese brush-and-ink painting. Championing the autonomy of photographic practice, with its unique emphasis on light, Liu wrote, 'If you say that the aim of photography is to reproduce painting, then you might as well study painting directly.'[15] For Liu, the primary subject was light. Photographers like Liu and his friends used contemporary visual technology and an aesthetic informed by China's literary and artistic past to create images inspired by everyday surroundings, images suited to artistic analysis and contemplation with no other function than to bring aethetic pleasure to the viewer.

In 1927 Chen Wanli, co-founder of the Light Society, went to Shanghai to participate in the Heavenly Horse Art Society's exhibition. Among the exhibitors was Chin-san Long (Lang Jingshan, 1892–1995), who had set up his own independent agency after many years working in the advertising department of *Shenbao*. With Chen Wanli and Huang Zhenyu as catalysts, the first Chinese art photography association in Shanghai was formed – the China Photography Association.[16] Most of the association's members worked in the publishing industry as art editors, illustrators or managers, and key participants included Chin-san Long, Hu Boxiang (1896–1989) and Ding Song (1891–1972). The latter two both worked for the British American Tobacco Company designing graphics for cigarette packaging, advertisements and new year calendar posters, many of which were based on photographs of Shanghai movie stars and celebrities. Huang Bohui (1894–1981), the owner of *Eastern Times*, was a photography enthusiast and a long-time friend of Chin-san Long, and provided exhibition and meeting space for the association, as well as access to the pages of his newspaper. The close alignment with business and the burgeoning media industry ensured that the exhibitions and activities of the Association were well funded and promoted. The group held annual photographic exhibitions, and following the second exhibition members of the public were encouraged to participate, something that indicated the expanding popularity of the medium as a creative art form.

In a work by Chin-san Long titled *Trying out the Horses*, a bird's-eye view of racehorses being walked by their trainers and jockeys in a pre-race warm-up, we glimpse the friendship and creative collaboration between Long and Chen Wanli (illus. 63). The first race meeting in Shanghai was held in 1848 and the Shanghai Race Club (for expatriates) was established in 1862. By the 1920s the racetrack, which was located in the international settlement, had attracted a good deal of Chinese interest and support, though Chinese could only be honorary members. News of the races were reported both in the Chinese and the Western media, and illustrated magazines often ran track-side stories including 'snapshots' of Chinese women in fashionable dress. In Long's photograph the horses and trainers – rendered in a soft-focus Pictorialist style – occupy the upper section of the image leaving an area of active void in the lower section where Chen has inscribed words of praise about Long's photograph, including the date (1928), signature and name seal. The vertical lines of calligraphy sitting on the surface of the paper create a tension with the depth of field of the photographic view that is accentuated by shadows, forcing the viewer to engage with contrasting visual languages and codes.

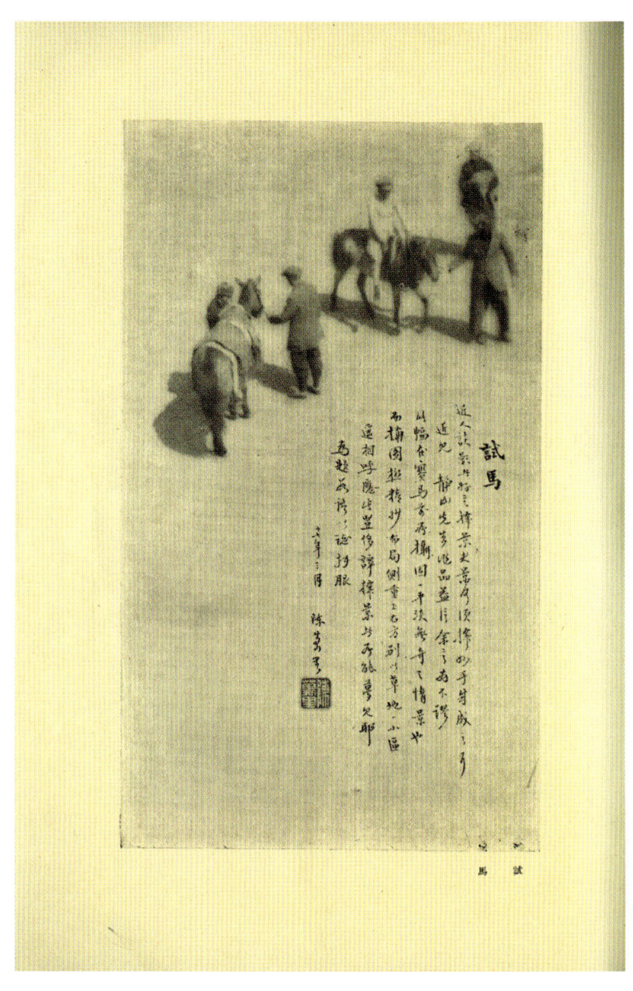

63 Chin-san Long, 'Trying out the Horses', with inscription by Chen Wanli dated 1928, published in *Jingshan sheying ji* (1929).

The photograph features in Chin-san Long's first volume of photographs, which appeared in 1929 and demonstrates his talent and versatility as a photographer. Long had begun his career in newspaper advertising and was hired as a part-time photographer by the *Eastern Times* in 1928 (the newspaper established a photo supplement in 1920 and was where Long's first image appeared). He also published photographs in leading pictorials including *Young Companion*, *Shanghai Sketch* and *Tianpeng*, a magazine dedicated to photography and the unofficial journal of the China Photography Association.

The Black and White Society, established in Shanghai in 1930 by the camera enthusiasts Chen Chuanlin, Nie Guangdi, Lu Shifu (1898–1983) and others, continued and expanded the activity of the China Photography Association. The society held its first exhibition in 1932 in the *Eastern Times* building, a fact that highlighted the close connection and creative tension that continued to exist between photography, commercial art and the media. Members included both professionals and amateurs and the Black and White Society grew to become the largest and most active of Republican China's modern photographic groups.

The society's name is explained by Lu Shifu in terms of physics: if an object scatters all wavelengths, it appears white, and if it absorbs all wavelengths, it appears black, making black and white the constituents of light, and of all colours. It's logo, a reworking of the traditional yin-yang symbol, conveyed the group's inclusive aspirations – a straight line rather than a curved line bisects the fields of black and white, and the two 'eyes' are positioned on one level, representing integrity and equality.[17]

From the outset members of the group had international ambitions, and works by Wu Zhonghang (1899–1976), Lu Shifu and Chen Chuanlin were included in exhibitions held in London, Paris and Chicago. The society's magazine *Black and White Pictorialist* introduced readers to the work of major modern photographers including Albert Renger-Patzcsh (1897–1966), Aenne Biermann (1898–1933) and László Moholy-Nagy (1895–1946), and foreign photography and art magazines such as *Das Deutsche Lichtbild*, *Photographie* and *The Studio*. It was supported by advertisements for Leica, Rollei, Kodak and Agfa, the manufacturers of which all had outlets in Shanghai.

During the 1920s life drawing had attracted considerable controversy in Shanghai and local authorities had at first attempted to ban the use of nude models at the Shanghai Art College. By 1927, however, painting, drawing and photographing nude models had become an acceptable, albeit avant-garde, artistic practice, though models were expensive and hard to find. Chin-san Long's nude studies were published in illustrated magazines such as *Art Life* and classified as 'art photography'. In *Figure Study* (1934) Chen Chuanlin adopts a high vantage point to look down on the model, accentuating the lines and planes of her body and at the same time concealing her identity (illus. 64). His approach to photographing a nude contrasts strongly with Heinz von Perckhammer (1895–1965), a German photographer working in China who published a book with the English title *Noble Nudity in China* (1928). Perckhammer posed his models in exotic, orientalizing tableaux that by comparison are overtly sexualized and provocative. A selection of Perckhammer's photographs was published in *Shanghai Sketch*, causing considerable controversy and a boost in the magazine's circulation.

Wang Yuhuai, the head of *Modern Miscellany*'s photographic studio, was also a member of the Black and White Society. *Two Petite Acrobats*, titled *Flight* in Chinese, was included in the group's first exhibition. It brings to mind the work of Moholy-Nagy. The double-exposure image features two female acrobats silhouetted against a Western-style circus tent and the sky. The trapeze and tent create a web of lines that frames the performers who are about to thrill a crowd with their high-altitude, high-risk act. Taken the moment before the trapeze artists launch into the air, the modernist image communicates latent movement and the physical drama that is about to unfold.

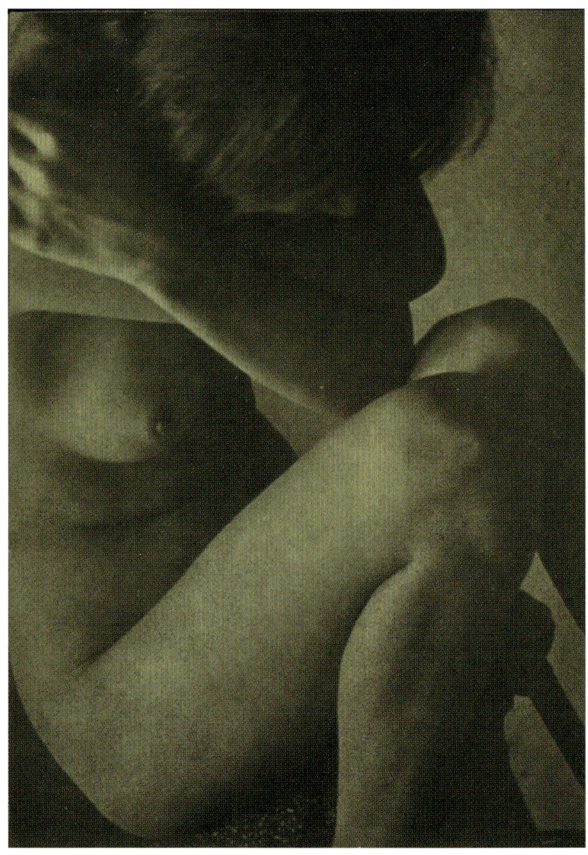

64 Chen Chuanlin, 'Figure Study', published in *Hei bai ying ji*, I (1934).

Wang's photograph may be compared with an image of a funeral procession taken by the German-born Hedda Hammer [Morrison] (1908–1991), who arrived in Beijing in 1933, having studied photography in Munich (illus. 66). Hammer was manager of the Hartung's Photo Shop (established in 1912) from 1933 to 1938 and lived on in the old imperial capital until her departure in 1946. Hartung's, located in the former Legation Quarter, was where expatriates and travellers acquired photographs, had their photographs taken and film developed and printed. It was also a place where people could buy German photographic equipment and supplies. Hammer was inspired by the built environment of the city and the drama of local performances but, unlike Wang Yuhuai, she chose to photograph a Chinese funeral. The airborne paper disks, representing money for use in the afterlife, contrast with the solid arcs of the tram tracks that convey the funeral party towards the viewer and the delicate tracery of overhead electric tram wires. Through Hammer's European-derived contemporary gaze, and Wang's modernist

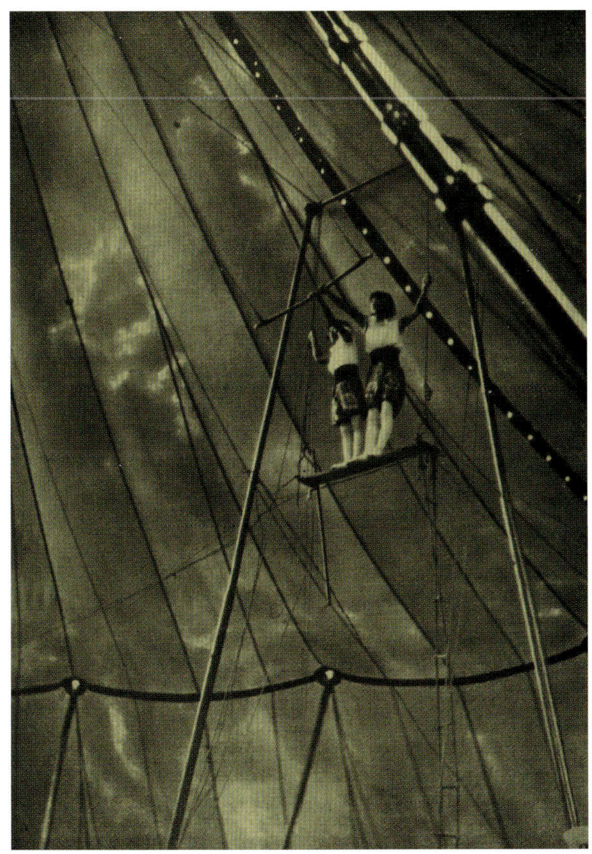

65 Wang Yuhuai, 'Two Petite Acrobats', published in *Hei bai ying ji*, I (1934).

aesthetic, photographs of documentary interest become works of art of considerable stature.

Another significant figure associated with the Black and White Society is the illustrator Ye Qianyu (1907–1995), whose *New Home* is a brilliant example of Shanghai Modern. This work captures a fashionable young woman in a *qipao* standing on the steps outside one of Shanghai's new Art Deco residential buildings (illus. 67). Ye Qianyu was one of Shanghai's leading illustrators and cartoonists, and editor of *Shanghai Sketch* (1928–30) with Zhang Zhenyu, and later of *Modern Miscellany* (1930–37). After 1949 Ye became known for his iconic brush-and-ink paintings of female dancers, many of them drawn from China's ethnically diverse population. Ye's lively figure paintings, the result of years of observation, drawing and photographic practice, are rendered with sure spare lines and intense colour. The ease with which Ye moved across art forms was not uncommon and is indicative of the cross-fertilization between commercial and fine art that energized early twentieth-century visual culture, not only in Shanghai.

Photographers, artists and designers working for the illustrated press created some of the most experimental and engaging visual imagery of the 1930s. *Young Companion* and *Modern Miscellany* were leading exemplars of visual communication. Eye-catching covers helped sell magazines. Artists applied colour to photographs of movie stars, improving on the original, or employed photomontage, a creative splicing and assembly of different photographs, for dramatic effect. Through embellishment and creative intervention, in part inspired by reference to Western pictorials such as *Vanity Fair* and *Vogue*, photographs were incorporated creatively into the cover's overall graphic design. Designers were also influenced by the experimental photomontage works of Dada artists such as Max Ernst and Hannah Höch, though

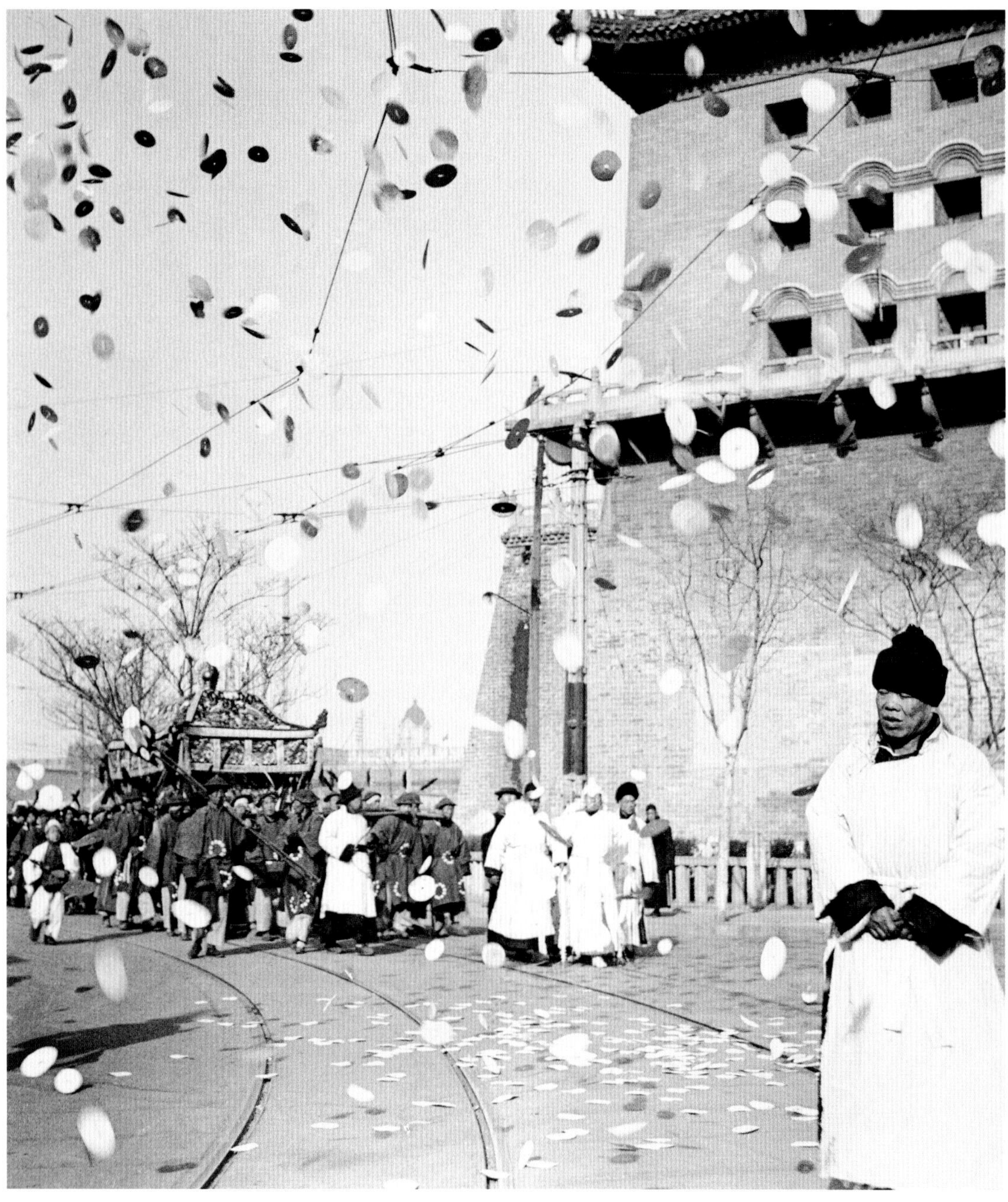

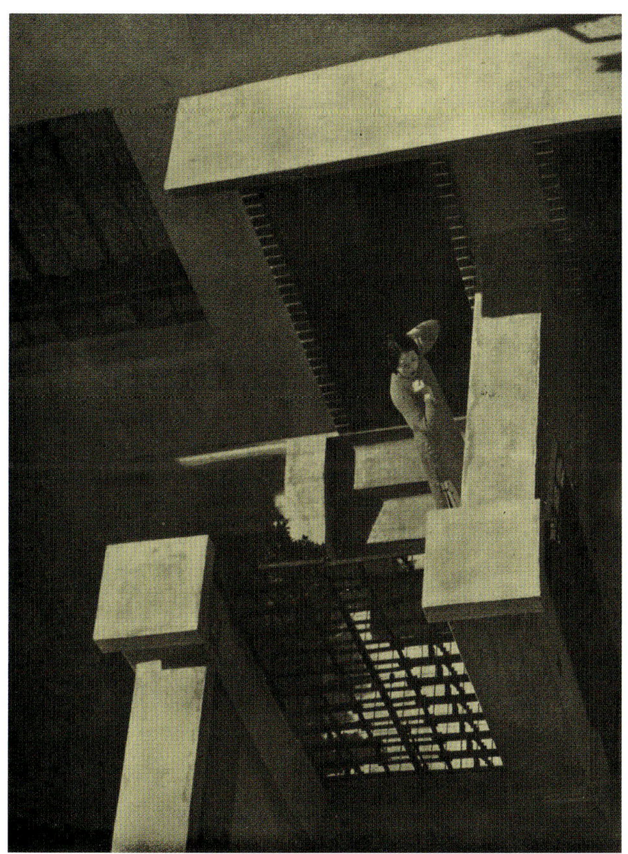

67 Ye Qianyu, 'New Home', published in *Hei bai ying ji*, II (1935).

66 Hedda Hammer [Morrison], *Funeral Procession at the Foot of Zhengyang Gate Watchtower*, 1933–46, gelatin silver print.

the visually arresting results of Chinese appropriations and adaptations were without the political edge of the originals.[18] It is easy to mistake style for substance in Republican-era Shanghai, where the creative milieu was the context for political arguments that would change China. Photography was the perfect medium for ambiguous times, a vehicle for experiment that made possible culturally complex play with surfaces and realities. Artists and editors engaged in a process that Lydia Liu calls 'interpretive translation', something akin to the interlingual practices and extensive translation of foreign texts into Chinese in the modern period.[19]

Chin-san Long carried the practice of photomontage over into his creative work and it became a defining characteristic of many of his later photographs. His 1932 portrait of *Chang Shan Tzu* uses the format of a painted hanging scroll and is reproduced with a couplet by the subject's brother, the artist Chang Da-chien (Zhang Daqian), to mark his 51st birthday, noting that the photograph features the famous Qiping pine tree and the Lion Forest of Mount Huang in Anhui (illus. 68). Long's friend, also an artist, poses as a Daoist immortal. In order to create the image Long selected features from different negatives and re-composed them during the enlarging process. The resultant image is like a Chinese painting with a vertically structured tripartite composition of foreground, middle ground and background that defies single point perspective. Long calls this style of working 'artistic photography'. Through a process of active intervention and manipulation Long overcomes the inflexibility of the camera and eliminates what he describes as 'unnecessary or detrimental effects'. What he strives for is a 'perfect scenery which may never exist in the real world'.[20]

In this fertile, tubulent atmosphere of Rebulican China, many writers and artists, including brush-and-ink painters, and intellectuals of all kinds took up photography as a hobby. As a means of creative expression it fed their practice in other media and their thinking about the world and how it might be changed. With careful editing and darkroom techniques such as masking, burning and dodging, fantastic images could be created that improved upon reality. The manipulation of negatives for creative purposes was a radical intervention that would have far reaching implications when applied to news photography. Darkroom techniques could be used to remove unnecessary or inconvenient details from an image, including individuals who had fallen from favour, or did not fit a particular story. Settings could be enhanced to create an impression that things were better than or different from actuality. Like advertisers, propagandists came to appreciate the malleability of the medium and the ease with which a composite version of truth could be made to stand for reality.

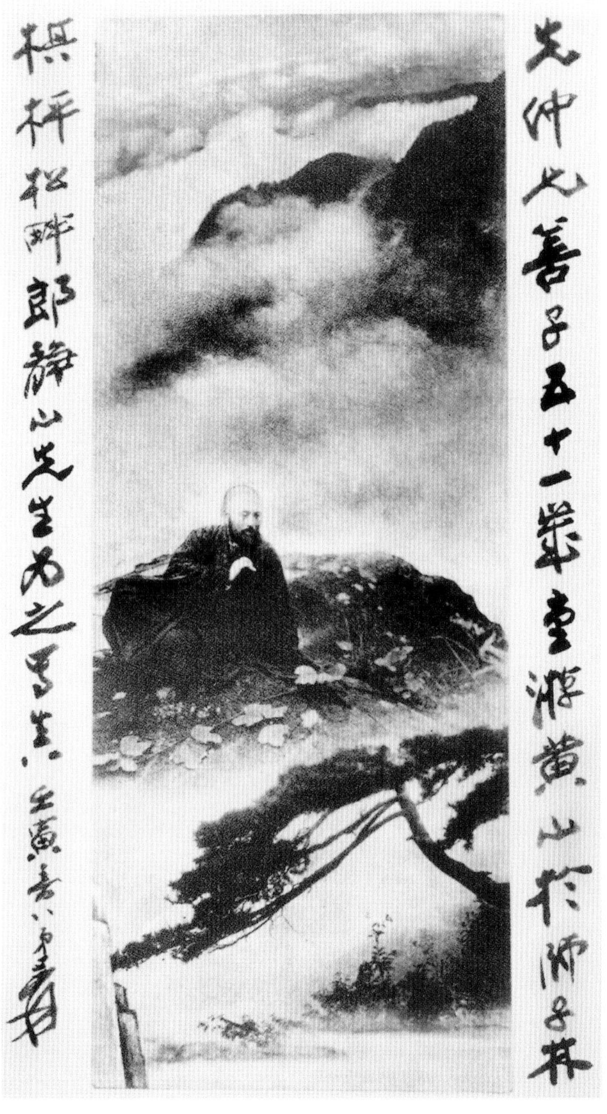

68 Chin-san Long, 'Portrait of Chang Shan Tzu', 1932, published in Hsiao Yong-sheng, *Hua-yi, Chi-chin, Long Chin-san* ('A Collection of Artworks by Long Chin-san', Taipei, 2004).

four

War and Propaganda

On 28 August 1937 the Japanese army bombed Shanghai South Station, where hundreds of refugees, including women and children, awaited evacuation. The Beijing-born photographer H. S. Wong (Wang Xiaoting, 1900–1981), known as 'Newsreel Wong', was the first to reach the scene of devastation. His image of a crying baby surrounded by wreckage was sent around the world via William Randolph Hearst's International News Service and 'News of the Day' newsreel, eliciting a strong emotional response. It was chosen by *Life* magazine as 'picture of the week', accompanied by the headline 'The Camera Overseas: 136,000,000 people see this picture of Shanghai's South Station', making it one of the most recognized images of Japanese atrocities and the Pacific War (illus. 69).[1]

Related photographs that show individuals attending the distraught baby in the chaos of the moment were published in *Look* magazine, causing Japanese nationalist groups to claim that Wong's photograph was staged.[2] Wong later said:

> I walked across the railway track, and made many long scenes with the burning overhead bridge in the background. Then I saw a man pick up a baby from the track, and carry him to the platform. He went to get another badly injured child. The mother lay dead on the tracks. As I filmed this tragedy, I heard the sound of planes returning. Quickly I shot my remaining few feet of film on the baby. I ran toward the child intending to carry him to safety, but the father returned. The bombers passed overhead. No bombs were dropped.[3]

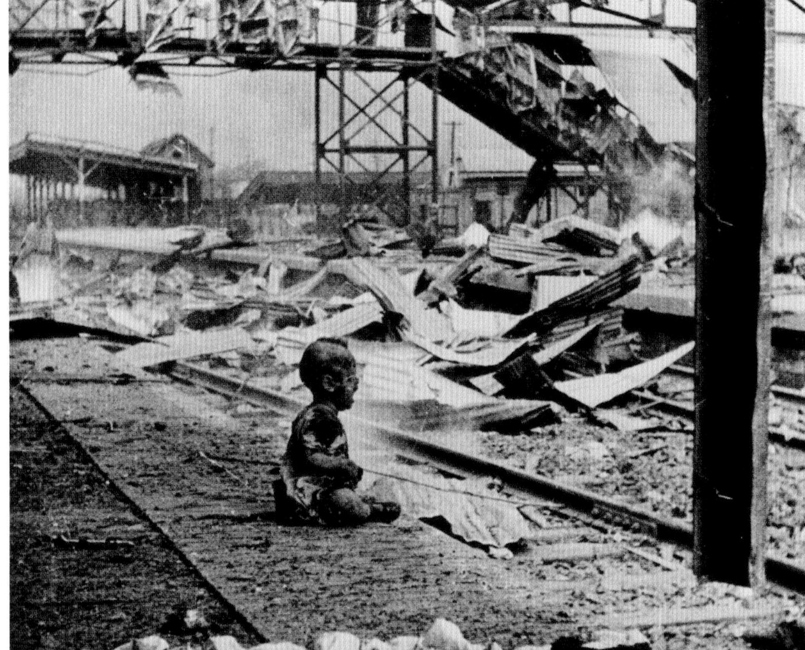

69 H. S. 'Newsreel' Wong, Chinese *Baby at South Station, Shanghai, 28 August 1937*, gelatin silver print.

Responding to the Japanese accusation of staging, the photographer and historian Gu Zheng observed: 'Photography is a special mode of remembering. Ever since its invention it has taken on the responsibility to resist forgetting. It is for this reason that images have been reinterpreted by different interests to fight against the possibility of remembering.'[4]

Another photograph that has an iconic status in the history of Chinese photography was taken in 1938 and shows three Communist soldiers perched on a mountain ridge alongside the Great Wall near Xifengkou, their artillery aimed at the invisible Japanese enemy. But it engages with a very different kind of remembering. This legendary image by Sha Fei (Situ Chuan, 1912–1950) encourages the viewer to create a visual and metaphoric link between the soldiers and the mountains and sturdy watchtowers that have stood guard over Chinese territory for hundreds of years. Created away from the combat zone, it was conceived to engender feelings of patriotism and a commitment to defend the motherland.

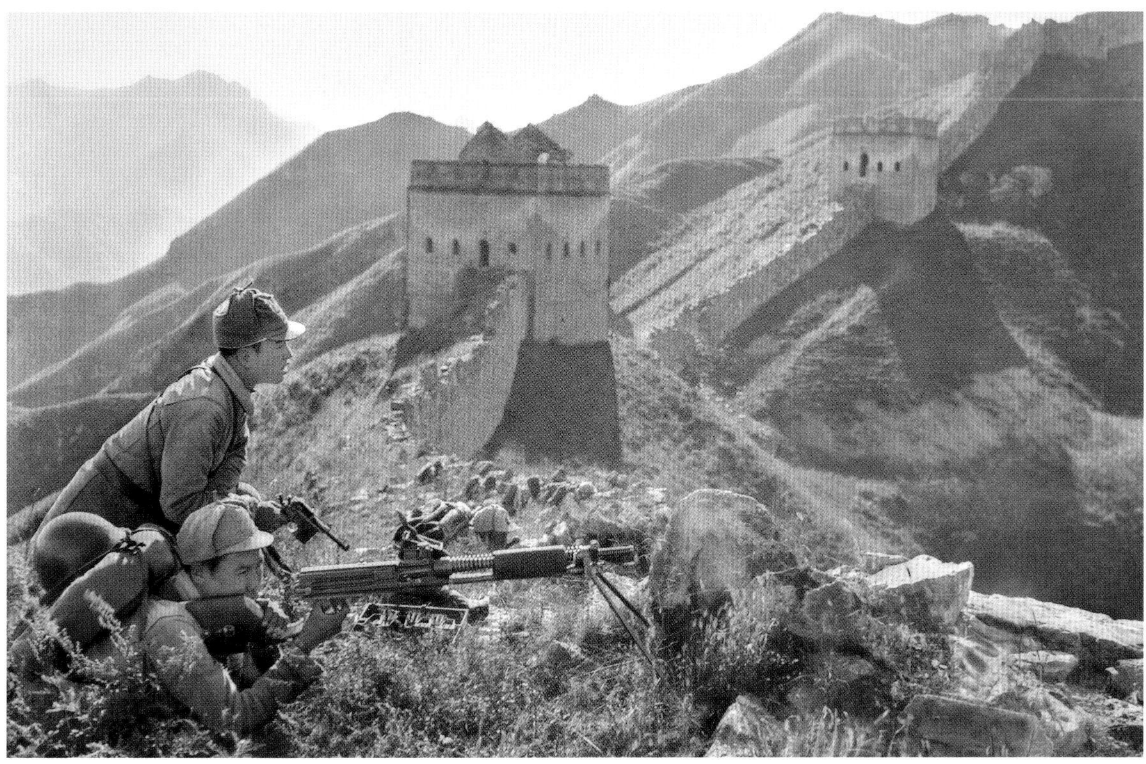

70 Sha Fei, *Fighting on the Ancient Great Wall*, 1938, gelatin silver print.

The photograph was included in an exhibition of the military achievements of the People's Liberation Army (PLA) in the Palace Museum, Beijing, in 1950. It outlived its creator, who was executed in March of that year, charged with the murder of the Japanese doctor who had been treating him for psychological problems and tuberculosis. Sha Fei worked as a radio operator in Guangdong before moving to Shanghai, where he became a member of the Black and White Society. After the outbreak of the Sino-Japanese War in July 1937 he wrote an article titled 'Photography and National Salvation' in which he articulated his growing political consciousness and belief in the power of photography to arouse patriotic sentiment. He joined the army and was assigned to document the war in northern China from the Communist Party (CCP) base in the Jin-Cha-Ji Border Region at the junction of Shanxi, Chahar (in present-day Inner Mongolia) and Hebei provinces.

His job was to train photojournalists and establish a news agency. The *Jin-Cha-Ji Pictorial*, a propaganda magazine, was the first of its kind to be produced in a Communist-controlled area (published 1942–7). Sha Fei's Great Wall photograph first appeared in the *Jin-Cha-Ji Pictorial* (volume 4, 1943). The news agency mounted photo exhibitions about recent campaigns in army camps, offices and schools, and on village and city walls, which became an important feature of cultural life in the so-called 'liberated areas'. Sha Fei's deputy, Shi Shaohua (1918–1998), took a series of photographs of the 'Wild Goose Plume' waterborne force, a local militia that patrolled Baiyangdian, the largest natural lake in northern China and home to many varieties of wild geese. The intention of the series was to promote awareness of the active role played by citizens in defence. A selection of the photographs were published in the *Pictorial* (volume 6, 1944).

71 Shi Shaohua, *Wild Goose Plume Force*, 1944, gelatin silver print.

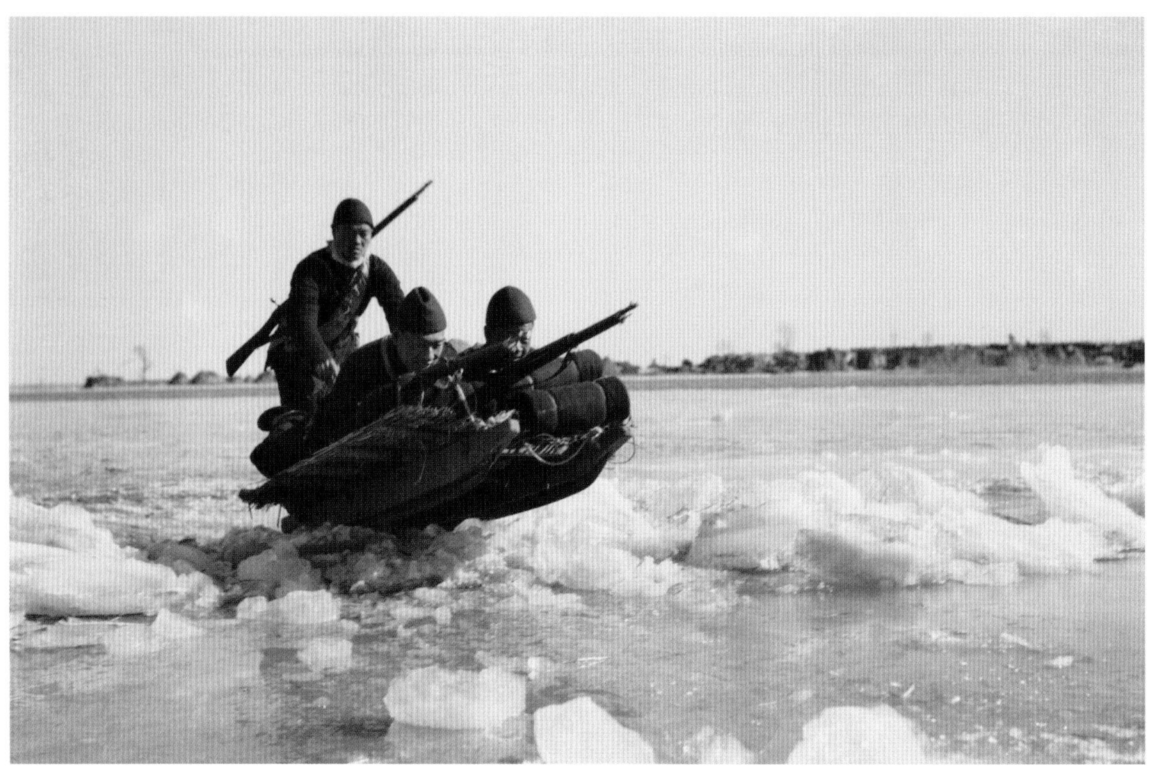

Another prominent propaganda photographer was Wu Yinxian (1900–1994) who, like Sha Fei, started out as a member of the Black and White Society. While studying at the Art Academy in Shanghai, he purchased a Brownie box camera and taught himself photography. In 1932 he went to work at the Tianyi Film Studio where he painted backdrops and wrote movie credits. Later he was the cinematographer for some of China's best-known early films including *Sons and Daughters of the Storm* (1935) and *Street Angel* (1937).

After the fall of Shanghai to the Japanese, Wu moved to the Communist base at Yan'an and became head of the technical and photography sections of the newly established Eighth Route Army film group. One of the movie cameras that would be used by Wu Yinxian was given to the group by the Dutch film-maker Joris Ivens (1898–1989). Ivens, himself a communist, travelled to China in 1938 with the combat photographer Robert Capa (1913–1954) as his cinematographer for *The 400 Million* (1939), a documentary about modern China and the war of resistance against Japan. Capa had photographed the Spanish Civil War and would go on to photograph the D-Day landing in Normandy. He was a driving force behind the formation of Magnum, an international photographic cooperative formed with Henri Cartier-Bresson (1908–2004) and others in 1947 in the aftermath of the Second World War. Ivens had hoped to film in Yan'an, where the American journalist Edgar Snow (1905–1972) had interviewed Mao Zedong and other leaders for his book *Red Star Over China* (1937), but was unsuccessful. Before he left China a clandestine meeting was arranged and Wu Yinxian was sent to collect the camera and some precious unused film stock. Iven's camera, a much-valued gift, was used by the film unit to produce many historically significant documentary films.[5]

One of Wu Yinxian's most widely published photographs shows Dr Norman Bethune (1890–1939) performing an operation on a wounded soldier at a field hospital set up inside a small temple not far from the battlefront near Laiyuan in Hebei (illus. 72). It was taken in October 1939 and published in the inaugural issue of *Jin-Cha-Ji Pictorial* (1942) as part of a double-page spread commemorating the work of Bethune, who died from blood poisoning a month later. A poignant long shot of the same temple-hospital, taken by Wu Yinxian and Sha Fei's close colleague, Luo

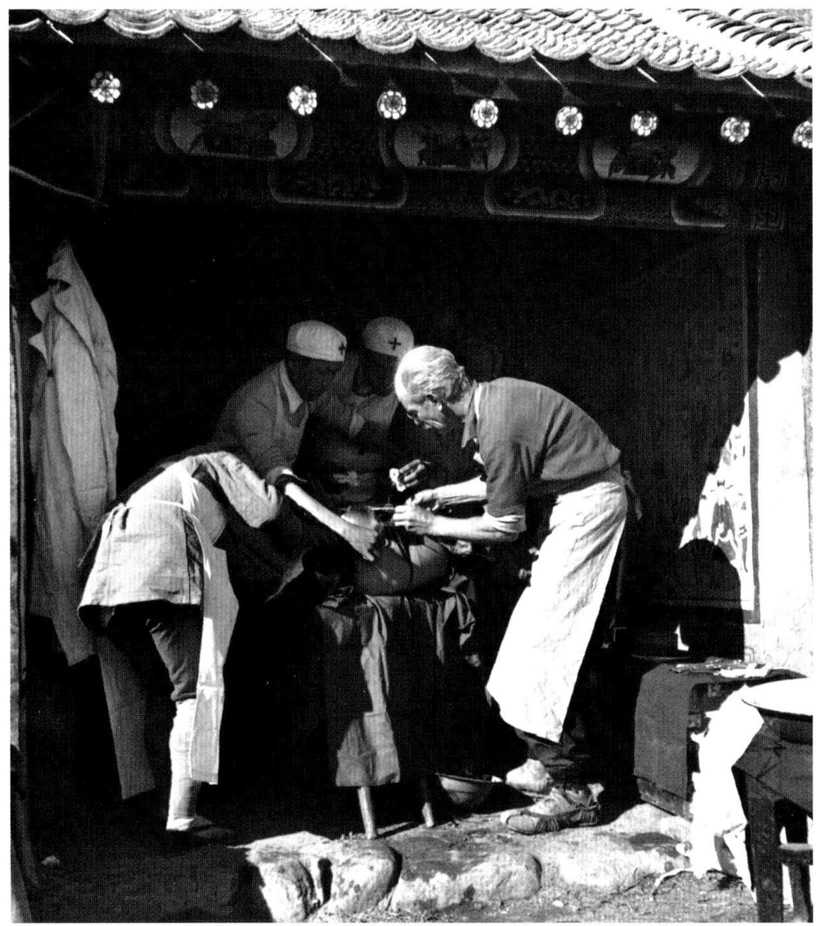

72 Wu Yinxian, *Dr Norman Bethune*, October 1939, gelatin silver print.

Guangda (1919–1997), shows a long line of wounded soldiers lying on makeshift stretchers, waiting their turn to be operated on. Bethune, a Canadian communist, had arrived at the Jin-Cha-Ji Border Region in June 1938 to work as an advisor on sanitation. Soon after Bethune's death Mao Zedong wrote a speech praising his selfless devotion to Chinese life and the Communist cause and hailing him as a role model. Bethune was a keen amateur photographer and his Kodak Retina II camera was bequeathed to Sha Fei. In the introduction to Wu Yinxian's book *General Knowledge of Photography* (1939), Sha Fei describes photography as 'a

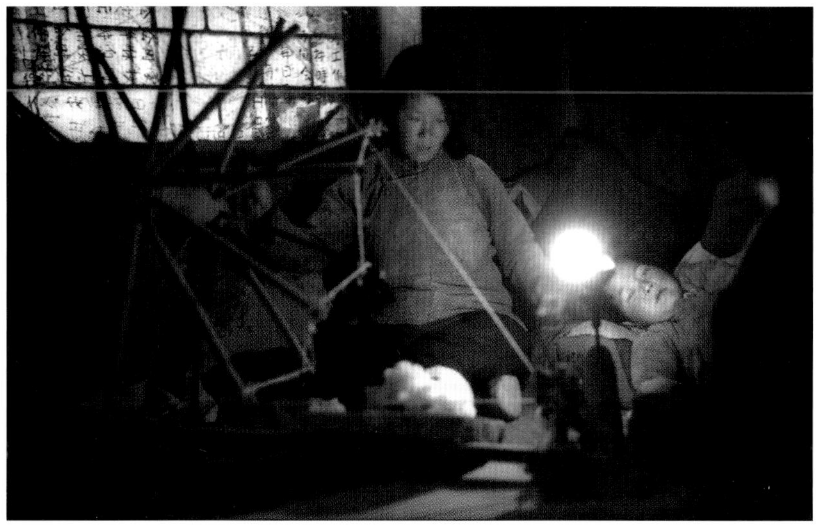

73 Li Tu, *Evening in a Farmer's Home (Spinning Cotton)*, 1943, gelatin silver print.

sharp weapon of combat' and a 'propaganda tool for recording news of great political significance that one is duty bound to report'. He emphasized the importance of artistic training, scientific knowledge and correct political consciousness, recognizing that the unique attributes of photography gave it the power to reach and influence large numbers of people. That view would enjoy a long legacy in China, exerting a significant influence over photographic practice in the ensuing decades.

Other kinds of photographs that have had an ongoing resonance in later image making are genre scenes. These include such works as *Evening in a Farmer's Home (Spinning Cotton)* by Li Tu (1911–1992), which shows a tireless wife working by an oil lamp, a young child lying at her side. The homely scene of rural life, chosen for the back cover of the third issue of the *Jin-Cha-Ji Pictorial* (1943), drew attention to a photo-essay about the heroism of women and children who were producing cotton and woollen yarn for use in the war of resistance. Li Tu's image contrasts strongly with the photographs of men at war, balancing activity and repose, age and youth to create a paean to a simple life guided by political ideals and a commitment to hard work.

In 1942 a photography group was established in Yan'an, led by Wu Yinxian, to train a new generation of revolutionary image makers who could use the modern medium rather than painting or woodcuts. It was a successful training model that was repeated for successive groups. After Mao Zedong was named chairman of the Politburo of the CCP Central Committee in March 1943, photographic images of Mao would become ubiquitous in the Communist-controlled regions of China. The September issue of the *Jin-Cha-Ji Pictorial*, for example, begins with a full-page photographic portrait, *Comrade Mao Zedong, Leader of the Chinese Communist Party*. This and other portraits of Mao were influenced by images of Joseph Stalin (1878–1953), General Secretary of the Communist Party of the Soviet Union Central Committee, and were intended to counter portraits of Chiang Kai-shek that circulated elsewhere in China and overseas.

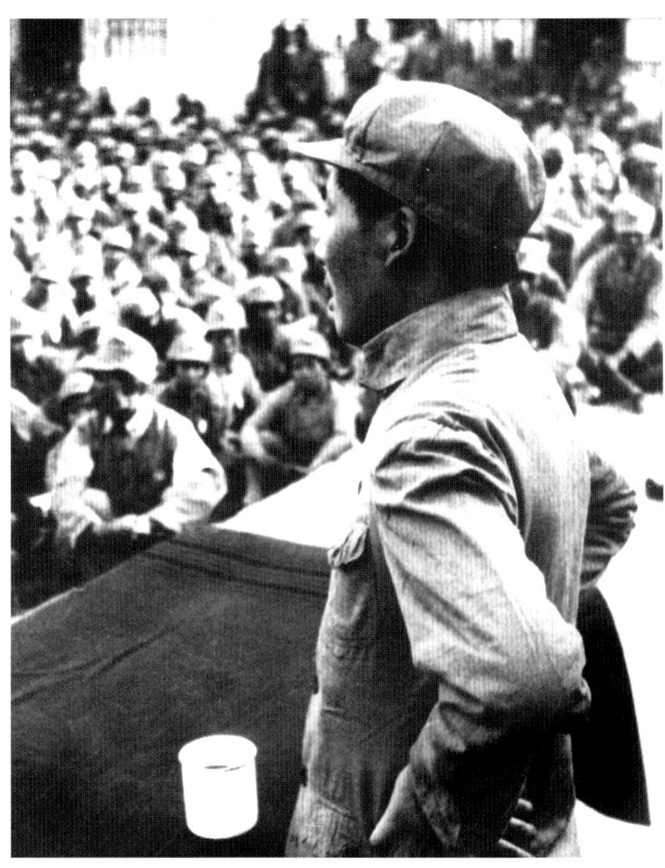

74 Xu Xiaobing, *Mao Zedong Making a Speech at Yan'an*, 1938, gelatin silver print.

Much earlier, in 1938, Xu Xiaobing (1916–2009) took a photograph of Mao that presaged his leadership of the country. Mao stands in profile to the right of the frame, his hands placed confidently on his hips, towering over a crowd of soldiers. The photograph, published in the *Eighth Route Army Military and Politics Journal* in 1940, was taken during a series of lectures titled 'On Protracted War' delivered to soldier-students at the Military and Political University for the War of Resistance Against Japan in Yan'an, in which Mao outlined his strategy for the war.[6] In China there is a tradition of depicting rulers and leaders using a frontal view in order to emphasize their integrity and authority, a practice that was further adapted to suit ideological needs after 1949. Xu Xiaobing explains the reason for the unusual side-on view: 'If I had stood in front [of Mao] I would have had to stand in the middle of the crowd . . . there really was nowhere to stand, so all I could do was move over to the side and take the shot.'[7]

The 1938 portrait of Mao was the first of many that Xu would make of the Communist leader over the coming decade. He also made many striking photographs of army life. One memorable image is that of a soldier standing in a tree staring out over a flat plain, his job to alert Communist forces of the approaching enemy. Like Wu Yinxian, Xu Xiaobing began his working life at the Tianyi Film Studio in Shanghai. In 1937, after the forced closure of another company where he was a cinematographer, he worked at the Northwest Film Company before joining the Eighth Route Army where he was assigned to work for the newly constituted Yan'an Film Company.

During the 1930s Japan continued to strengthen its military and cultural control over many parts of China, most notably Taiwan, which it had occupied in 1895, and Manchukuo, annexed in 1931. In 1934 the Manchukuo News Agency, run by Tokyo to control news and information in the new state, issued a series of official photographs to mark the ascension of Puyi, the dethroned Qing emperor, as Emperor of Manchukuo (1934–45). One of the most influential Japanese photographers working in Changchun was Fuchikami Hakuyō (1889–1960), a key member of the Manchuria Photographers' Association and chief editor of the *Pictorial Manchuria* magazines (1933–44), published by the powerful South Manchurian Railway Corporation, which contained sophisticated propaganda about life in the colonized domain.

75 Teng Nan-kuang, *Ferryboat on the Tamsui River*, 1940, gelatin silver print.

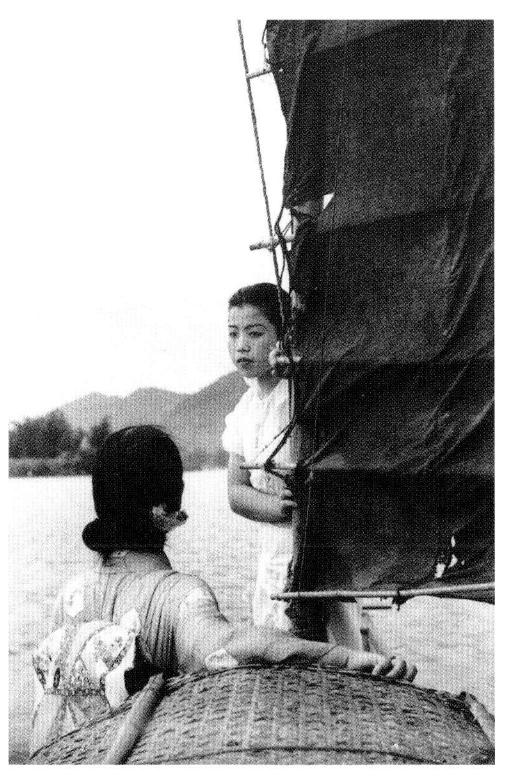

In Taiwan Japanese language and dress was introduced to build a sense of Japanese identity in the population. One of the best-known photographers to document life on the island in this period was Teng Nan-kuang (1907–1971), who had taken up photography as a hobby while studying economics in Japan. Teng participated in the inaugural International Photography Exhibition held in Shanghai in 1934 and had work published in Japanese photographic magazines. After returning to Taiwan in 1935 he opened a camera shop in Taipei. Teng travelled extensively on the island to create a visual archive of life at that time. In *Ferryboat on the Tamsui*

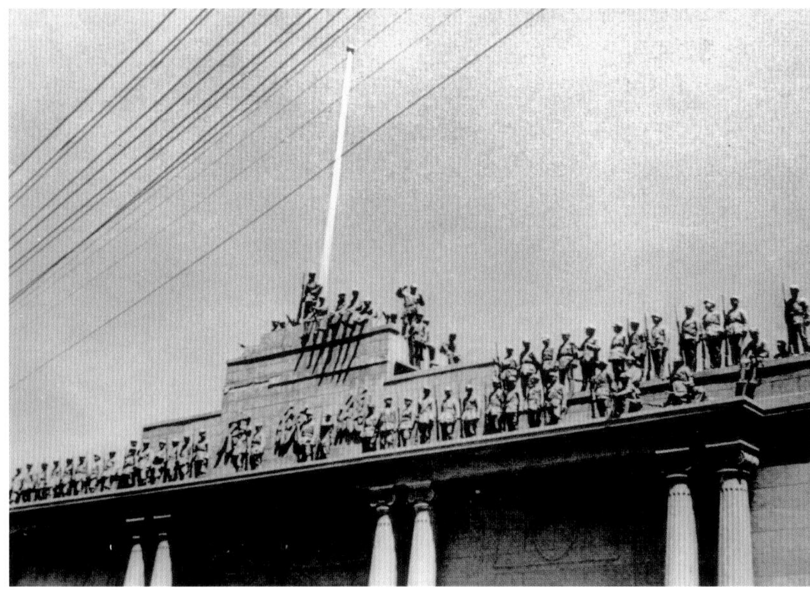

76 Zou Jiandong, *Victory Nanjing*, May 1949, gelatin silver print.

River, taken in 1940, a local woman in Western dress looks back in the direction of the camera, while another, wearing a Japanese kimono, looks straight ahead. Using the metaphor of a boat Teng evokes the uncertain future of the island. Two other important photographers who were active in Taiwan during this period are Chang Tsai (1916–1994) and Lee Mingtiao (*b.* 1922). Together with Teng Nan-kuang they are known as the 'Three Swordsmen of Taiwanese Photography'.

The United Front between the Nationalist and Communist forces collapsed with the surrender of Japan and the end of the Second World War, and the battle for political control of China took over. Brokered by the United States, negotiations between Chiang Kai-shek, leader of the Nationalist Party, and CCP chairman Mao Zedong, produced an agreement but no lasting peace, and civil war was declared in 1946. The United States withdrew troops and cut military aid to the nationalist government and, after heavy fighting and great loss of life on both sides, the Communist Party claimed victory.

The Communist capture of the nationalist capital of Nanjing is chronicled in a famous photograph by Zou Jiandong (1915–2005).

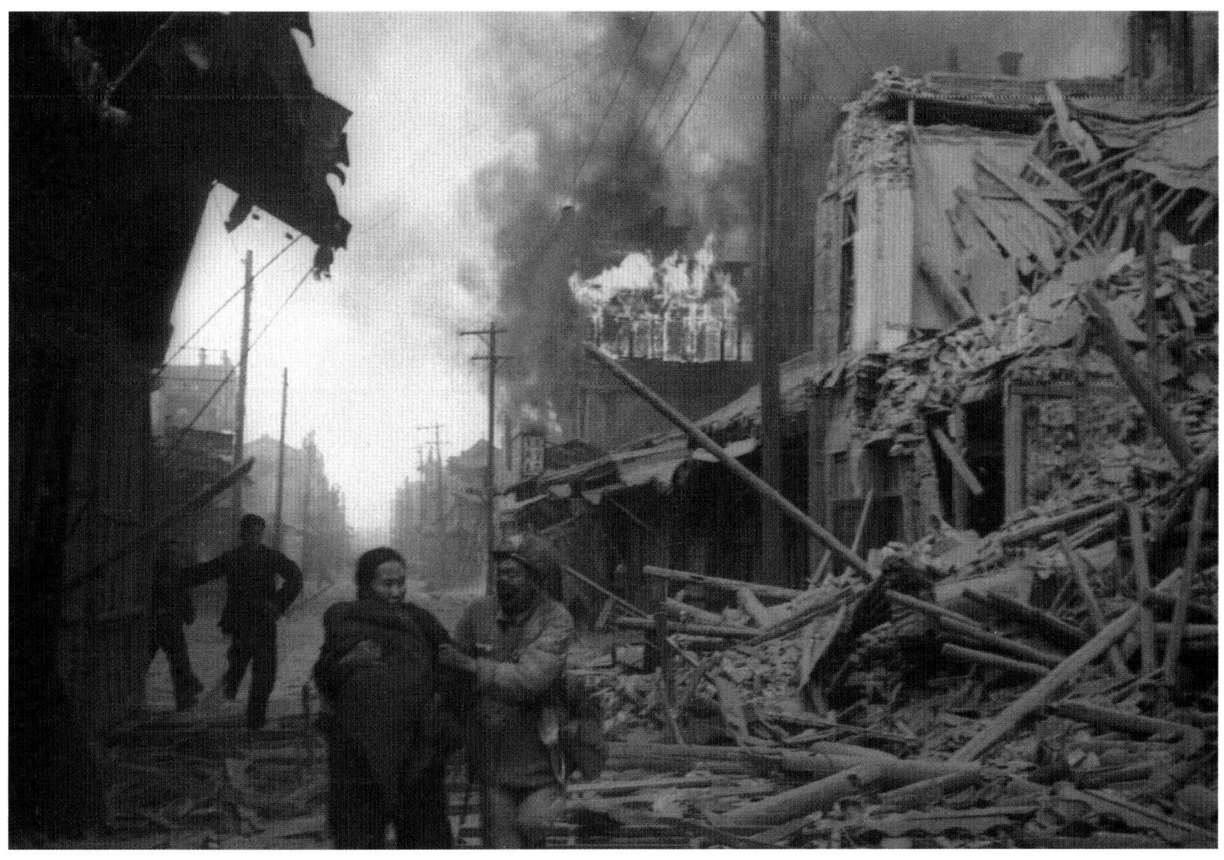

77 Yuan Ling with Xiao Chi, *Rescue*, April 1949, gelatin silver print.

Triumphant soldiers stand under a bare flagpole on top of Chiang Kai-shek's presidential palace, their forms echoing the solid masonry columns below. As there were no photographers with the military unit that overran the palace, permission was sought to film and photograph a reenactment two days later.[8] The photograph was later titled 'Heroically overturning heaven and earth', a line from Mao's poem about the capture of Nanjing, and is a fine example of an image constructed in order to evoke a particular historical moment.

Another widely circulated civil war photograph was taken in April 1949 after the PLA broke through the final line of resistance in Taiyuan, Shanxi. A PLA soldier leads a mother and child through a scene of urban devastation after the retreating nationalist army torched Willow Lane, one of the busiest streets in Taiyuan, in a failed attempt to block Communist forces. The photograph by Yuan Ling (*b*. 1924), the chief photographer attached to the Political Department of the 19th Corps (assisted by Xiao Chi, *b*. 1928) was published in the *North China People's Liberation Army Pictorial* in 1949. Since then it has featured in many publications and exhibitions to illustrate the duty of PLA soldiers to 'Serve the People'.

The establishment of the Central People's Government announced by Mao Zedong on the rostrum above Tiananmen, the Gate of Heavenly Peace, on 1 October 1949 was one of the most significant events in twentieth-century Chinese history and marked the end of decades of international and civil war. Chen Zhengqing's photograph of the foundational moment was published in the *People's Daily* on 2 October and in newspapers and magazines across the country. Chen Zhengqing (1917–1966), who was in Beijing as the special correspondent for the influential *Northeast Pictorial*, became deputy director of the News Photography Bureau under the State Office of News and Publishing of the new government. He had joined the Party in 1937, the year after his graduation from Shanghai's Datong University. After studying in Yan'an and working in northwestern and northeastern China, he was appointed in 1946 to head of the photographic department of the newly established *Northeast Pictorial*.

Hou Bo (*b*. 1924), who rose to prominence as one of the most trusted of Mao's photographers, was also assigned to document the 1 October announcement on the rostrum. In her compelling image Mao gazes out to the assembled crowd, whereas in Chen's photograph the chairman's eyes are downcast as he reads from the declaration. Born into a family of intellectuals, Chen Zhengqing was vilified at the start of the Cultural Revolution. His life ended tragically in 1966 when he and his wife He Hui (1920–1966), a Party photographer and archivist, committed suicide. Hou Bo's longevity (she was the wife of Xu Xiaobing) and a renewed interest in historic photography have brought her public prominence in recent decades. Hou and Chen's photographs, with their focus on history-making, contrast strongly with the images of Henri Cartier-Bresson who, while on assignment for *Life* magazine, took many photographs of people

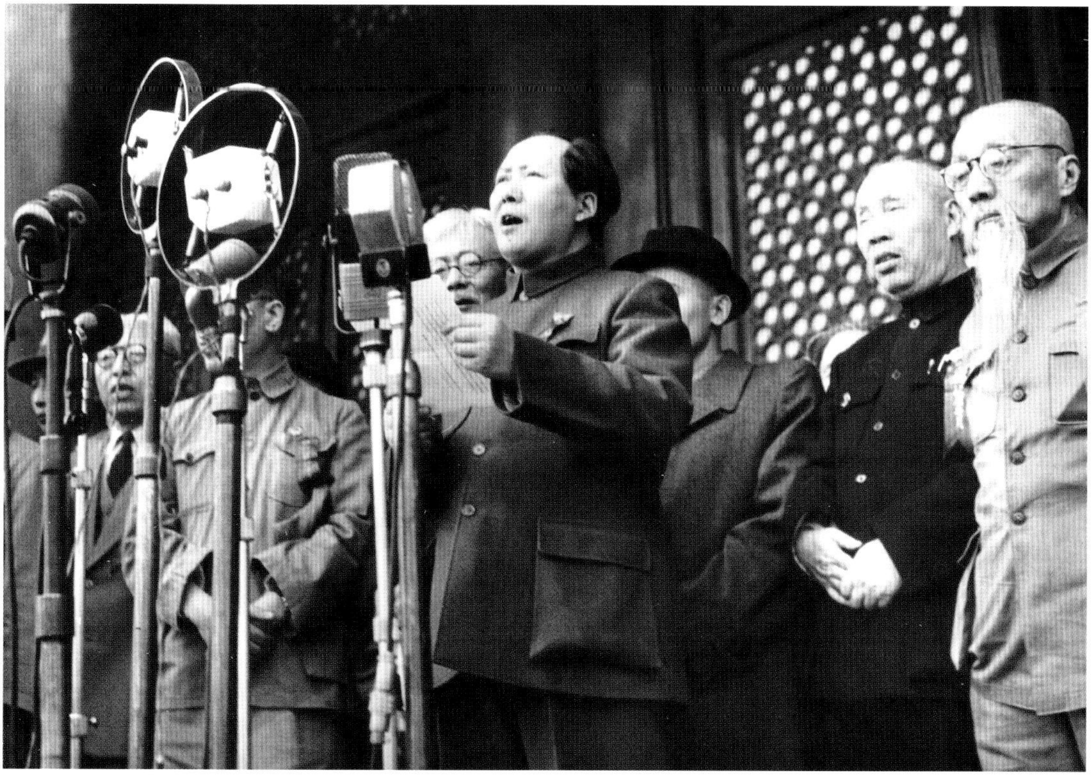

78 Hou Bo, *Founding Ceremony, the People's Republic of China*, 1 October 1949, gelatin silver print.

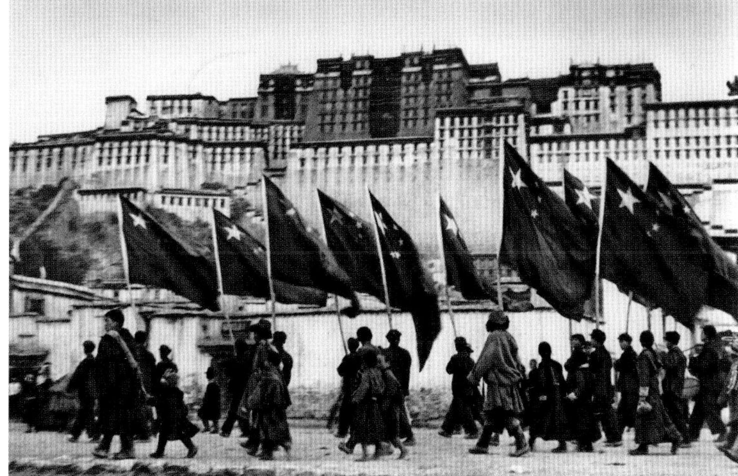

79 Jiang Xiande, *Entry of Advanced Detachment into Lhasa*, 1951, gelatin silver print.

and street life in cities across China in the period immediately before and after the Communist victory.

Soon after the establishment of the People's Republic of China (PRC), the CCP moved to extend its rule over the resource-rich territory of Tibet. Jiang Xiande (*b*. 1927) photographed the entry of Communist troops into Lhasa on 9 September 1951, after Tibetan officials were forced to signed a controversial agreement on the 'Peaceful Liberation of Tibet', claiming Chinese sovereignty over the Tibetan domain (illus. 79).[9] Three years later Hou Bo photographed Mao Zedong flanked by Tibet's spiritual leaders, the young Dalai Lama and Panchen Lama, in Beijing in September 1954 on the occasion of talks coinciding with the First Meeting of National Representatives. Later, in 1959, the Dalai Lama fled from Tibet during an uprising against Chinese rule.

Photography played an important role in the CCP's propaganda offensive to win hearts and minds across China. The photographers who shaped the role that photography would play in New China were trusted individuals who had worked under difficult conditions during the long war years. Shi Shaohua effectively ran the News Photography Bureau in the State Office of News and Publishing and in 1952 became director of the News Photography Department of the Xinhua News Agency. A book called *News Photography* published in 1953 refers to the 'political task' of news photographers 'to reflect glorious scenes of struggle by the Chinese people to create a new historic epoch'. The author, Mao Songyou (1911–2000), a photographer working at the agency, makes it clear that news photography could not be divorced from politics (he published an 'Introduction to Photojournalism' in the *Black and White Pictorialist* in 1936–7[10]).Together with other print media photography would play an active role in the ideological moulding of the population. Photographers, Mao said, take photographs from life, applying artistic processes in order to influence the thoughts, feelings and actions of viewers. The reason why photography could be used to 'educate' people was because of its 'power to move people's emotions'. He called for 'photographic workers to increase the beauty of their images such that they sing the praise [of New China]'.[11]

A photograph of construction workers fixing a chimney at the Anshan Steelworks in northeastern China taken by Cai Shangxiong

80 Cai Shangxiong, *Repairing the Coal Chimney at Anshan Steelworks, Liaoning*, 1954, gelatin silver print.

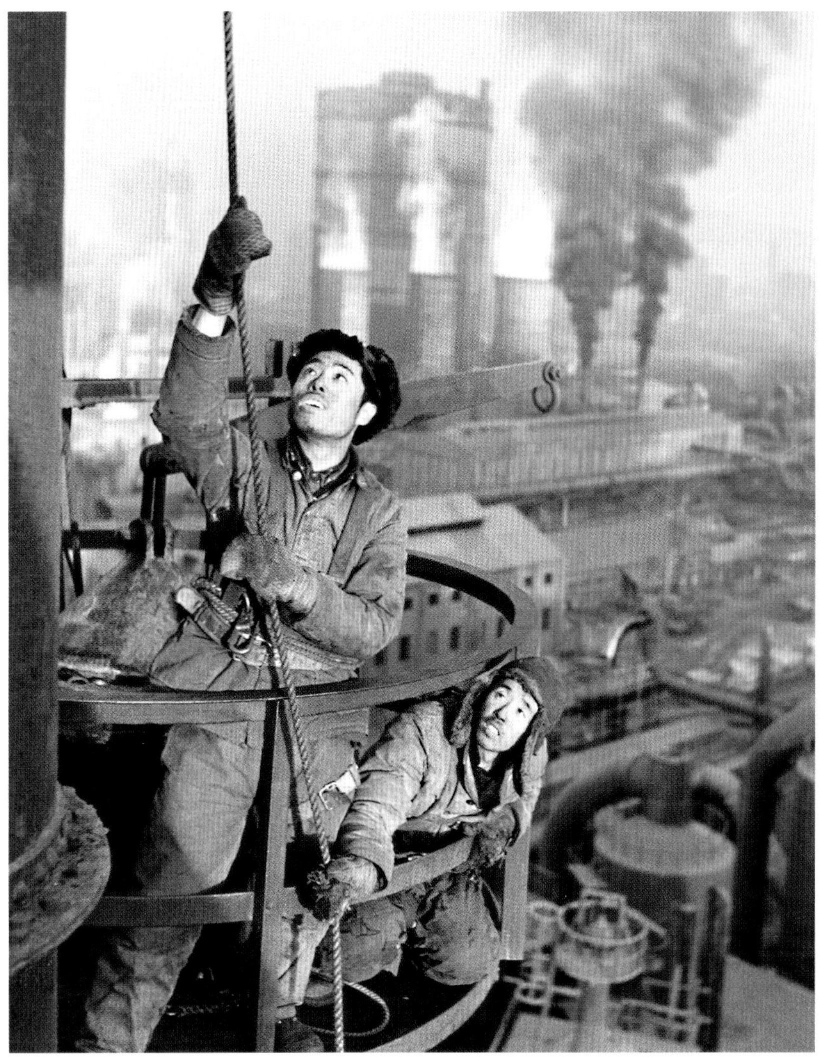

(*b*. 1919) in 1954 is an iconic work of this kind. Cai had worked as a photographer with the *Jin-Cha-Ji Pictorial* and was sent by the News Photography Bureau to report on the Korean War. He was assigned to the *People's Pictorial*, established in 1950, where he rose to become deputy general editor. In Cai's photograph two young workers 'heroically' carry out repairs on a chimney so that steel production can resume. The

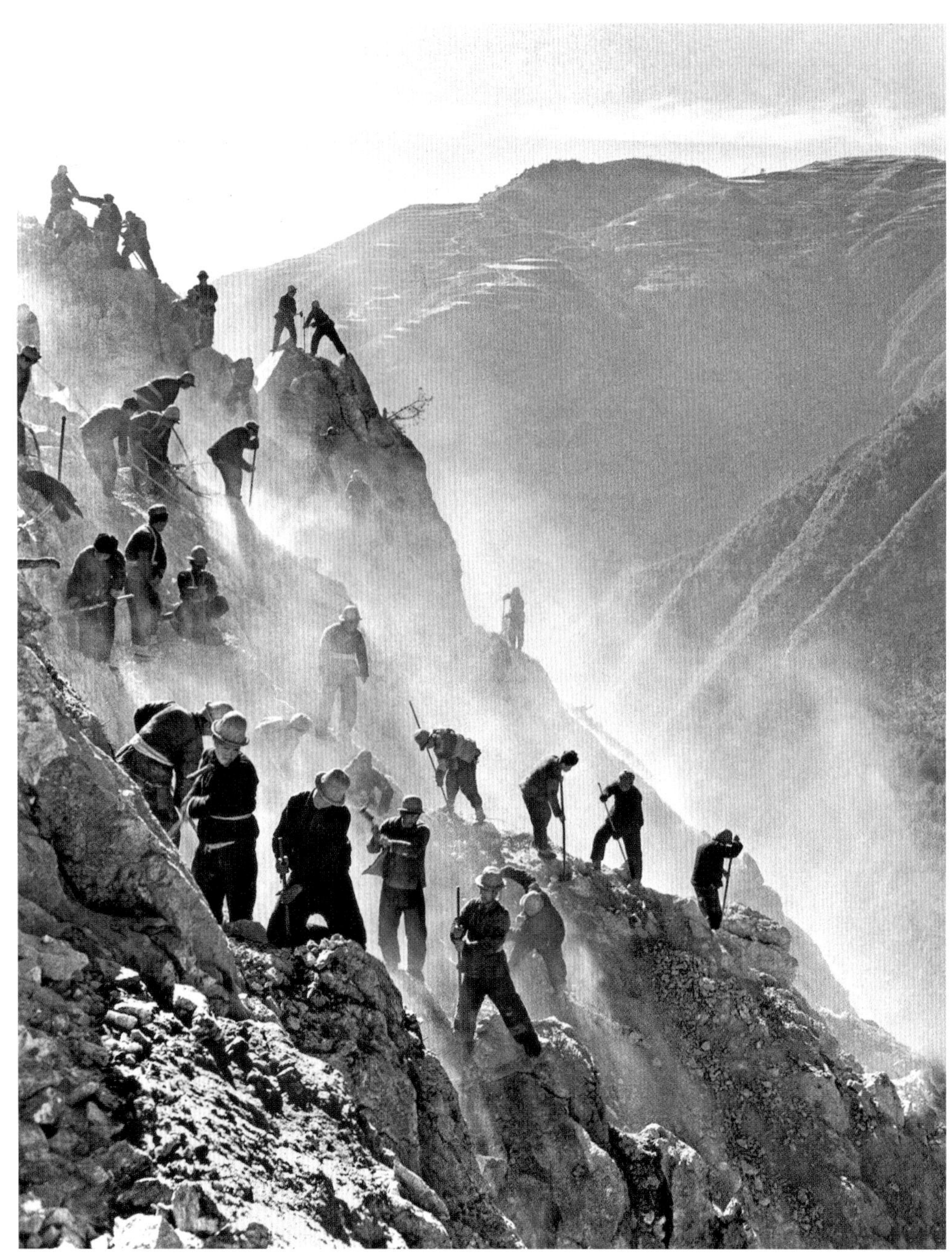

Anshan Steelworks, dating back to 1916, represents a proud story of the revival of heavy industry in New China. It became a model factory and steel workers became the most representative of all workers.

In 1956 the Chinese Photographers Association was established with Shi Shaohua, the head of the Xinhua News Agency photography department, as its chairman. The CPA was a professional association for photographers and carried out the directives of the Party. In his inaugural address Shi outlined the organization's plans, which included exhibitions (group and solo, national, regional and overseas), a national magazine and a photography annual. The following year the magazine *China Photography* was launched and the First National Exhibition of Photographic Art was held in Beijing, drawing on entries from photographers across China, and from Chinese overseas. This show formed the basis of the *First Photography Annual* (1958) with the stated objective of reflecting 'our great Socialist construction, the life of workers, peasants and soldiers, natural scenes of striking beauty, and rich and diverse products'.

One of the construction projects that received widespread publicity during the Great Leap Forward, Mao's attempt to boost industrial and agricultural productivity, was the creation of a canal on top of a mountain range in Lintao, Gansu, in China's arid northwest. Thousands of people laboured to achieve the seemingly impossible: to divert water from the Tao River up and over the mountain range to enable the expansion of agriculture. A striking photograph of the high-altitude construction site was taken in 1958 by Ru Suichu (*b.* 1932), a photographer for the *People's Pictorial*. In this new-style landscape image, workers take the place of rocks and trees, plumes of dust replace languid mist, and terraced agricultural fields can be seen in the distance, anticipating future productivity.

A proud achievement of the New China was the production in 1958 of the first limousine, the Red Flag. A striking photograph of a worker sitting in the engine cavity under the bonnet of a sedan surrounded by fellow workers who are illuminated by great shafts of natural light celebrates the glory of the accomplishment. The photograph was taken by Liu Entai (*b.* 1934) at the First Auto Works in Changchun, a flagship Party enterprise established during the first Five-Year Plan with the assistance of Soviet experts.

81 Ru Suichu, *Diverting Water from the Taohe River to the Mountains, Lintao, Gansu*, 1958, gelatin silver print.

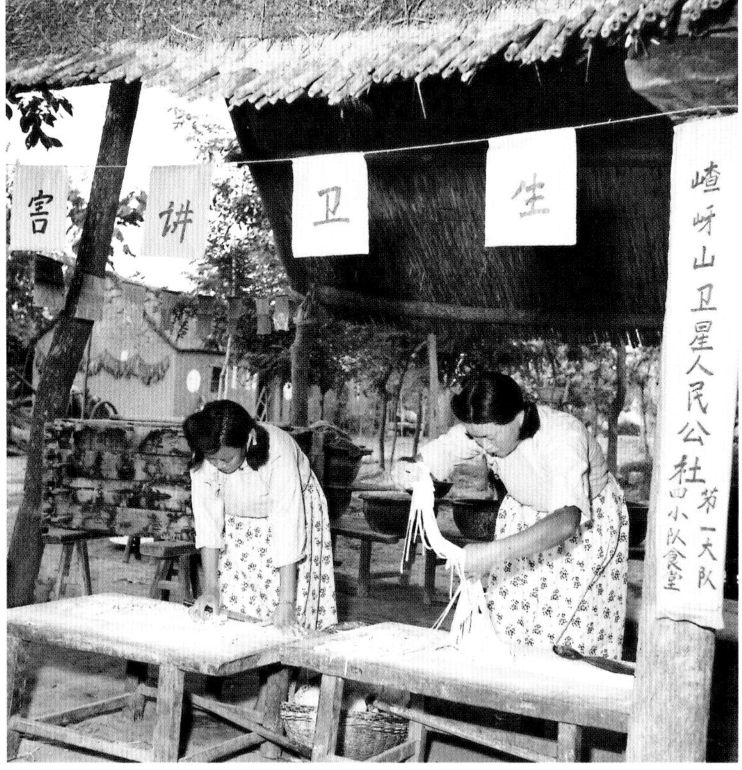

82 Wei Dezhong, *Preparing Noodles for Lunch at the People's Commune, Suiping, Henan*, 1958, gelatin silver print.

In 1957 Wei Dezhong (*b*. 1934), a young photographer from Henan, was assigned to work as a photojournalist at the *Henan Daily* in Zhengzhou. The following year he photographed the first People's Commune. His photograph shows two women making noodles in a newly constructed outdoor kitchen. After the Communist land reform policies intensified, confiscation of land, forced collectivization and the formation of People's Communes had taken farmers away from individual farming. The combination of political change, with farmers obliged to attend meetings rather than grow crops, misguided policies and a series of natural disasters produced the Great Famine (1958–61) in which between 15 and 45 million people died. Most of China's grain was grown in the provinces of Henan and Hebei where photographs of Mao Zedong and other Communist officials were taken as they admired 'bumper harvests' during the Great Famine, but few

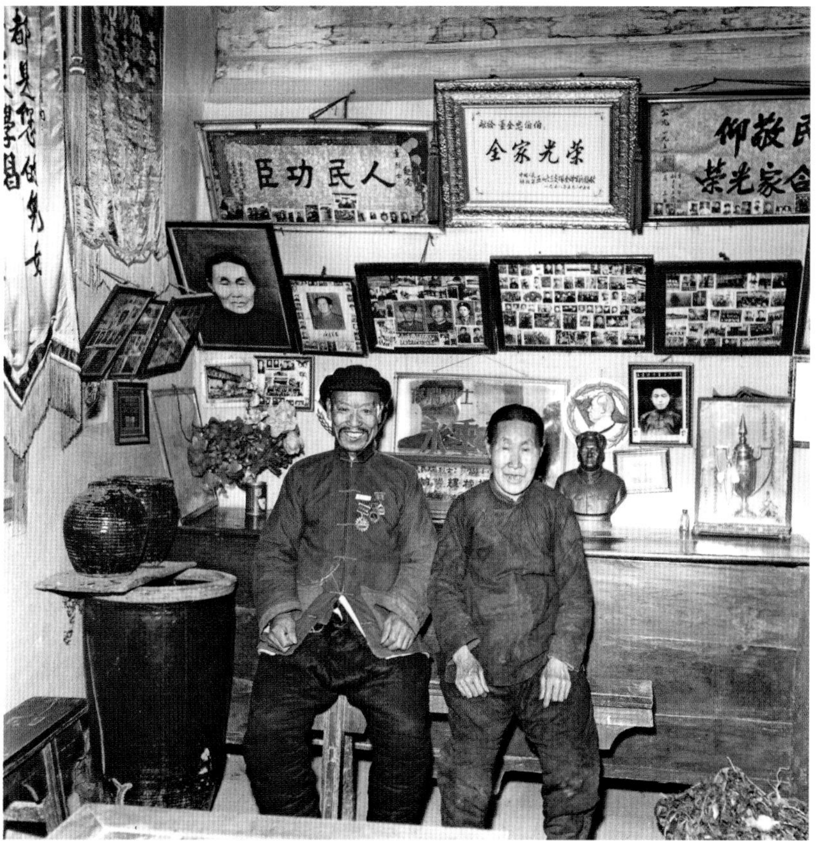

83 Zhang Zudao, *A War Hero's Parents, Huailai, Hebei*, 1958, gelatin silver print.

images have yet come to light that record the devastating reality that gripped much of China during the period euphemistically termed the 'Three Years of Natural Disasters'. Photographs that were published and circulated in newspapers and pictorial magazines at the time told stories that presented the Party and its government in eulogistic terms.

During the 1950s positive news also included stories of self-sacrifice. The smiling elderly couple in a photograph by Zhang Zudao (*b.* 1922) are the parents of a young soldier, Dong Cunrui (1929–1948), who famously gave up his life for the Communist cause.[12] Taken in their modest home in Huailai, Hebei, in 1958, Zhang places the young man's parents against the family shrine that commemorates their son. The father proudly

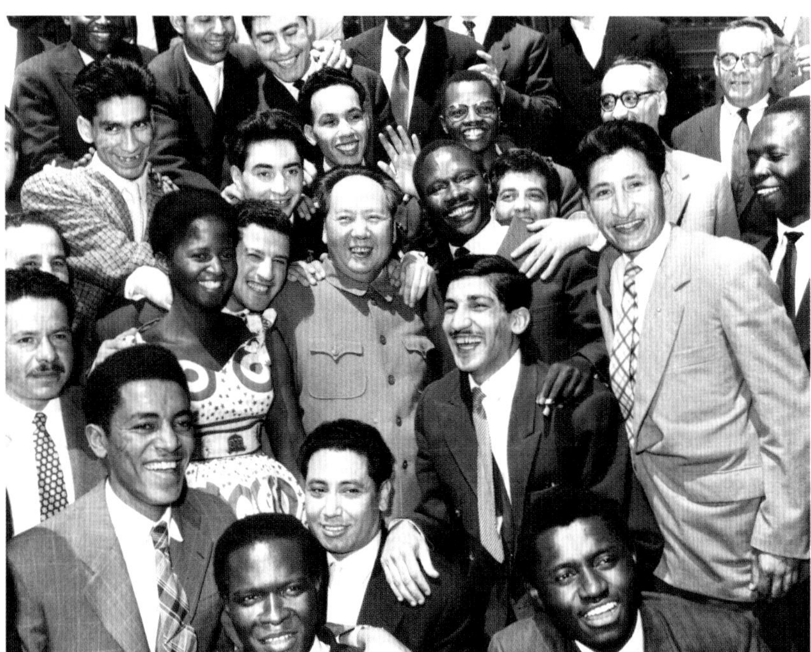

84 Hou Bo, *We Have Friends All Over the World*, 1959, gelatin silver print.

displays medals awarded to his son for bravery. The small black and white photographs, carefully arranged like patchwork within large glazed frames, are typical of those taken at the time, their size indicative of the relative expense and scarcity of photographic materials.

The smiling face of Mao Zedong standing at the centre of a group of foreign delegates is the subject of a photograph by Hou Bo, variously captioned 'Chairman Mao meets with VIPs from Asia, Africa and Latin America' or 'We Have Friends All Over the World'. In 1959 some 700 representatives from international trade union, youth and women's organizations were invited to Beijing for Labour Day celebrations that marked a decade of China's 'liberation from oppression'. The photograph, taken inside the leadership compound of Zhongnanhai on 15 May 1959, is one of many that Hou Bo took during the Labour Day celebrations as part of her job as photographer to Mao and Party leaders. Writing about works in the Third National Exhibition of Photographic Art, her colleague Chen Zhengqing praised the image as an 'outstanding news photograph', noting 'the appropriate choice of angle in order to suit the requirements of the subject', thus 'strengthening the subject', fitting for the depiction of the great leader. Accompanying technical information shows how the image was cropped for dramatic effect and states that Hou Bo used a flash to make the photograph lighter, ensuring that Mao's smile radiated out from the centre of the image, appearing larger, paler and more prominent than the others.[13]

Like all official photographs from the period, images that were submitted for use were the property of the news agency and not the individual photographers and were manipulated according to official requirements. It was common practice to enhance Mao's appearance. He was a heavy smoker and there was a person dedicated to the task of retouching copy negatives to whiten his teeth. Through negative editing, dodging and burning, images were improved, the positions of people were altered or they were removed. Re-editing could occur numerous times as individuals went out of favour, sometimes with the result that an image bore little relationship to the original scene.

In 1964 the Swiss-born Magnum photographer René Burri (*b*. 1933) was invited to China by Pakistan International Airways (PIA) to document the inauguration of the PRC's first air link with the outside world – the arrival of a PIA Boeing 720B aeroplane from Karachi, indicating the increasing closeness of diplomatic and security relations between the two countries. The detonation of China's first nuclear bomb, five months later, on 16 October, at the Lop Nur test site in Xinjiang, was a milestone of an altogether different order. Nuclear capability would prove China's standing as a world power. The test, code named 596, referred to June 1959, the date when the Soviets stopped assisting China with their nuclear programme after the collapse of relations. The PLA photographer Meng Zhaorui (*b*. 1930), who was assigned to document the detonation, used colour film (Agfa) to record the ball of fire, and black-and-white film for the mushroom cloud from a distance of some 30 kilometres (illus. 85). After he had completed the assignment a directive was issued stating that the image of the mushroom cloud would be released in colour.[14] Rising to the challenge, expert colourists carefully tinted the mushroom cloud, setting it against a clear blue sky, translating the black-and-white photograph into a fantastic technicolour-like image. The PLA conducted subsequent nuclear tests in 1965 and 1966 and Meng's photographs of all three tests were published in the *People's Daily* on 1 October 1966, China's National Day. Some months earlier, on 16 May, Mao had launched the Great Proletarian Cultural Revolution, unleashing an unprecedented period of violence carried out by radicalized activists who came to be known as Red Guards.

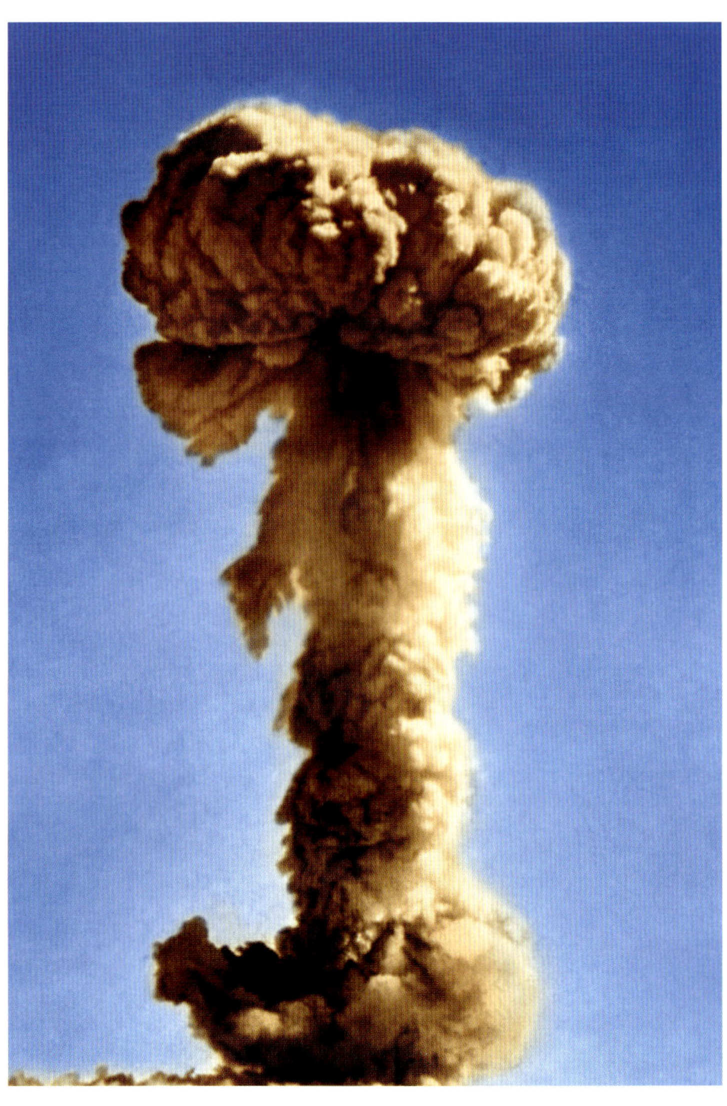

85 Meng Zhaorui, *China's First Successful Nuclear Test*, 16 October 1964, hand-coloured gelatin silver print.

Weng Naiqiang's photograph of Mao Zedong reviewing Red Guards from the rostrum at Tiananmen on 18 August 1966 is a quintessential image of the early Cultural Revolution. Mao holds out his army cap to the crowd who were chanting 'Long Live Chairman Mao', to which he replied 'Long live the People'.[15] In Weng's photograph he appears like a helmsman charting a course through a sea of adoring masses, bringing to mind the song 'Sailing on the Ocean Requires a Steady Hand', written in 1964. Weng Naiqiang (*b*. 1936) was born in Jakarta, Indonesia, where his father ran a photographic store and produced feature films. He was one of many patriotic overseas Chinese who 'returned' to China to contribute their expertise to the new society. Weng studied oil painting at the Central Academy of Fine Arts in Beijing and after graduation was assigned to

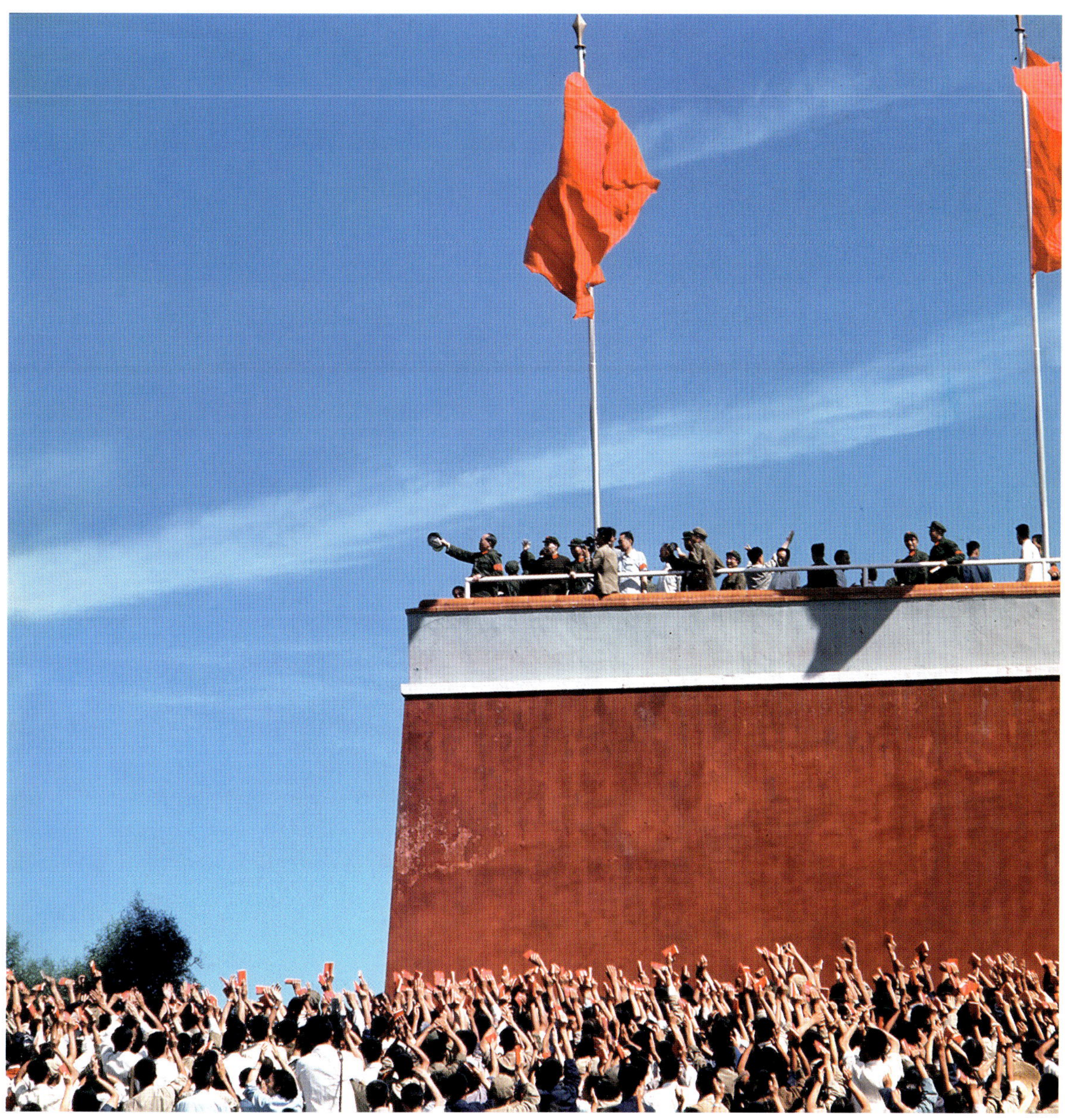

86 Weng Naiqiang, *Mao Reviewing the Red Guards*, 18 August 1966, chromogenic print.

work at the Foreign Languages Bureau. With his facility in languages he was assigned to the Japanese-language edition of the *People's Pictorial* magazine, initially as art editor and later as a photojournalist. On 18 August 1966 Weng was told that there would be 'a major event' and was allocated some Kodak colour film, which was expensive and a privilege to use. He took a number of photographs of Mao reviewing the Red Guards, but they were never published. Instead a heavily reworked close-up of Mao Zedong holding out his hat to the crowd by Lu Xiangyou (*b*. 1928) appeared on the cover.

Mao reviewed the Red Guards in Tiananmen Square on eight separate occasions, making it a site of Communist pilgrimage. At that time few people owned cameras. Visitors to Tiananmen Square could have a commemorative picture taken by a 'Worker, Peasant, Soldier' photographer. It was fashionable to pose for the camera wearing a Mao badge and holding a 'Little Red Book' of the quotations of Mao Zedong, with the rostrum in the background. Some people had more formal photographs taken in newly established or renamed studios such as Beijing's 'People's Photography Studio', or 'Eternally Red Photographic Studio', where you could have a quotation from Mao Zedong printed on the white surround and the edges cut with scissors to create a decorative 'frame'. Photographic studios had backdrops painted with revolutionary themes, like the 'Worker, Peasant, Soldier Studio' in Qiqihar, in far northeastern China, where three young men had their photograph taken on 19 April 1971 as if sitting on a beach with a navy ship speeding across the ocean. Photographs of babies taken to commemorate their first birthday were hand-tinted to highlight healthy red cheeks and lips and the ubiquitous Mao badge. And a photograph of a young boy taken at the Torch studio in Beijing on the occasion of his third birthday in 1969 shows him wearing a Mao badge and riding a tricycle, with Mao's signature and the phrase 'assiduously succeed in struggle, criticism and reform' printed on the frame. What is striking about these photographs is their small size. They were affordable, could be printed in multiples, sent in the post, or placed under the glass cover of a work desk, or together with other family photographs in a large hanging frame. With the help of photographers, people of all ages performed in front of the

Opposite page clockwise from top left:

87 Portrait, Eternally Red Photography studio, Beijing, 1972, photograph from a Cultural Revolution photo album.

88 Portrait, Torch studio, Beijing, 1969, photograph from a Cultural Revolution photo album.

89 Group portrait, Worker Peasant Soldier Photography studio, Qiqihaha, 19 April 1971, photograph from a Cultural Revolution photo album.

90 Souvenir portrait from Tiananmen, Beijing, November 1966, photograph from a Cultural Revolution photo album.

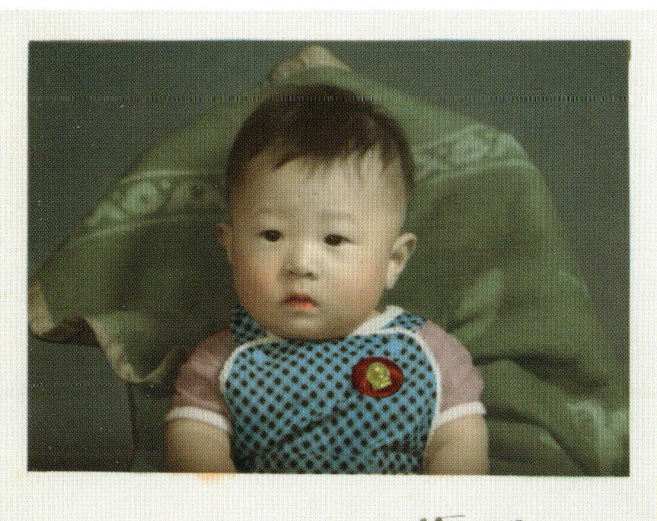
永红照相 1972

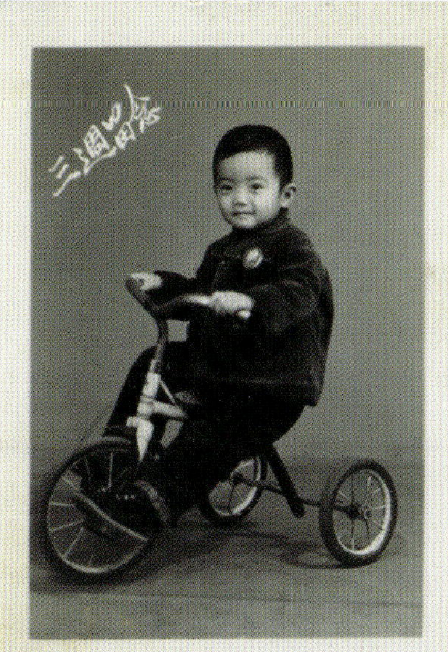
三週留念
认真搞好斗批改。
毛泽东
北京 火炬 1969

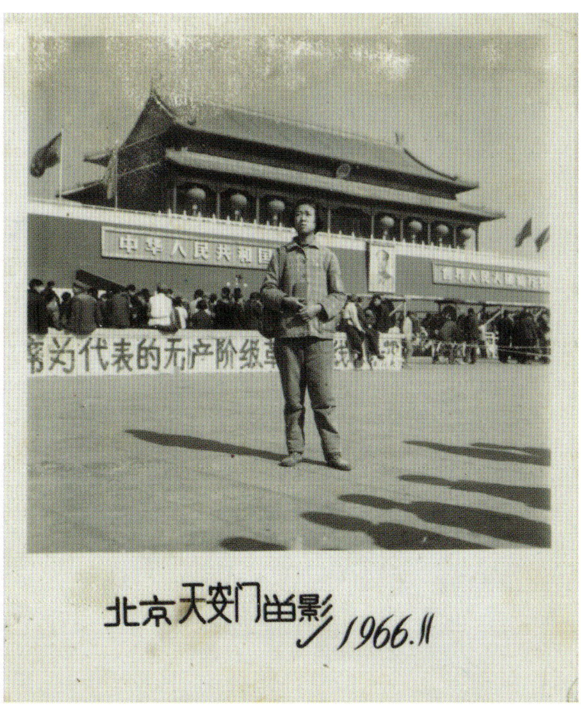
北京天安门留影 1966.11

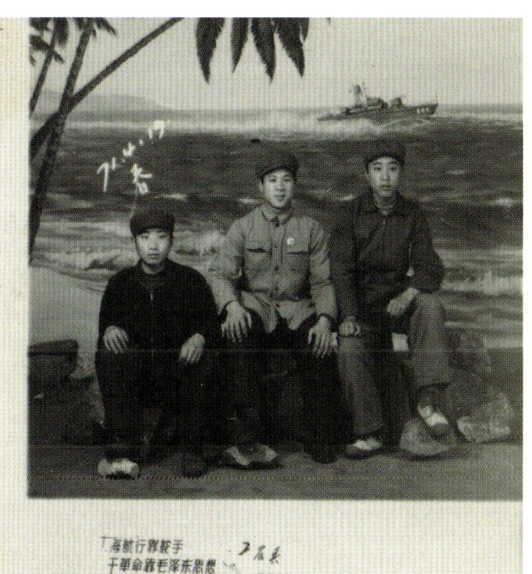
海航行靠舵手
干革命靠毛泽东思想

camera, aspiring not only to look their best but to be the best, acting out contemporary ideals that conformed to a collective consciousness.

Among the most stylized images produced during the Cultural Revolution are still photographs of the model revolutionary operas initiated by Jiang Qing (1914–1991), Mao Zedong's wife, a former actress and enthusiastic amateur photographer. The revolutionary operas adapted movements from Peking opera and Western ballet, combining them with rousing music and new moralizing narratives that placed workers, peasants and soldiers centre stage. During the filming of the revolutionary operas and ballets, photographers were called upon to create still images for use in promotion. Photographers from the Xinhua News Agency assigned to this task were Chen Juanmei and Zhang Yaxin, with Shi Shaohua as overall supervisor.

Imagery had to comply with strict political guidelines regarding lighting, colour, composition and expression. Primary subjects were required to be 'taller, larger and more complete' than other figures in a composition, and convey ideals that were 'red' (patriotic), 'bright' (like Mao Zedong's thought) and 'shining' (emanating positive rays, like the sun). While the photographers shot scenes using black-and-white and colour film, the images were designed to convey the energy and atmosphere of a live performance in which colour played a central role. Given the political significance of the operas, colour film, still a luxury in China, was made available to the photographers in unrestricted quantities. Scenes were enacted over and over again to capture perfect compositions and characterizations on film. Once photography had been completed (each opera took about six months), the film was sent to the Cultural Group of the State Council, led by Jiang Qing herself, for approval. Only then could the images be published. The photographs were used for a wide variety of propaganda purposes including movie posters, new year prints, children's picture books, postage stamps and publications intended for distribution overseas.

While the great majority of photographs taken during the Cultural Revolution were self-conscious and staged, some photographers working as official photojournalists also documented the darker side of life. Li Zhensheng's (*b.* 1940) harrowing photographs of the Cultural Revolution

91 Shi Shaohua, *Still from the modern revolutionary opera 'Red Detachment of Women',* 1970, chromogenic print.

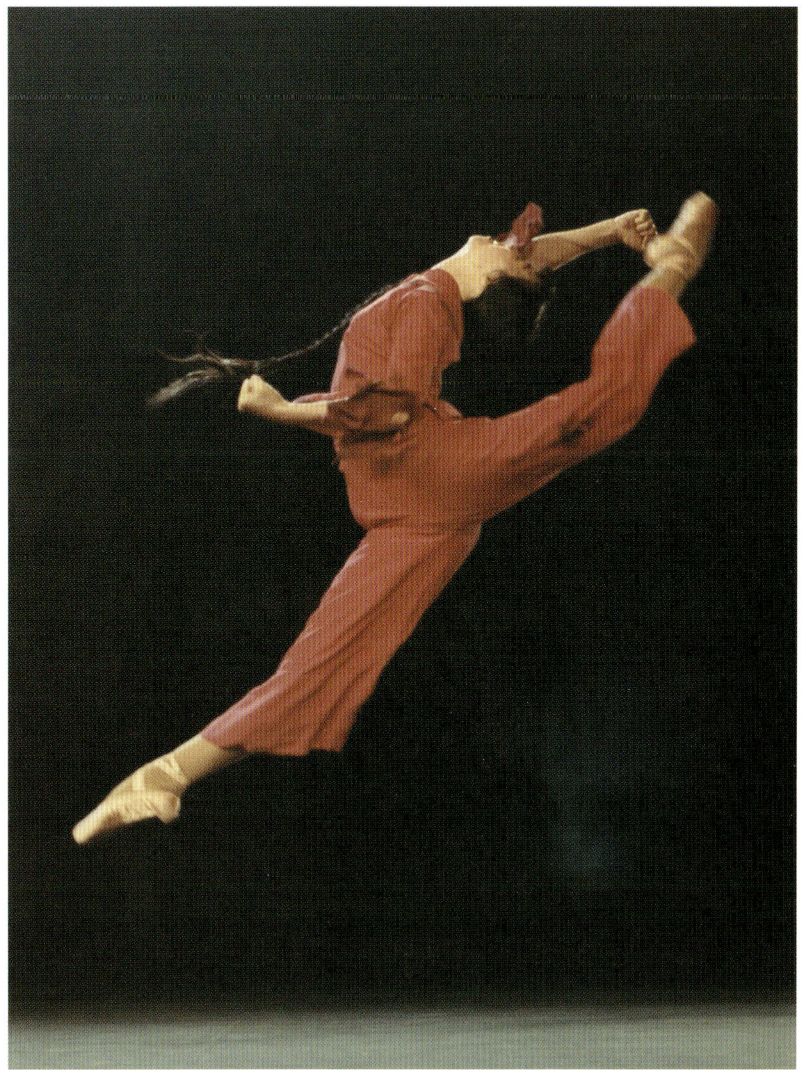

stand in stark contrast to the 'red, bright and shining' images that were so widely reproduced. Li was a photographer for the *Heilongjiang Daily Newspaper* and took a series of photographs recording the denunciation and vilification of the former governor of Heilongjiang, Li Fanwu. In one image a placard hangs from his neck bearing his name and crime as a

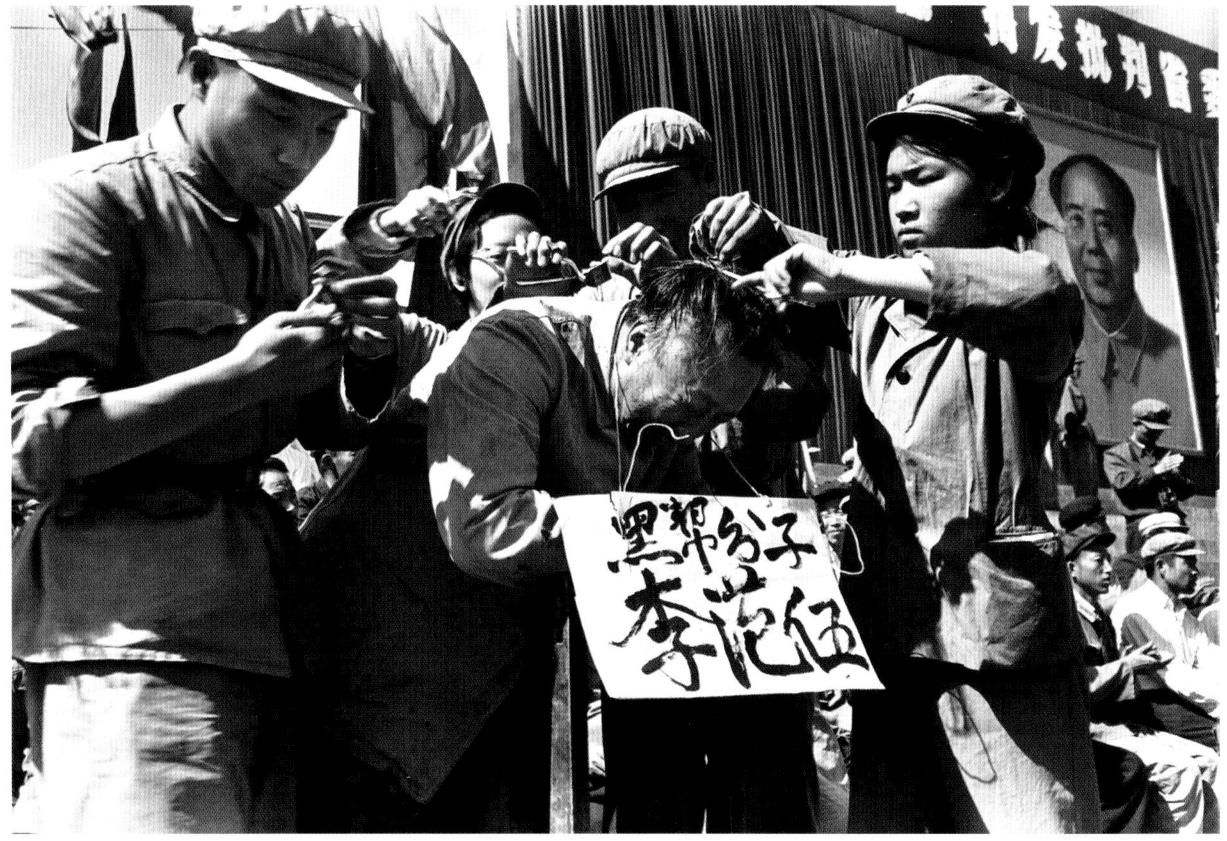

92 Li Zhensheng, *Humiliation of Li Fanwu*, 12 September 1966, gelatin silver print.

'black element', while a young woman violently cuts his hair (he was accused of looking like Mao Zedong). Other photographs by Li show the smashing of Buddhist statues and the burning of books regarded as corrupt because of their perceived 'feudal' or 'bourgeois' content.

During the Cultural Revolution many officials and intellectuals committed suicide or died as a result of their treatment. In the absence of any kind of justice some brave individuals took it upon themselves to record what was happening to their loved ones. Wang Jingyao, for example, took photographs of his wife Bian Zhongyun, the vice principal of a girls' middle school in Beijing, after she was beaten to death by students on 5 August 1966. He photographed the interior of their home plastered with big-character posters (*dazibao*) vilifying Bian, and her daughters washing their dead mother in an attempt to restore her dignity. The photographs document the demise of a wife and a mother, offering proof and seeking redress. They have since formed the basis of the documentary *Though I am Gone* (2006) by independent film-maker Hu Jie. It was shot on digital video and posted on the Internet, and has been widely screened in museums and galleries around the world.[16]

The practice of using visual language to portray positive images of leaders and nation building that was established earlier in the twentieth century was intensified dramatically during the Cultural Revolution. As with any language, the CCP's visual lexicon had to be learned. The extent of control over image making during this period can be gauged by the official Chinese response to Italian film director Michelangelo Antonioni's television documentary *Chung Kuo* (China). Antonioni, a committed socialist, was invited to visit China in 1972. The film opens with children singing 'I love Beijing's Tiananmen', and a sequence showing people having their photographs taken by 'Worker, Peasant, Soldier' photographers in Tiananmen Square. Antonioni, who narrates the film, says he is in China with his camera to observe this great laboratory of gestures, voices and movements. When it was shown in China in closed sessions, the film was denounced. A *Peoples' Daily* editorial on 30 January 1974, headlined 'A Vicious Motive, Despicable Tricks', accused Antonioni of not including enough 'good or progressive scenes' and too many 'inferior, old and backward scenes'.

Antonioni focused on 'the people', but his roving, impressionistic camera style did not imbue places and people with the grandeur and dignity expected by his hosts. His framing lacked symmetry, order and decorum, and was interpreted as being undermining and disrespectful. His combination of reportage and artistic expression was wholly foreign to China at that time. 'There are sometimes long-shots, sometimes close-ups, sometimes from the front and sometimes from behind, at one moment throngs of heads and at another legs and feet moving helter-skelter. These shots are intended to make [Tiananmen] Square look like a boisterous market place. Is this not aimed at defaming our motherland?' blasted *People's Daily*. Propaganda officials could not tolerate Antonioni's probing, free-form camera work. The visiting director had also got caught in factional crossfire, an oblique attack on Premier Zhou Enlai, who had approved the film. It was not until 2004 that *Chung Kuo* had a limited Chinese release in the Beijing Film Festival in honour of Antonioni's contribution to cinema, three years before his death.

five

Reportage and New Wave

1976 marked the beginning of 'people's photography', photography by individuals – many of them from families of political or cultural influence – who had experienced the trauma of the Cultural Revolution and, no longer content merely to witness history, wanted to record their own perspectives and life experience. In that watershed year the premier Zhou Enlai died on 8 January, a massive earthquake devastated Tangshan in northeastern China on 28 July, and on 9 September the death of Mao brought about the fall of the Gang of Four and an end to the Cultural Revolution. This tectonic shift ushered in a period of mourning, soul-searching and tentative openness.

After the death of Zhou Enlai people came to Tiananmen Square to place white flowers and wreaths containing his photograph on the steps of the Monument to the People's Heroes. By 4 April, the traditional day for commemorating the dead, the base of the monument had been covered with tributes. Despite a prohibition, large numbers of people had gathered in the square. Luo Xiaoyun (*b*. 1953), a keen amateur photographer, was among those who recorded the mass outpouring of emotion. Using her Leica camera she photographed Li Tiehua, a director at the Beijing Red Flag Peking Opera troupe, talking to the crowd (illus. 93). Raised above the people, but still very much one of them, he takes Tiananmen Square as his stage. Li's speech, like the poems pasted on the Monument to the People's Heroes, was critical of Mao's radical allies and he was arrested.

Early on the morning of 5 April the authorities declared the end of commemorations and moved to suppress the crowds, beating and arresting people, and clearing the Square of tributes. Later that morning a huge

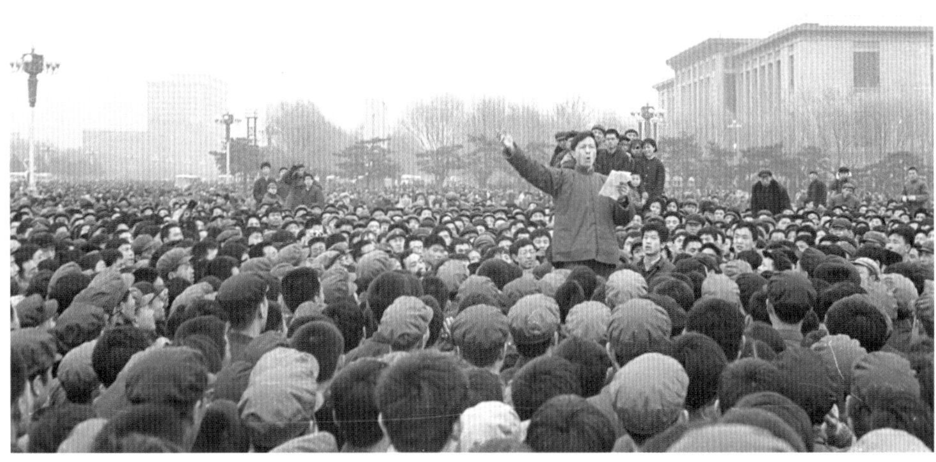

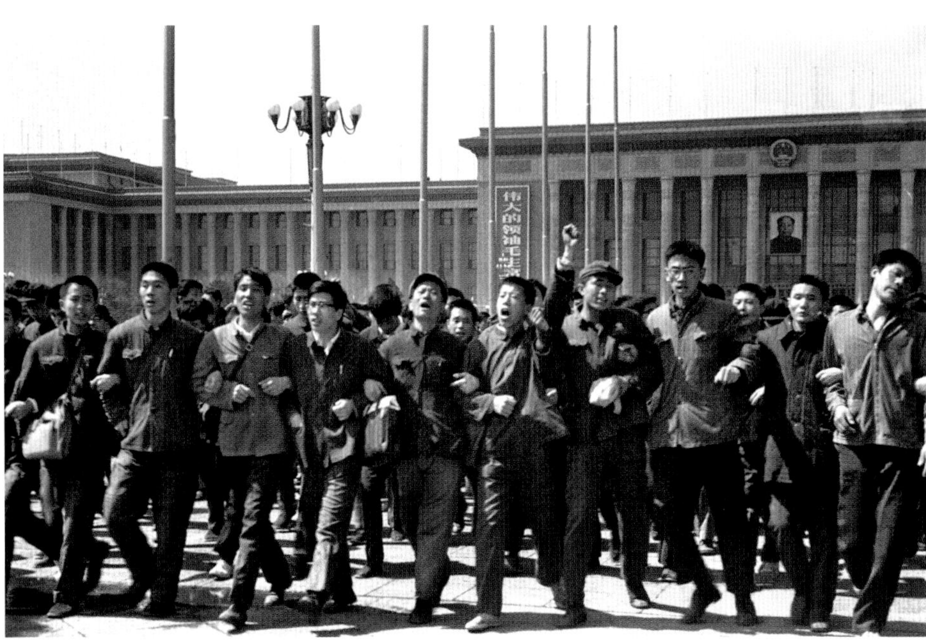
伟大的领袖毛

crowd of angry people assembled outside the Great Hall of the People, demanding the return of their wreaths and the release of those who had been detained. In a show of defiance protesters locked arms and marched towards the nearby command centre for workers and the people's militia, singing 'The Internationale'. Wu Peng's iconic image of people power, which was given the caption 'Unity is Strength that will Lead Us to Tomorrow' when it was published in 1979, shows a line of young men walking away from the Great Hall. Wu Peng (*b*. 1948) was a railway worker and self-taught photographer who also repaired cameras. He had been visiting the Square regularly from the day Zhou died, taking photographs with a second-hand Soviet Kiev III camera that he had bought in Beijing some years earlier. Security officials confiscated many cameras and film from photographic studios across Beijing in an attempt to control the circulation of unauthorized images but Wu managed to develop his own film and hide the negatives in secret locations. Determined that the photographic evidence be seen, he made an album of prints and got it to Zhou Enlai's widow, Deng Yingchao. Other photographers did likewise. Wang Zhiping's album, *Funeral of a Nation*, circulated privately.

In December 1978 the Communist Party of China's Central Committee overturned the assessment of the Tiananmen Incident of 5 April as a counter-revolutionary movement. The leadership announced an end to 'class struggle' and the beginning of 'socialist construction and modernization', acknowledging the need to 'liberate thinking, free people's minds, and seek truth from facts'. Following this significant policy shift in which Deng Xiaoping (1904–1997) played a key role, a book titled *The People's Mourning* (1979) was published with Wu Peng as special executive editor. The publication drew on thousands of images by unofficial and official photographers. Wu was also involved with a related exhibition at the China National Art Gallery (later known as the National Art Museum of China or NAMOC). The 'people's photographers' had achieved their objective in having their work published and displayed for the benefit of the public. What had begun as a people's project, however, was now part of party-sanctioned historiography, linked to political campaigns that promoted the new chairman Hua Guofeng and repudiated the Gang of Four.

93 Luo Xiaoyun, *Mainstay*, 4 April 1976, gelatin silver print.

94 Wu Peng, *Unity is Strength*, 5 April 1976, gelatin silver print.

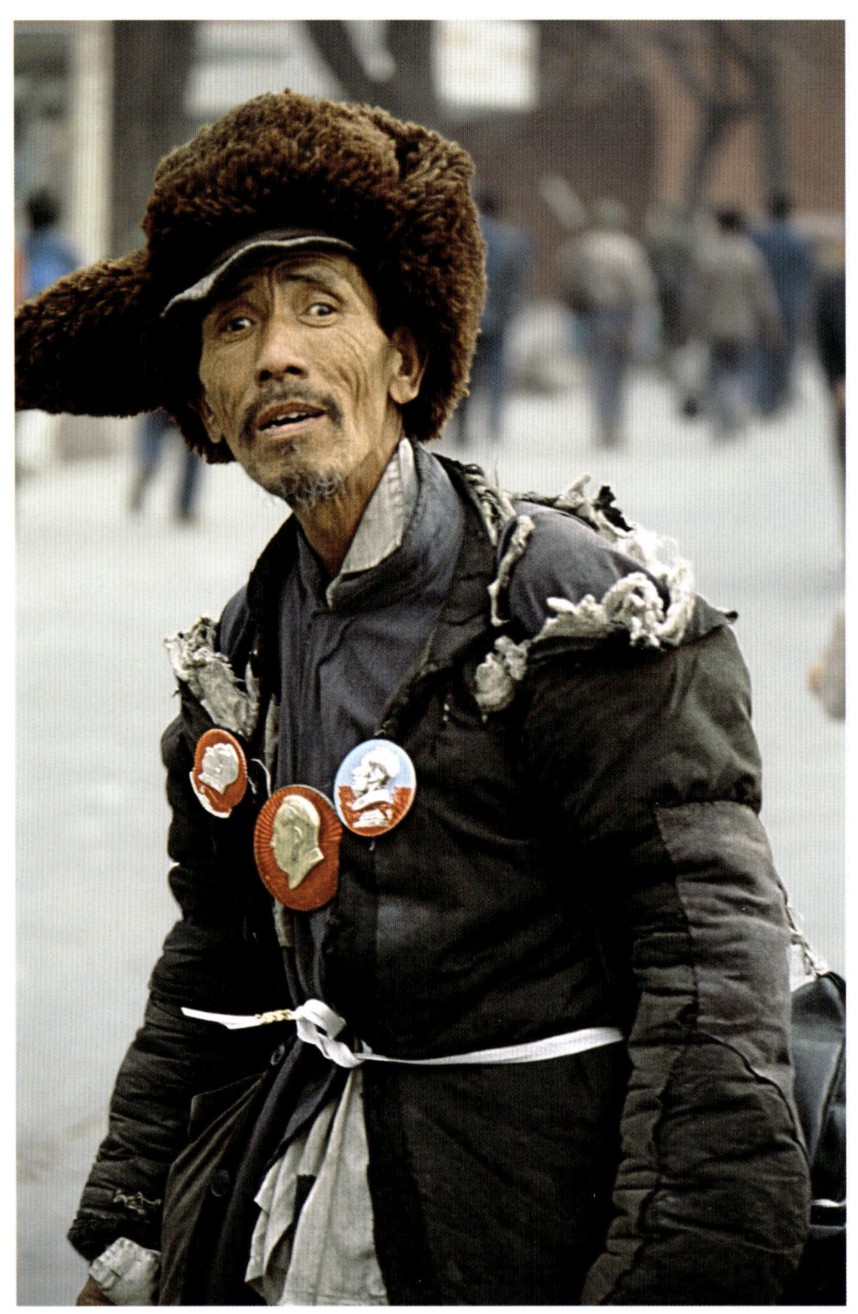

One of the most poignant images of the period is a photograph of a petitioner by Li Xiaobin (*b.* 1955) taken in November 1977. Individuals who had grievances and were unable to get a fair hearing in their hometown travelled to Beijing to plead with higher authorities for justice. According to Chinese government estimates there were some 30 million cases of miscarriages of justice arising from the Cultural Revolution. Li lived close to the Department of Public Security and the courts where petitioners gathered in makeshift camps, and worked at the Museum of the Chinese Revolution on the edge of Tiananmen Square. He was deeply moved by their plight.

Li too had photographed the mourning for Zhou Enlai and had helped assemble material for *The People's Mourning*.[1] On the day he photographed *Petitioner*, a friend who worked at the Beijing Foreign Trade Bureau gave him some highly prized imported colour film which he loaded into his Seagull camera, fitted with a borrowed Leica 135-mm lens. Riding his bicycle by the Forbidden City, Li came across the old man, his tattered jacket fastened with a home-made clasp fashioned from shining Mao badges. The badges were a commemoration of the figure who had shaped the old man's life, a marker of loyalty perhaps, tinged with despair. Li rode ahead, stopped, waited for the old man to get close, then turned and took three photographs in quick succession. He did not dare to talk to his subject, fearing that he might be suspected of photographing a person whose appearance implied disaffection. Li waited until early 1978 to develop the film and exhibited the photograph for the first time in 1986. He describes the image as 'lacking in artistic pretension, coarse and not beautiful', a style of photography that was problematic even with the changing political mood.[2]

Another young photographer who was active in the Square in April 1976 was Wang Wenlan (*b.* 1953). Drawn to the Square for 'reasons of personal conscience/spirit', he dressed in plain clothes rather than his army uniform.[3] His photographs, carefully concealed until it was safe, were also included in *The People's Mourning*. Wang was sent to report on the devastating earthquake that hit the industrial city of Tangshan, near Tianjin, on the morning of 28 July 1976. According to official Chinese sources the quake measured 7.8 on the Richter scale, killing hundreds of

95 Li Xiaobin, *Petitioner*, November 1977, chromogenic print.

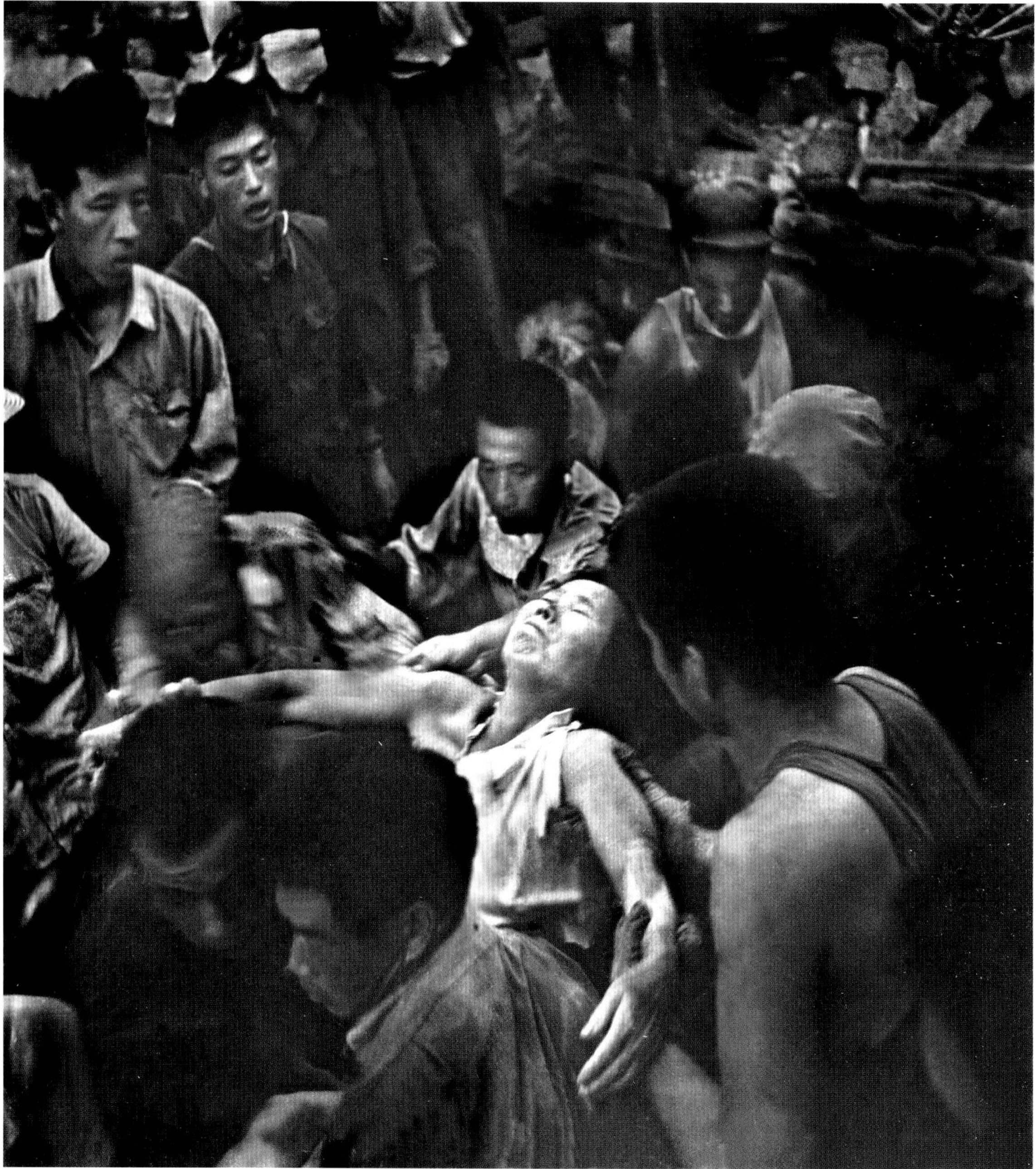

thousands of people. China was determined to handle the disaster alone and refused international aid. Some ten official photographers were assigned to 'report' on the natural disaster, but their activities were restricted to recording rescue scenes, not the dead. On 9 August a 46-year-old woman, Lu Guilan, was pulled out of the rubble alive after being trapped for thirteen days. It was reported that she had drunk her own urine to survive. Wang took his photograph of Lu at around 7 p.m. in low light using a Seagull 120 camera.[4] In the masterfully composed image a diagonal line is traced by the trajectory of her passage from the earth as if she is being raised from the dead. Wang Wenlan became head photographer of the English-language newspaper *China Daily* when it was established in 1980. He contributed significantly to the role that photographs have played in official print media since that time.

He Yanguang (*b*. 1951) is another pioneering photojournalist. Back in 1976 he was a factory worker, imprisoned for his activities in Tiananmen Square. After his name was cleared, he was transferred to the Central Committee of the Communist Youth League, and became a reporter at the *Beijing Youth Newspaper* (published by the League) when it resumed publication in 1981. In 1980 he photographed elderly women praying in Beijing's South Cathedral, a Jesuit church that dates back to the early seventeenth century. Titled *Celebrating Easter Once Again*, the photograph documents the reopening of Christian churches in 1979. In a companion image He Yanguang photographed a gathering of cadres and intellectuals who met regularly to sing, celebrating their 'Second Liberation' through their rehabilitation from alleged crimes (illus. 97). Taken with a Hasselblad camera belonging to the newspaper but not published at the time, it too is a pathos-filled image, recording a historic moment for ordinary people, survivors of the Cultural Revolution.

In 2008, looking back over 30 years of photojournalism, He observed:

> Photography is not just about looking, sometimes it is also about resisting forgetfulness. People often ask me why I would take a photograph of something if it will not make it into the paper? My response is unequivocal. When you take a photograph the image becomes eternal, you don't have to worry about waiting, the day will

96 Wang Wenlan, *The rescue of Liu Guilan who had been trapped for 13 days after the Tangshan earthquake on 28 July 1976*, gelatin silver print.

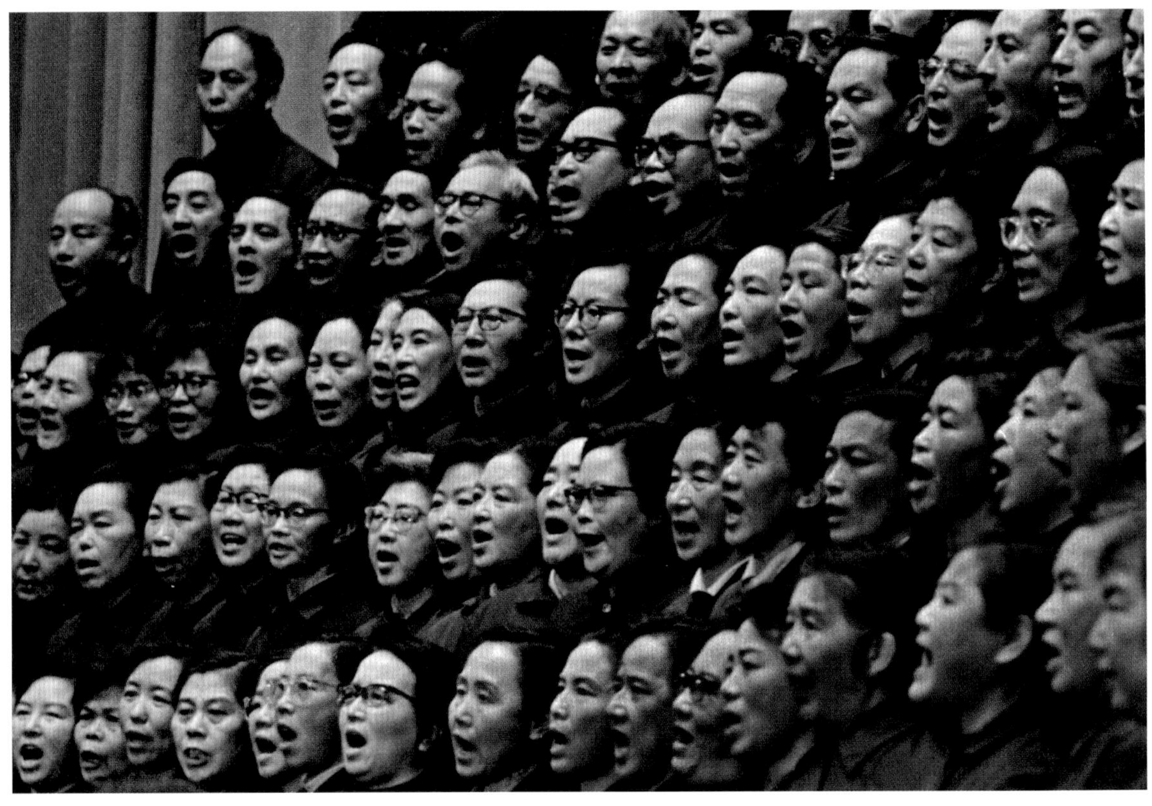

97 He Yanguang, *Second Liberation*, 6 December 1980, gelatin silver print.

> come when it is possible for it to be seen by readers . . . I have the patience to wait. History is so long, no matter what kind of prohibition there is, there is an inexorable movement towards disclosing the truth and revealing the real situation.[5]

Liu Heung Shing (*b*. 1951), a contemporary of He Yanguang's, was born in Hong Kong and in 1971 moved to New York to study political science and journalism. After graduation he secured an apprenticeship as a photojournalist at *Life* magazine. His mentor there was the action photographer Gjon Mili (1904–1984) who, Liu said, 'taught me how to interpret human experiences and capture them in two-dimensional images with warmth'.[6] In 1976 Liu travelled to China, on assignment for *Time* magazine, to cover the funeral of Mao Zedong, but was prevented from journeying beyond

Guangzhou. Three years later he returned as *Time*'s photographer in China (he later joined the Associated Press) and in 1983 published his now classic book *China After Mao: Seek Truth From Facts*.

One of Liu's photographs that captures the mood of growing liberalism is of a youth skating past a giant statue of Mao Zedong, taken at the Dalian Institute of Technical Management in 1981 (illus. 1). Liu's double portrait juxtaposes the living and the dead. The anonymous skater glides past the statue, propelling himself forwards through space that appears as boundless as the sky in an action of apparent fearlessness, as if he has broken free.

Liu's background as an outsider, and an insider with 'contextual understanding', gave him a unique position within the foreign news corporations. He describes his experience of being a photojournalist in China in the late 1970s and early 1980s and contrasts his approach with that of his mainland Chinese colleagues. He recalls an instance of looking through the viewfinder of his camera and seeing the hand of a Xinhua News Agency colleague reaching out to reposition and then remove an ashtray from view, as if to tidy up reality.[7] On-the-job contact between Chinese photographers and foreign journalists provided opportunities for interaction. After looking at Liu's photographs in *China After Mao*, Wang Wenlan says he began to realize that it was possible to take photographs with his mind as well as his eyes, and to actively engage with history.[8]

In April 1979 a landmark exhibition titled Nature. Society. Man was held in Beijing. The exhibition was organized by the April Photography Society, which took its name from the protests in Tiananmen Square in April 1976 that members of the society made it their mission to record. The exhibition was the first such event staged by an independent community arts organization since 1949 (it is earlier than the No Name and Stars art group exhibitions) and attracted large crowds. In the foreword to the catalogue, Wang Zhiping, one of the organizers, articulated his hope for a new kind of photography, one motivated by an artistic impulse to explore beauty and feeling rather than to reflect ideology:

> News photography cannot replace photographic art. Content is not the same as form. Photography as a form of art has its own special

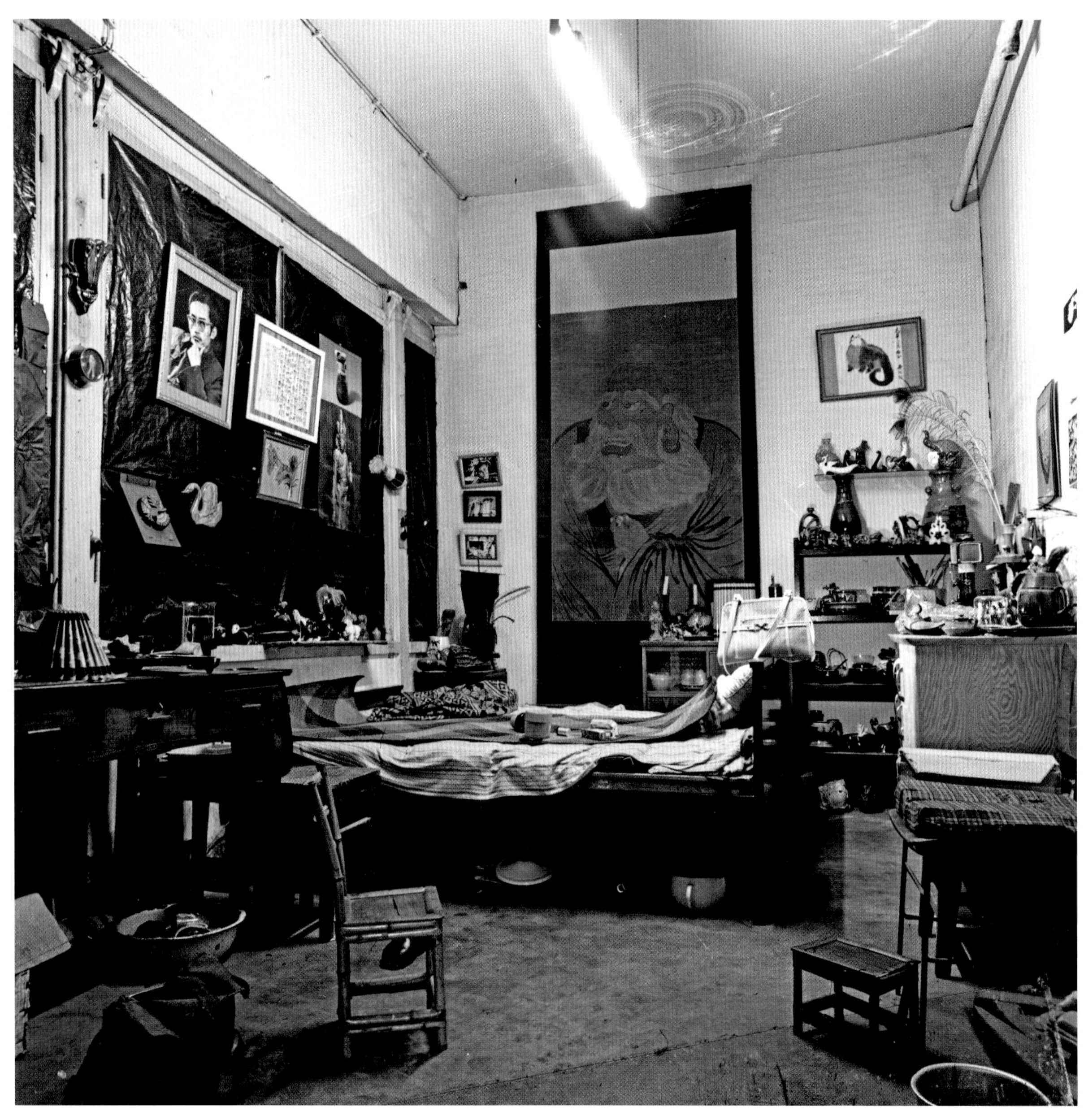

98 Wang Zhiping, *Home*, 1978, gelatin silver print.

> language. The time has come. Just as economic means should be used to manage economics, so artistic languages should be used to research art. The beauty of photography lies in the rhythms of nature, in the realities of society and in the emotions and interests of people. Increasingly it will not have to exist in 'important subject matter' or 'official ideology'.[9]

Wang appealed to individuals to use photography to explore their own relationship to natural, social and human worlds. He had studied set design at the PLA Art Academy, and among his photographs in Nature. Society. Man was a view of his modest single-room dwelling, the windows covered with black plastic sheeting so it could double as a dark room. Located in a once-imposing courtyard house, Wang's tiny allotment was typical of the congested living conditions created by Cultural Revolution politics, when strangers were moved into other people's houses. The home, however, remained a private realm, a place of retreat from the outside world. Members of the society met at Wang's home to select photographs for the Nature. Society. Man exhibition. While the subject of the photograph is significant, Wang creates a pleasing composition of abstracted black and white shapes and focal lines, dominated by the horizontal bed and the vertical hanging scroll on the rear wall.

Nature featured prominently in the exhibition and was used to evoke feelings and emotions: there were tender images of pairs of ducks and swans on ponds, kittens and young willow leaves silhouetted against shimmering sunlight. There were photographs too of carefree children, and people reading translations of foreign books in a way that had not been possible during the Cultural Revolution. Some images were more direct in their critique. An image of young boys peering at a caged monkey, by Wang Miao (*b*. 1951), a photographer working at the Cultural Relics Bureau Publishing House, was accompanied by the text: 'I am free, you can also do as you please, so who is actually inside the cage and who is outside?' In another work Wang Miao uses seasons to evoke the changing political climate. *Cold and Hot* is a bird's-eye view of a couple seated on a park bench gazing out across a thawing lake. The water's edge

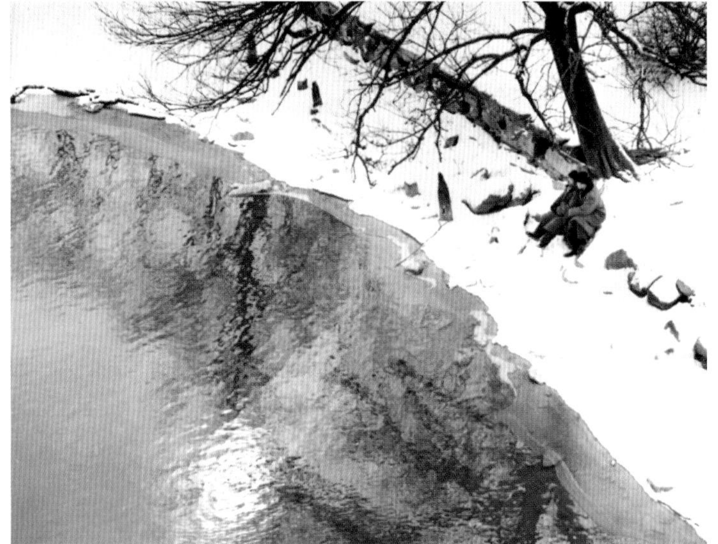

99 Wang Miao, *Cold And Hot*, November 1974, gelatin silver print.

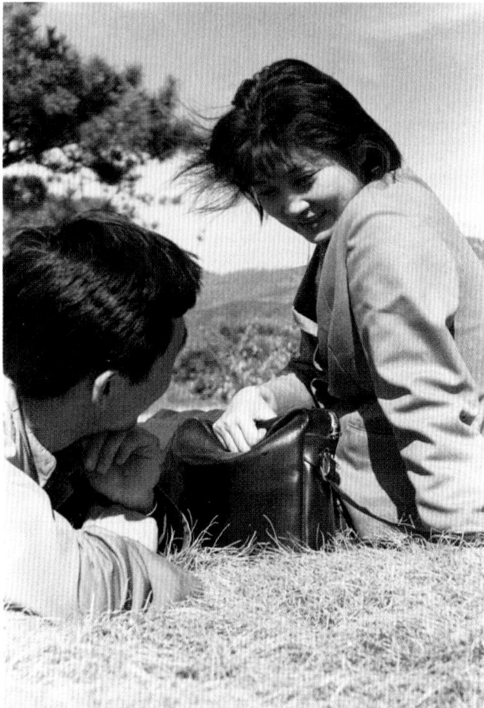

100 Li Xiaobin, . . . *OK?*, 1976, gelatin silver print.

creates a diagonal arc that bifurcates the image into black and white zones, evoking the diagram of yin and yang, a traditional symbol of harmony and balance.

The future is also the subject of Li Xiaobin's . . . *OK?*, a portrait of a young couple enjoying each other's company during a trip out of town. The photograph was taken in the grounds of the Temple of the Reclining Buddha in the Western Hills outside Beijing. The man lies on the grass, a light breeze plays with the woman's hair, and a pine tree (symbolic of longevity) can be seen in the background. As viewers we feel as though we have been brought into the intimacy of a private moment. Our eye is led in a circular motion around a central area of void: a future waiting to be written.

101 Li Jiangshu, *The Artist Shi Lu*, 26 April 1977, gelatin silver print.

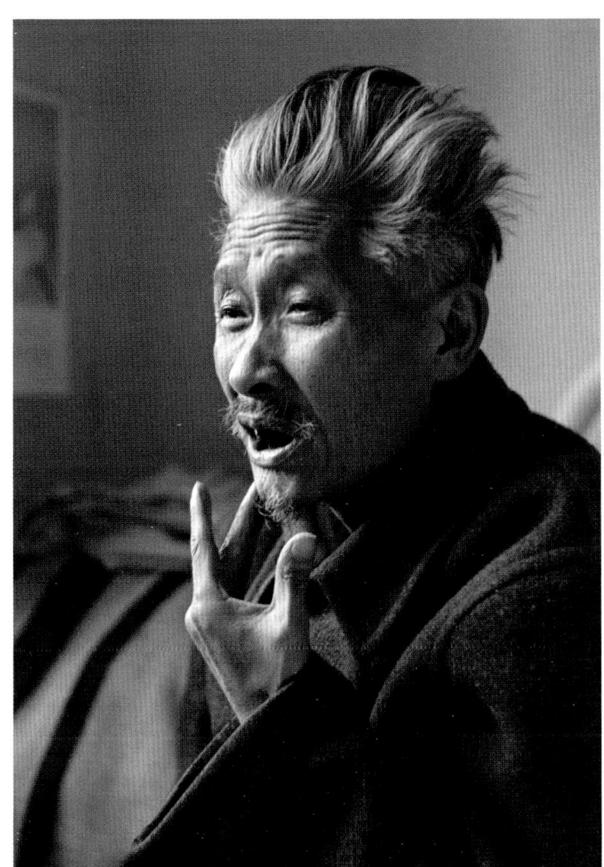

One of the most poignant portraits in the exhibition was Li Jiangshu's (*b*. 1954) portrayal of the brush-and-ink painter Shi Lu (1919–1982), taken at the end of the Cultural Revolution after his release from imprisonment for medical treatment in Beijing. Shi Liu's open mouth and dishevelled hair suggest the tragedy of his life. A member of the Party and a highly regarded artist from Xi'an in Shaanxi, during the Cultural Revolution he was criticized for his 'wild, weird, chaotic and black' paintings. Shi Lu suffered a mental breakdown and was beaten and imprisoned. Those artists who survived the torture and humiliation of the Cultural Revolution often bore physical and psychological scars for the rest of their days. In Li Jiangshu's portrait the artist appears to emerge from the darkness, his face and hand catching the light, the circular area of void between his mouth and fingers acting as a space for words that are spoken but inaudible. An extant copy of the photograph bears an inscription by Shi Lu on the reverse: 'Crazed portrait of heavenly wrath, but in fact the old man has no teeth'.[10]

The April Photography Society mounted two further exhibitions, in 1980 and 1981, which also toured nationally, indicating official acceptance of the work in an increasingly liberal atmosphere. The photography that attracted the most interest in the group's final exhibition at the China National Art Gallery was a series by Zhang Yimou (*b.* 1951), who was then studying at the Beijing Film Academy. Titled *Ah, A Generation of Youth!* (1979), each of the large, dark images illuminated a detail of a person such as an eye or a clenched fist. Like Shi Lu, Zhang Yimou was from Shaanxi. Zhang had taken up painting and photography while working in rural Shaanxi during the Cultural Revolution. He was over the age limit, but was able to persuade the Academy to accept him on the basis of a strong portfolio of photographs. A rear view of a young woman taken after having completed his first year at film school reserves her long black plait against a white field while removing all other traces of her lower body, demonstrating Zhang's technical accomplishment and his ability to create powerful contemporary images that resonate with tradition. It was published in the *China Youth Newspaper* in 1980.

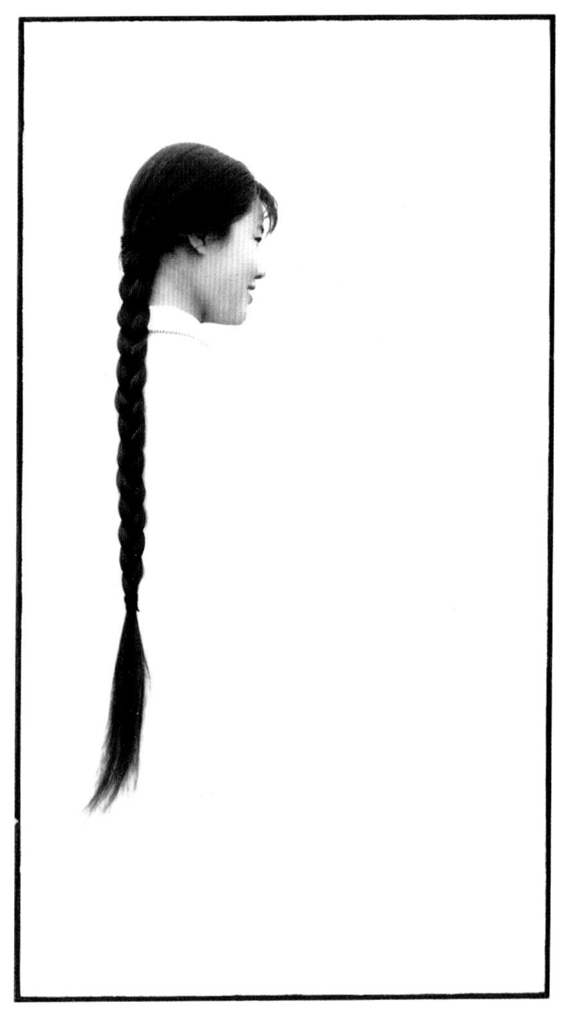

102 Zhang Yimou, *Chinese Girl*, 1980, gelatin silver print.

A group of Li Xiaobin's documentary photographs was also included in the exhibition, displayed in defiance of Wang Zhiping and other members, whose work had increasingly tended towards the artistic. Li's images were accompanied by an explanatory text:

> In my opinion content is also form. With regard to the work, content and form are equally important. I strive to use the unique characteristics of photography to express the beautiful, or what is not necessarily beautiful but is real and natural – what I regard as beautiful . . . Taking spontaneous shots of people going about their daily life, I do not want to embellish them in any way. Because I do not know or understand

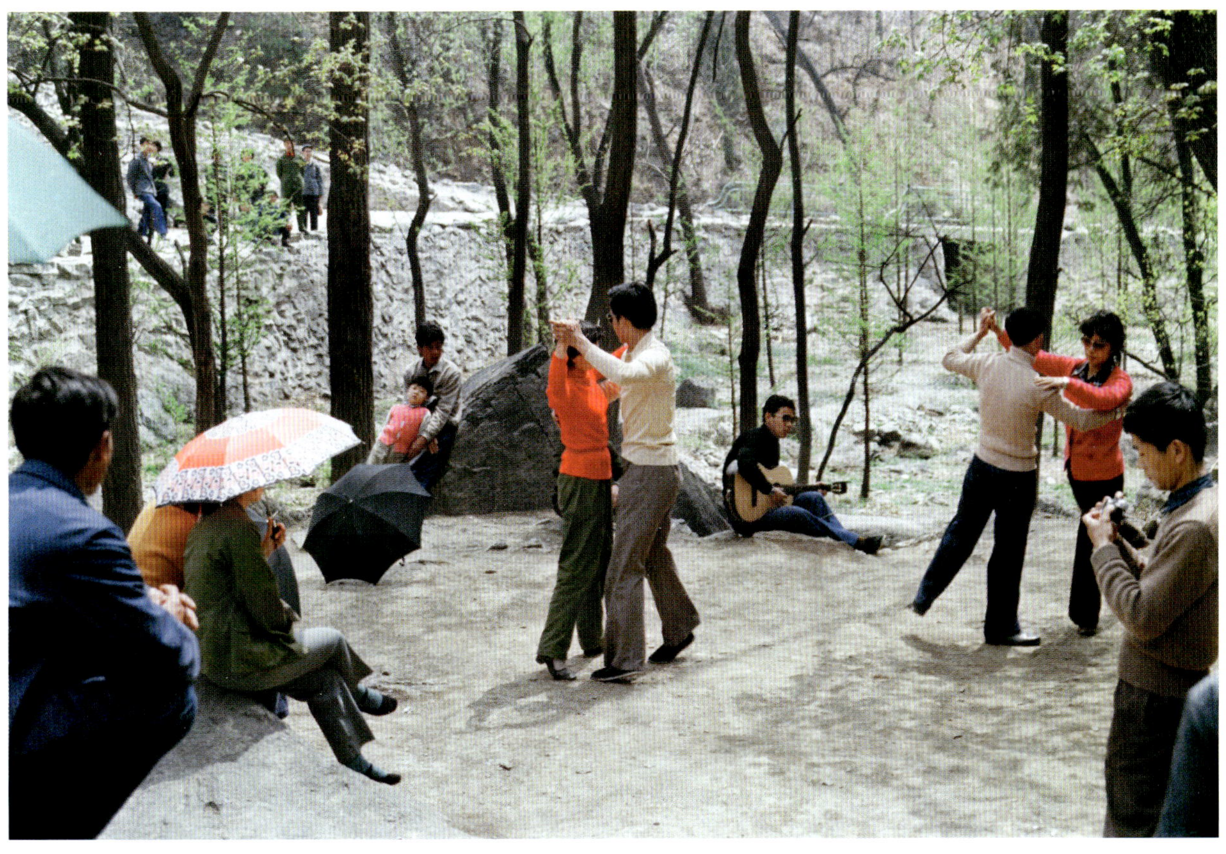

103 Li Xiaobin, *Dancing In The Park*, 2 May 1980, chromogenic print.

> them, all I want to do through the forms within the photographs is to convey a feeling.[11]

With this statement Li exposed a growing tension between practitioners of artistic and documentary photography. At the time, Li's carefully observed snapshots of people dancing in parks, wearing fashionable brand-name sunglasses and embroidered cardigans, were criticized as ordinary and lacking in technique, the kind of photograph that anyone could take. But he persisted: 'Today, we find ourselves in a period of great change and transformation', he argued. 'This period and its particular look is different from what has gone before and from what is to come . . .

if we cannot capture it with our cameras in a timely manner we will be creating a gap in our history, creating a loss that is difficult to make up.'[12]

During this period one of the most active photojournalists in southern China was An Ge (Peng Zhenge, *b.* 1947), who took up photography at the age of 32 after spending seven years as a rusticated youth in Yunnan, and then four years working in a factory, before being transferred to the Xinhua News Agency in Guangzhou. It did not take him long to realize that few of his experiences were reflected in photographs of 'buildings, bridges, factories, schools . . . hand shakes, gatherings, meetings and ribbon cutting' published in the mainstream media. It was time, he said, to photograph 'new people and new things, in their contexts', to capture on film 'a feeling that resonates with my contemporaries'.[13]

An Ge was a member of the Everybody Photography Society, established in Guangzhou in 1979, not long after the April Photography Society. The group held its first exhibition the following year. One of An Ge's classic early photographs is a rear view of three government officials squatting by the kerb at a busy intersection in Guangzhou. As they relax, probably smoking, we look over their shoulders and experience the bustle of Guangzhou in 1982, one of China's most dramatically modernizing cities at the time.

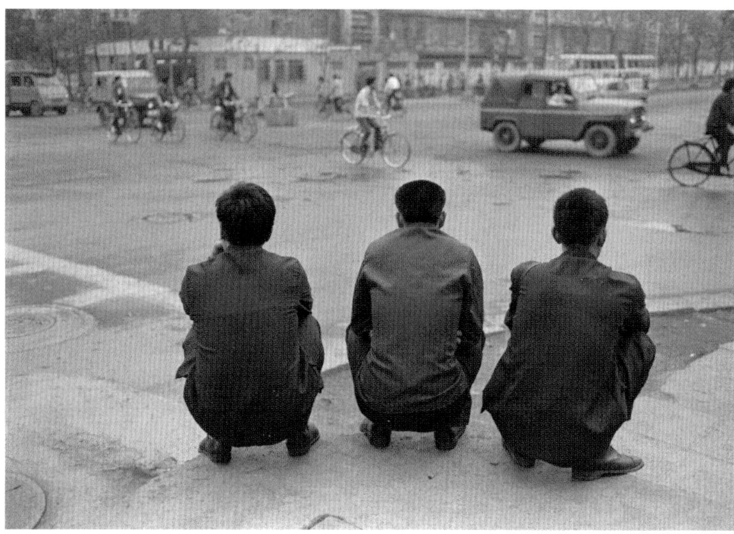

104 An Ge, *Three Men Squatting*, 1982, gelatin silver print.

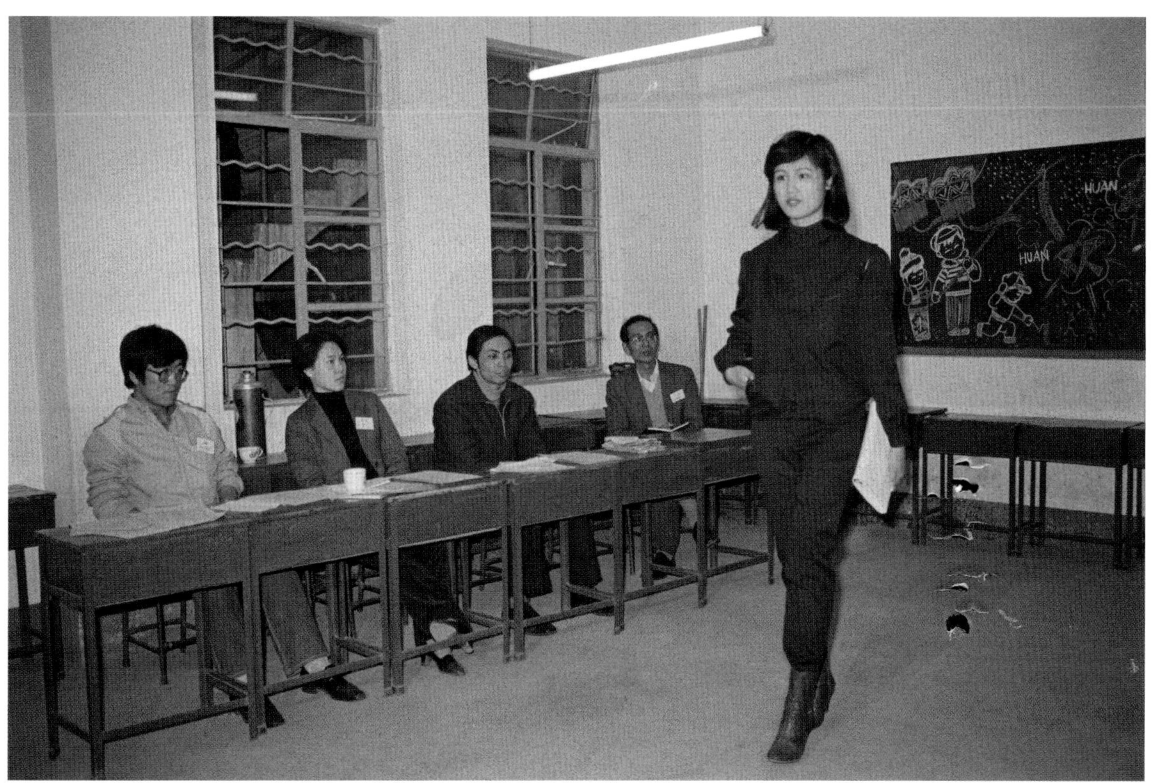

105 An Ge, *Beauty Contest*, 1985, gelatin silver print.

In 1985, in response to an official directive to promote morality, politeness and good behaviour, the Communist Youth League in Guangzhou initiated a beauty contest, the first since 1949. An Ge's photograph of the pre-selection parade, held at a local primary school, shows a fashionably dressed young woman being scrutinized by judges. It was immediately picked up by the Hong Kong press, but mainland coverage of the event was restricted to a few lines in Guangzhou's *Yangcheng Evening Newspaper*. China's door was opening to the outside world in a slow, controlled way.

At around this time, photographers from the April Photography Society joined Yang Shaoming (*b.* 1942), a photographer working at the Xinhua News Agency and the son of PRC president Yang Shangkun, to form the China Modern Photo Salon. The group held its first exhibition

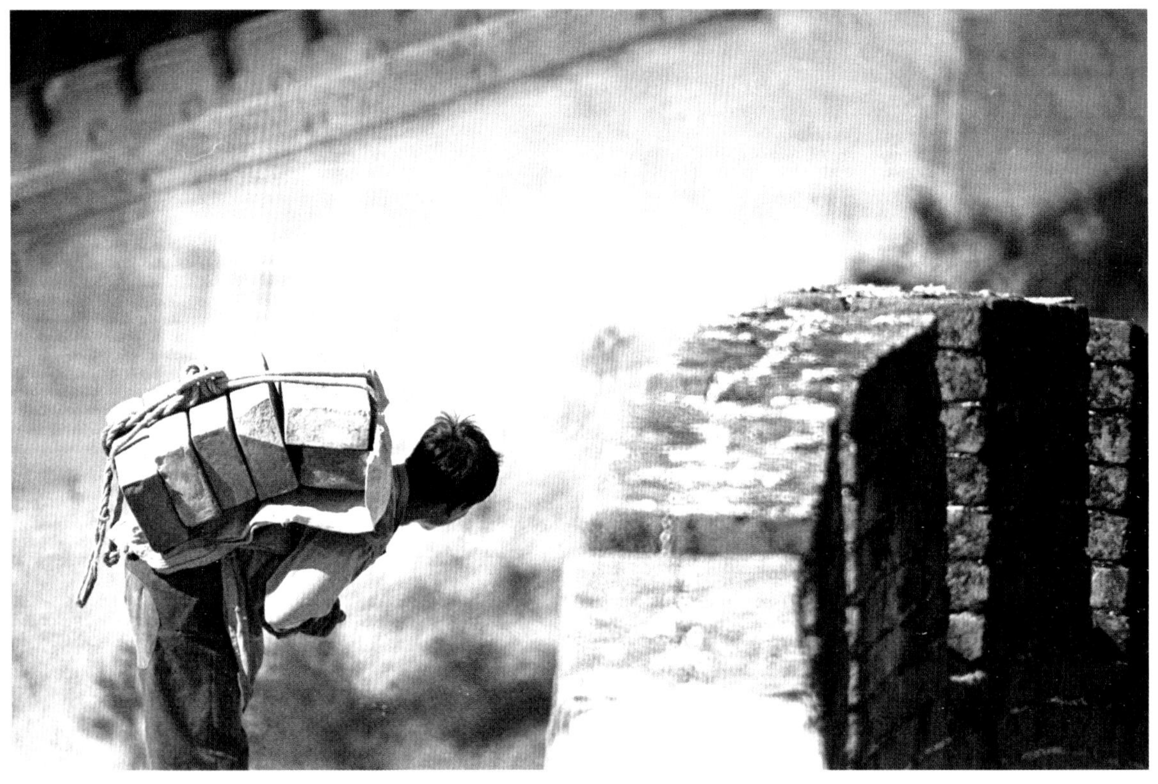

106 Wang Wenlan, *Burden on the Spine*, 1984, gelatin silver print.

in Beijing in May 1985, for which a lavish colour catalogue was printed in Hong Kong. The group's official nature is evident in the inclusion of two photographs by Yang Shaoming showing Deng Xiaoping, father of a modernizing China, as a relaxed family man playing cards and blowing out candles on a birthday cake.

A powerful image in the same exhibition, *Burden on the Spine* by Wang Wenlan, documents the restoration of the Great Wall at Badaling in 1984. The massive, ancient structure built to keep China secure from barbarian tribes on its northern border was being refurbished for Chinese and international tourists in the wake of economic reforms and the expansion of foreign trade. Conveying the back-breaking labour of the anonymous worker, the black-and-white photograph also alludes to the burden of China's past.

The second exhibition of the China Modern Photo Salon, Flashback, was a retrospective of the decade since 1976:

> Ten years ago we held cameras in our hands and recorded the stormy events of April 5. Over the past ten years we have continued to use the cameras in our hands to remember, apprehend and understand the great changes that have occurred . . . We seek to use new methods and new angles to get closer to the truth, and to conscientiously respond to questions posed by history through the reality of life and real life.[14]

While looking back to their roots as chroniclers of a mass movement that led to sweeping reforms, these photographers were also looking forward, conscious of a need to build on their achievements and embrace a wider network of practitioners. The exhibition again included a diverse array of works, ranging from Li Xiaobin's iconic photograph of the petitioner, seen in public for the first time, to He Yanguang's 1984 photograph of a crowd of people celebrating the Chinese National Day in Tiananmen Square with a banner inscribed 'Hello Xiaoping', using Deng Xiaoping's given name with unusual familiarity.

In many parts of China photographers began to take an active interest in the lives of ordinary people. In Xi'an, the Square City Photography Group, established in 1980, held an exhibition in an underground air-raid shelter underneath the ancient city. Members of the group, who went on to become the Shaanxi Group, were concerned with documenting local environments. Hu Wugong (*b.* 1949), for example, was assigned to work as an army propaganda artist and photographer when he graduated from the Xi'an Academy of Fine Arts Preparatory School. He took photographs of military activities in Ningxia and Gansu in northwestern China and in his home province Shaanxi. In 1975 he was transferred to the publishing house attached to the Shaanxi News agency. He describes the confusion and bewilderment in the early years of his professional life resulting from having to make photographs in compliance with the official dictates. Like others of his generation, Hu sought to extricate himself from this restrictive framework. At a conference on photography theory held in Guilin in 1981 Hu promoted the idea of truth in photography. His image of police

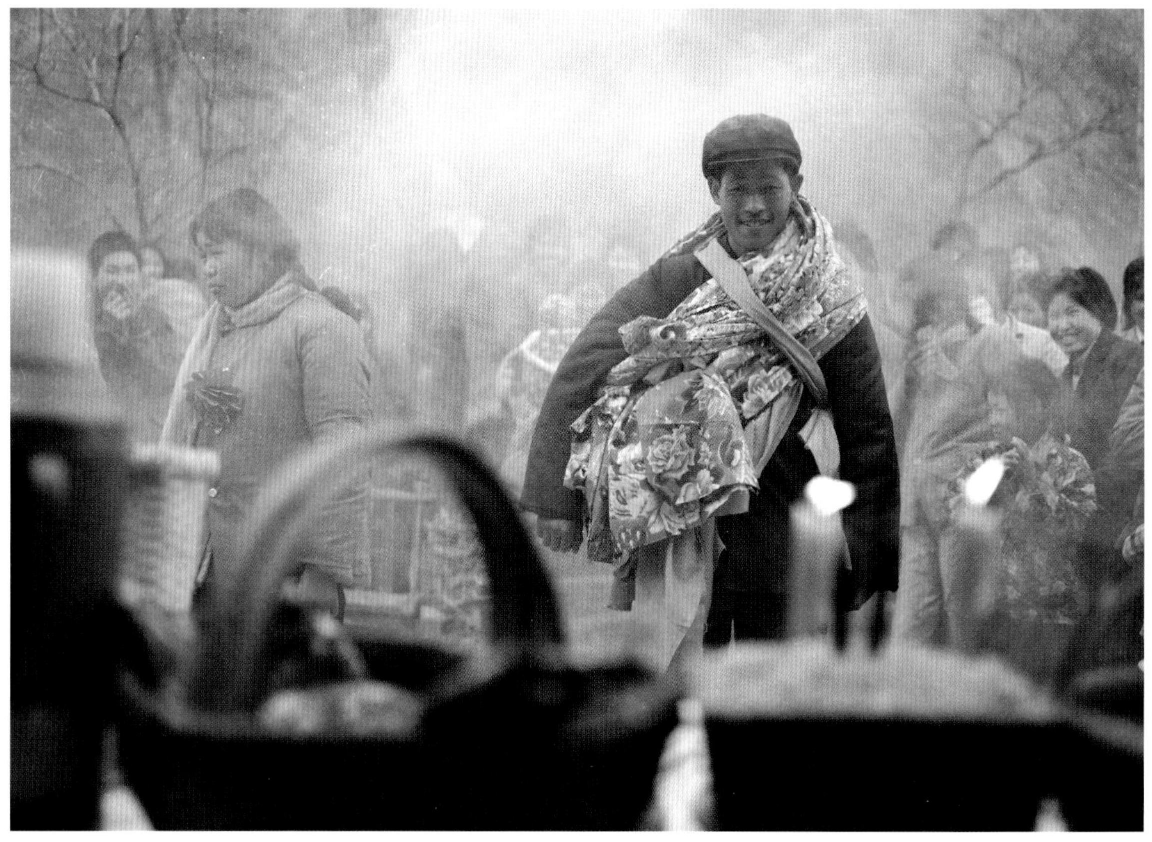

107 Hu Wugong, *Groom*, Lantian, Shaanxi, 1985, gelatin silver print.

rescuing people from floodwaters in 1983 was declared the best news photograph at the inaugural awards of the China News Photography Association and was featured on the cover of *China Daily* and the inaugural issue of *Photography Newspaper*.

But over time Hu became less interested in reporting topical events for a mass audience and chose to pursue a documentary photography that was not driven by a journalistic narrative. His award-winning photograph *Groom*, taken with a Mamiya camera in Lantian, Shaanxi, is typical of his documentary practice. The groom smiles warmly as he faces the camera, bedecked in lengths of cotton cloth printed with auspicious patterns that will brighten up the marital home, while the bride, designated by her peony flower, turns away. Hu photographs a rite of passage for a couple who remain nameless, reflecting 'ordinary events in ordinary settings . . . the most fundamental aspects of Chinese lives, which may seem outmoded, crude or evolving, but that are real expressions of Chinese civilization.'[15] Framed by the altar and candles, the photograph is a quietly powerful image of the resilience of individuals and local customs.

The photograph relates to a larger cultural interest in the ancient loess plateau region of Shaanxi, the subject of Chen Kaige's first feature film *Yellow Earth* (1984). The cinematographer for *Yellow Earth* was Zhang Yimou and the art director He Qun. Chen, Zhang and He were in the first group of students to graduate from the Beijing Film Academy after the Cultural Revolution. At that time, the early 1980s, an influx of foreign culture inspired developments in literature, music and art. 'Then, all of a sudden', according to Zhang Yimou, 'there was a surge of solidarity that compelled everyone to reflect on our own cultural tradition, our historical past . . . people worked from the primitive, basic principles to rediscover the value of human beings'.[16]

108 Hou Dengke, *Itinerant Wheat Harvesters, Guanzhong, Shanxi*, June 1993, gelatin silver print.

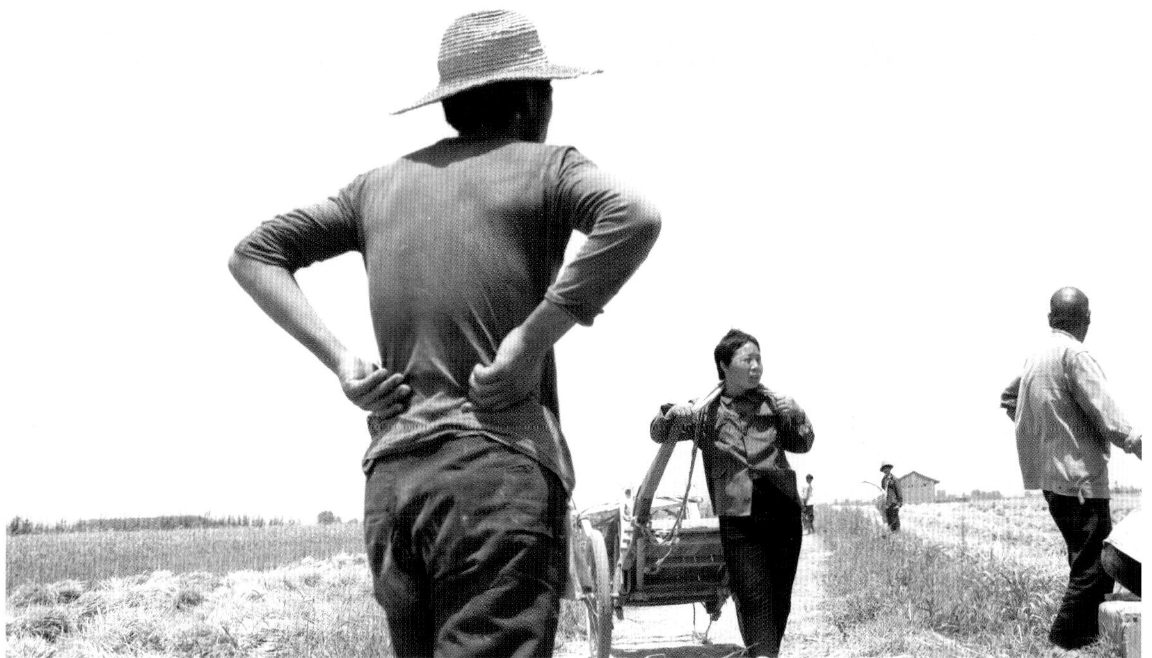

In 1988 Hou Dengke (1953–2003) and members of the Shaanxi Group initiated a major photography competition directed at releasing photography from didactic propaganda to address reality and human suffering. The resulting exhibition at the China National Art Gallery, called An Arduous Passage, was a sprawling array of works, culled from 20,000 images received from photographers across the country, organized into categories: news photography, documentary photography and creative photography. The exhibition showed work that for the first time addressed some of the more sensitive topics in the history of the PRC: Shi Panqi (*b.* 1932) on the Anti-Rightist Movement; Li Zhensheng (*b.* 1940) on the Cultural Revolution; Li Xiaobin on the Beijing Spring; and fake photographs created for propaganda purposes. The subsequent publication, *Forty Years of Chinese Photography*, refers to the exhibition as a 'gift' to mark the 40th anniversary of the founding of the PRC.

Wu Jialin (*b.* 1942) is an important photographer who emerged at this time and whose work is driven by a humanist impulse to document his native area. He was born in Zhaotong, on the high plateau in north-eastern Yunnan, a once prosperous area located on the historic trade route connecting China with Southeast Asia. Wu is a self-taught photographer who worked for the Yunnan News Photo Agency, but had mixed feelings about making his subjects dress up and smile. Wang Zhiping and Wang Miao's photographs of Tibet had an impact on him (local exotica became a focus in the absence of opportunities for foreign travel). 'Their photos mitigated the hypocrisy and made-up images of the popular photography of that time, which mainly served the Party's political ideas; their photos reflected the truth of life.'[17] Wu then faced, as he says, the 'sacred truth of life' and 'began [his] photographic life anew'.[18]

With his interest in the relationship between people and place, which was part of a larger cultural trend of 'searching for roots', Wu does not provide narrative-style captions for his images, only a place name and a date. The bare terrain of Zhaotong is starkly portrayed in a photograph from 1989 depicting a man walking on the main road out of town carrying two tree trunks, which seem to catch him in a pincer movement. The man's downcast determination suggests the effort required to carry the difficult load and draws attention to the complex interdependency of human beings and

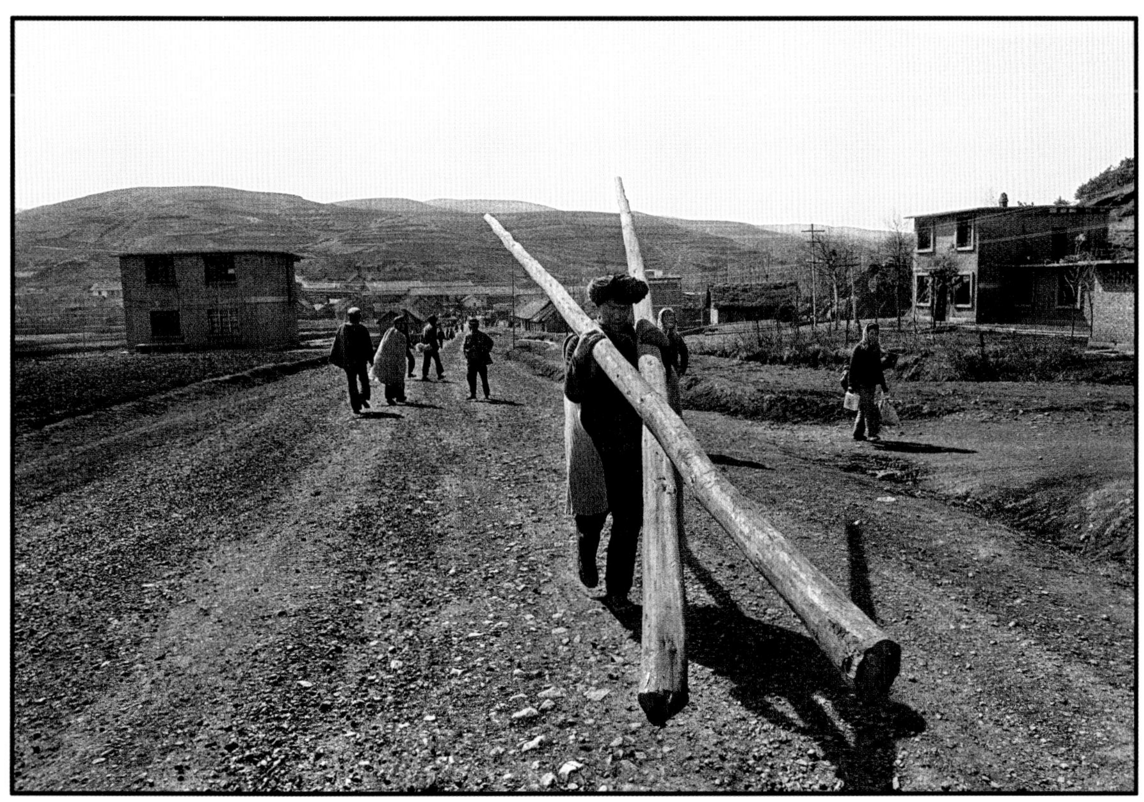

109 Wu Jialin, *Zhaotong, Yunnan*, 1989, gelatin silver print.

nature. Later Wu wrote: 'I consider myself not a documentary photographer but rather an artist, observing life with my own personality, my vision, and my strong subjective ideas . . . Photography to me is an activity of the emotion . . . my method is to walk, observe, discover, emerge, disappear, and photograph real things with true emotion.'[19]

The year he took the Zhaotong photograph, Wu Jialin saw the work of Magnum photographer Marc Riboud (*b*. 1923), a Frenchman who had spent close to four months in China in 1957 and returned for extended periods in 1965 and 1971. Riboud's work was published in the magazine *Photography* (*Sheying*). In 1993 the two photographers met in Shenzhen and Riboud helped Wu shape a selection of photographs that would be published later that year under the title *Mountain Folk in Yunnan*. While

Riboud did not formally exhibit in China until 1996, solo exhibitions of work by his Magnum colleagues Robert Capa and Henri Cartier-Bresson, whose photographs have also been significant in creating an image of China for the West, were held at the China National Art Gallery in 1985 and 1987 respectively. Exhibitions of work by Walker Evans (1980), Ansell Adams (1983) and Robert Doisneau (1983), and survey shows of photography from around the world including Canada (1978), Australia (1981) and Italy (1982), invariably part of official cultural exchange programmes, provided important opportunities for Chinese photographers to see works by influential international photographers, and in some cases meet them face to face.

In the 1980s delegations of Chinese press photographers also regularly travelled overseas, and conferences and exhibitions relating to photojournalism were held in China. In 1988 the Museum of the Chinese Revolution hosted an exhibition of 30 years of the Amsterdam-based World Press Photo Contest (1956–86), which toured to Guangzhou, Shanghai, Xi'an and other cities, and attracted large crowds. An even more ambitious project was A Day in the Life of China. Following a model applied in the United States, Japan and other countries, organizers brought 61 foreign photographers and 29 local photographers together on 15 April 1989 to record a period of 24 hours in cities and villages across China. International participants included Magnum photographers Bruno Barbey (*b*. 1941), René Burri (*b*. 1933), Mary Ellen Mark (*b*. 1940) and Sebastião Salgado (*b*. 1944), *National Geographic* photographer David Alan Harvey (*b*. 1944) and *Life* magazine photo editor John Loengard (*b*. 1934). On the Chinese side were Yang Shaoming from the Xinhua News Agency, He Yanguang, then director of photography for *China Youth Daily*, Wang Wenlan, director of photography at the *China Daily*, Wang Miao, a photographer for the Hong Kong-based magazine *China Tourism*, and many military photographers. Although the event was officially managed, the intention was to create a relatively candid view of life in China. Some foreign photographers were prevented from taking the photographs that they wanted, and Chinese photographers also encountered difficulties. He Yanguang was initially barred from a hospital for the criminally insane in Jinhua, Zhejiang. His published photograph shows a group of inmates awaiting trial, peering out from behind the bars of their communal cell in Jinhua (many people languished in jail waiting for lawyers and proceedings). It contrasts with Yang Shaoming's photograph of Deng Xiaoping, chairman of the Military Commission and effective leader of China, who appeared to be relaxing at home with his wife Zhuo Lin and grandson.[20] But it is unlikely that Deng would have been putting his feet up with his family that evening as Hu Yaobang (1915–1989), a liberal who had been removed from his post as General Secretary of the Communist Party two years earlier, had passed away in the early hours of 15 April, the 'Day in the Life of China'. By the time the project photographers returned to Beijing that evening people were gathering in Tiananmen Square to mourn Hu Yaobang's passing.

The last photograph (uncredited, but taken by a Chinese photographer) in the subsequent publication shows two 'big character posters' freshly posted onto a wall at Beijing University:

> All Beijing University mourns!
> See who prospers, who despairs.
> In 40 years, China has failed to rise.
> In 70 years, democracy remains unfulfilled.
> Deng Xiaoping still has his health at 84.
> Hu Yaobang dies first at 73.
> The politicians come and go.
> Can there be no cure?[21]

The poster presages the sentiments of people who came to Tiananmen Square to mourn the death of Hu Yaobang and express their frustration with the leadership. 1989 was the 40th anniversary of the PRC and the 70th anniversary of the May Fourth Movement, when students protested against China's treatment in the Treaty of Versailles, which ended the First World War, and the Chinese government's weak response. After seven weeks of non-violent demonstrations in Tiananmen Square, force was used against civilians, and on the evening of 3 June tanks and artillery moved into the centre of Beijing, killing an unknown number of people. An image that has become iconic of the stubborn bravery of civilian

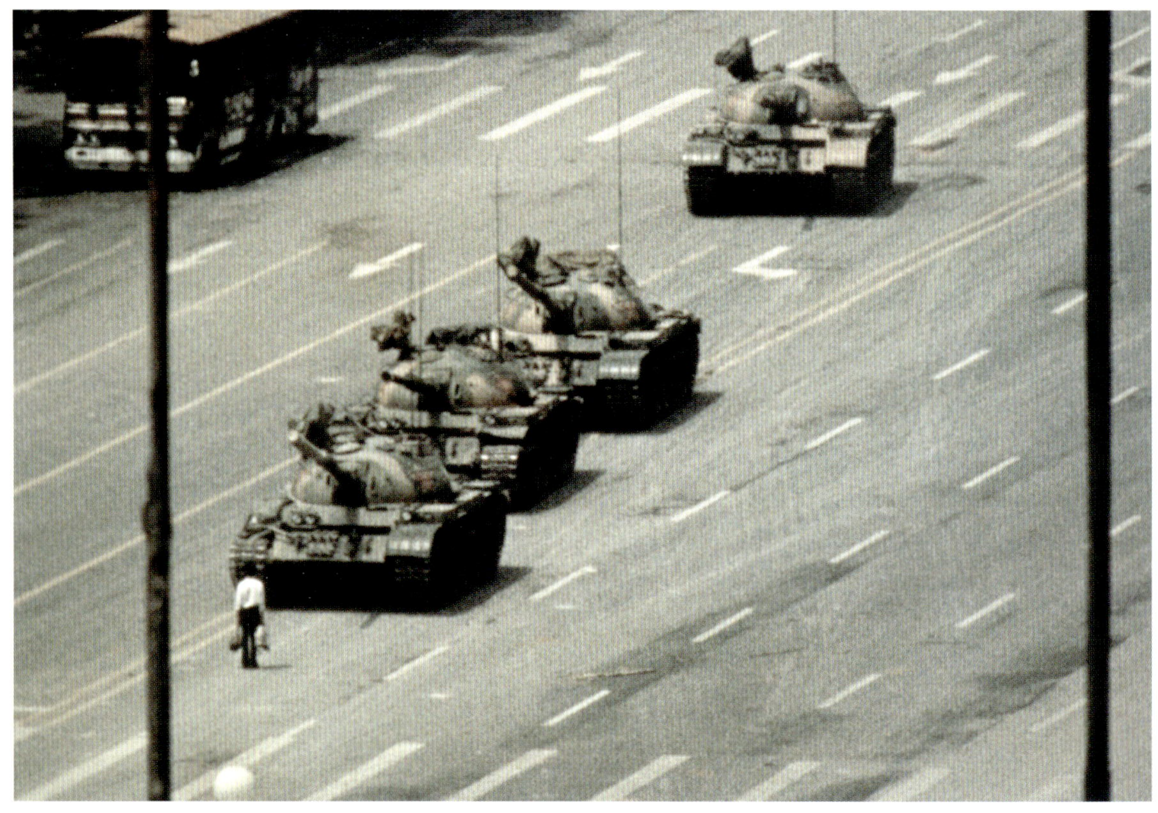

110 Arthur Tsang Hin Wah, *Tank Man*, 1989, chromogenic print.

protesters in the face of a formidable military presence on 4 June is the 'Tank Man', a lone individual staring down a row of tanks in the middle of Chang'an Boulevard, immediately to the east of Tiananmen Square. From film footage that is now etched in the minds of people around the world, we know how the 'Tank Man' waved his bags in the air and manoeuvred to prevent the tanks from passing, climbing onto a tank to talk with those inside, before disappearing into the crowd never to be seen again.

Four photojournalists working for international news agencies, located on the balcony of the Beijing Hotel, captured the event: Charlie Cole (*Newsweek*); Stuart Franklin (*Time*); Jeff Widener (The Associated Press); and Arthur Tsang Hin Wah (Reuters). Hong Kong-born Arthur Tsang Hin Wah (*b*. 1951) was a photographer for United Press International and later

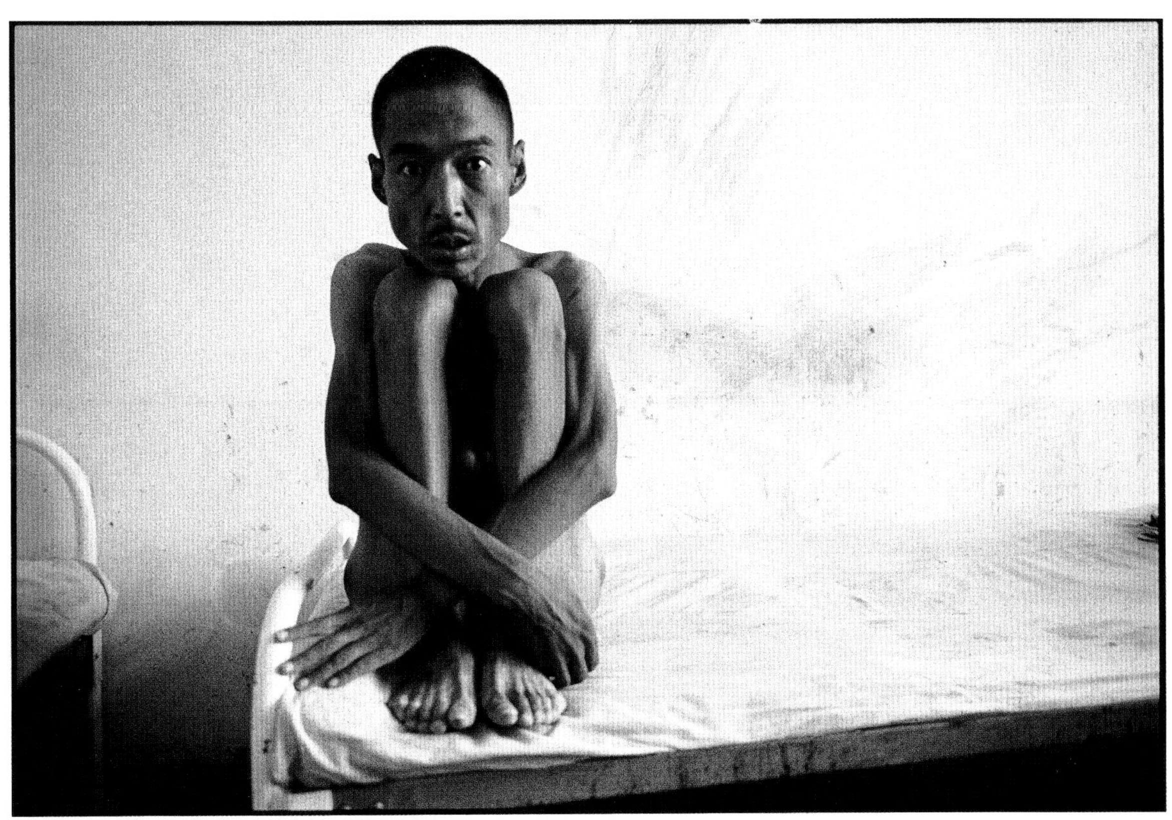

111 Lü Nan, *Yang Jun, Mental Hospital, Tianjin*, 1989, gelatin silver print.

Reuters, covering regional news in Southeast Asia. His photograph, taken from the eleventh floor of the hotel, was the first of the four to be taken. The photographs, charged with symbolism, record one of the most remarkable performances by an individual in recent Chinese history.

While the New York-based photojournalist Mary Ellen Mark photographed patients in the Second Mental Hospital in Chongqing on 15 April 1989, she was unaware that her work had exerted an influence on contemporary Chinese documentary photography. In 1989, after the events of Tiananmen, photographers Lü Nan (*b.* 1962) and Yuan Dongping (*b.* 1956), colleagues working at the *Minorities Pictorial* in Beijing, began independent projects to investigate the lives of people with mental illness in China. Lü Nan was inspired in part by Mark's portraits of women in

Ward 81, the maximum-security section of Oregon State Hospital, which he had seen published in the Taiwanese magazine *Lion Arts* (Hsiung-Shih Mei-Shu). For Lü Nan it was a two-year project, photographing patients in hospitals, at home and homeless. In October 1989 he quit his job working in the darkroom at the *Pictorial* where he had worked for five years, and has travelled extensively since then photographing people living on the margins of society.

Lü Nan's remarkable photograph of a male patient sitting naked on the edge of his bed was taken in a mental hospital in Tianjin (illus. 111). The patient, Yang Jun, was 35 years old and had been hospitalized for ten years. In 1986 he was diagnosed with tuberculosis and placed in quarantine without medication. With no family he was dependent on the state. He died two months after the photograph was taken. Unlike Mark, who was given permission by family members and the Oregon State Hospital to photograph patients on condition she did not reveal names or case histories, Lü Nan captions his photographs with brief but vital information. The text, he says, is intended to confer respect on the individuals who are stigmatized by their mental illness and have been abandoned by society.[22] His portrait of the encounter with humanity stripped to its barest essentials might function as a metaphor for Chinese society as a whole.

Lü Nan's photographs were first presented to the public as a slide show at the Pingyao Photography Festival in 2005 (as part of his 'trilogy' of portraits including Chinese Christians and Tibetans) and two years later exhibited at the Songzhuang Art Museum in Beijing. In his introduction to the publication *The Forgotten People: The State of Chinese Psychiatric Wards* (2008) Li Xianting, the art critic and director of the Songzhuang Art Museum, frames Lü Nan's work as art. The art gallery provided a space where visual narratives that run counter to the mainstream can be presented, unlike the outlets available for journalism, which remain closely controlled.

Lü Nan is one of many independent documentary photographers who, after 1989, began to turn their cameras onto marginalized and dispossessed people, responding to the failure of investigative journalism and in the process systematically exposing dark, controversial or shocking aspects of Chinese society. He is the only mainland Chinese photographer associated with Magnum (he is a corresponding member). He says of his work: 'My job is caring about people; my focus is also people.'[23]

In 2003 a landmark exhibition, Humanism in China: A Contemporary Record of Photography, was held at the Guangdong Museum of Art. The chief organizers were An Ge and Hu Wugong, pioneers of people-centred photography in China, and Wang Huangsheng, director of the Guangdong Museum of Art (2000–2009), who supported the nationwide project and acquired the some 600 works of the exhibition for the museum's collection. Another key participant was fotoe.com, an independent Guangzhou-based web platform representing numerous agencies and the work of some 3,000 Chinese documentary photographers. In the introduction to the exhibition Hu Wugong refers to documentary photography as 'sincere', reflecting people's lives, society, and the ebb and flow of history. It is, he says, 'about responsibility, respect and integrity'.[24]

Since the 1990s the blurring of the boundary between documentary and artistic photography has been a dominant characteristic of contemporary Chinese photography as photographers use the medium to open up divergent narratives, including exposing cases of inequality, injustice and environmental degradation.

In 2009 the freelance photographer Lu Guang (*b.* 1961) was awarded the W. Eugene Smith Grant in Humanistic Photography for a series of powerful and shocking photographs titled *Pollution in China*. The following year Lu received a grant from *National Geographic* magazine to work on a project to document pollution in China and its impact on people's lives, indicating global interest in China's social and environmental problems. Photographers like Lu continue the humanistic tradition of people's photography, using the camera to record the effects of China's rapid economic growth.

six

U-Turn

In the decade leading up to 1989 photography moved into the artistic vanguard while retaining its social edge. Beijing artist Wang Youshen (*b.* 1964) began to experiment with photography while he was studying oil painting at art school. In 1987 he teamed up with Bi Jianfeng, Chen Shuxia and Hong Hao to form the Central Academy of Fine Arts Student Photography Group. Their manifesto, printed in the *Photography Newspaper,* declared their interest in photography as art:

> using the camera as a paint brush, and photographic paper as canvas, we use our own imagination, ideas and feelings in our works . . . We use what is unique to us as our point of departure . . . and use our unique perspective, to examine objective reality, and through our arrangements give expression to the abundance of our feelings. Art is creative practice, photography is also creative practice. Both require our dedication.[1]

After his graduation in 1988 Wang Youshen was assigned to work as an art editor at *Beijing Youth Daily*. Working at the newspaper he had ready access to cameras and equipment. Among the works included in the landmark China/Avant-garde exhibition at the China National Art Gallery in 1989 – now famous for its ironic logo 'No U-turn' – was an early example of conceptual photography by Wang Youshen and Yang Jun, also a graduate of the Central Academy. The joint work titled '✓' comprised a grid of black-and-white photographs adhered to a panel propped against the gallery wall and extending onto the floor. The photographs were taken in Wangfujing, Beijing's busiest shopping street, using a camera mounted on a tripod, set with an automatic timer to shoot a photograph every minute. A court 'Notice' used to publicize the names of criminals who were to be executed, and a large red painted '✓' (official shorthand that an offender had been put to death), were superimposed over the photographs. The artists were forced to remove the red tick and cover the court notice, effectively censoring the installation.

Wang Youshen and Yang Jun's work, and the action of Xiao Lu firing a gun at her installation *Dialogue* in February, which forced the closure of the China/Avant-garde exhibition, were portentous works that unintentionally presaged the violence and bloodshed that would unfold in June that year. The events were a culmination of, and temporarily brought to a halt, over a decade of artistic innovation.

From the late 1970s artists, writers and photographers had been experimenting with the expressive and conceptual potential of their respective media, combining new artistic ideas with newly learned techniques. Early examples of experimental photography include Chen Fan's 1979 portrait of the prominent Stars group artist Wang Keping, in which positive and negative images are overlaid; Liu Shizhao's *Lights from ten thousand homes*, an image of light refracted on a window pane; and Xu Zhuo's *Modernity*, a constructed image employing double exposures, composite negatives and painted motifs. As the reform era advanced, individuals came together to share new ideas. In 1986 Gu Daxiang, Li Mingzhi and Yu Xiaoyang became known as the Rupture Group for the bold artistry of their images, incorporating collage, projection, soft focus and slow exposure. And the following year five Xiamen photographers – Li Shixiong, Chen Yongpeng, Xie Ping, Zhou Yuedong and Cai Ming – held an exhibition at the Hong Kong Arts Centre titled Five in One, the first by an unofficial group of amateur photographers from the mainland. In Shanghai members of the North of the River Alliance used the city as a subject to express feelings of isolation, confusion and unease, employing a variety of lenses and camera angles, and striking juxtapositions of imagery. They held an exhibition at the Paris Café in Shanghai's Huaihai cinema in 1986, followed by an exhibition in Beijing called Explorers, indicating the new territory they were charting in Chinese photographic practice. Their mission was 'to understand the world that we all face with eyes that cannot be substituted by those of anyone else'.[2] Gu Zheng, a key member of the group, became a leading historian and theorist of contemporary Chinese photography. He worked in the Seagull camera factory in Shanghai and regards photography as an integral part of life. His camera, like a notebook, is always at hand.

In Guangzhou, Zhang Hai'er (*b.* 1957) also pursued city-based photographic work that broke free from the strictures of straight realism. He came to photography out of disillusionment with painting, having studied and worked as a set designer and art director at Guangdong Television, and enrolled as a graduate student at the Guangzhou Academy of Fine Arts. In 1984, the year before he entered the art academy, he began to experiment with photography, and found it to be a medium that 'satisfied a deep internal need. I had been searching for a more direct medium that had a capability for quick response.'[3]

Zhang Hai'er's early photographs were taken in his immediate environment of Guangzhou; snatched shots of places and people going about their lives: riding bicycles, getting out of mini-vans, screaming, walking in the street. Invariably people, or traces of people (including the photographer) are a blur in the corner of the image, as if they are moving into or out of the frame by chance. He used a wide-angle lens to expand the field of vision to include the periphery, like the eye. Early on Zhang Hai'er rejected Cartier-Bresson's concept of the 'decisive moment'. The movement of the camera was conscious, a way of making visible his presence: 'The movement of a subject is a natural outcome of the photographic process, whereas movement caused by your action [as a photographer] is an expression of your existence'.[4]

A dynamic, tightly framed photograph of fashionably dressed young women holding hands was chosen for the cover of the inaugural issue of *Photography* (August 1988). The moving camera creates flares of light (like ectoplasm) imbuing the photograph with a feeling of transcendence. The magazine called for 'photography of real significance' that would connect with modern cultural developments and in the process elevate the position of photography within Chinese art.[5] The photographs, by Zhang and others, have no captions and stand alone without

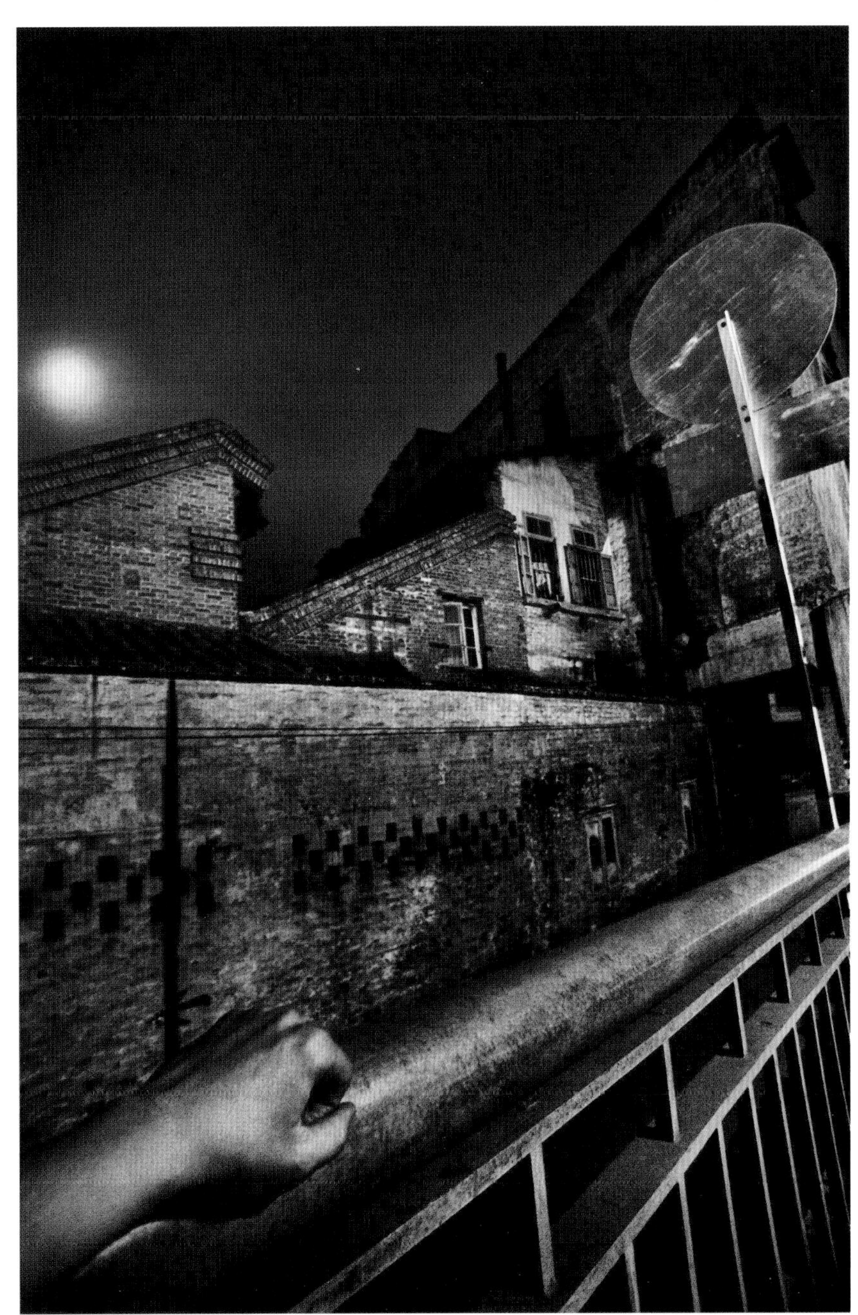

112 Zhang Hai'er, *Night Scene with the Photographer's Left Hand, Guangzhou*, 1987, gelatin silver print.

interpretive text, highlighting their status as works of art rather than photojournalism.

Fulfilling its vow to 'face the international cultural mainstream with an attitude of true frankness and openness', the inaugural issue featured translations of foreign writings on photography, and images from *Red Series* (1979) by the Swiss artist and photographer Christian Vogt, which were reproduced in colour and had a dramatic impact on a wide range of visual artists. The editors included Li Mei, who had been involved with an earlier publication *Modern Photography* (1984–8), and Yang Xiaoyan. Shenzhen, the base for both magazines, was designated a Special Economic Zone in 1979 and developed rapidly as a showcase of China's experiment with market capitalism.

Zhang Hai'er was one of five young Chinese photographers featured in Rencontres d'Arles (1988), one of the world's most important photography festivals. A striking photograph taken in 1989 after his return from Europe and variously titled *Miss Lin* or *Bad Girl* is from a series exploring urban working women in China's fast-changing society, a subject that has since been pursued by many other photographers. Rather than use a detached documentary style, Zhang comes up close, decontextualising the subject and increasing the intensity of his and our voyeuristic gaze. Dramatic lighting creates an image of starkly contrasting black and white.

Beijing-born Liu Xiao Xian (*b*. 1963) came to photography via a very different route. Disillusioned with the prospect of working in an optical factory for the rest of his life, he decided to conduct light-based experiments for himself. Liu's earliest photographic works were created with a Minolta single lens reflex camera that belonged to his older brother, Ah Xian (Liu Jixian), a self-taught artist with close links to the Stars art group. Liu started by creating moody portraits of artist friends and Cubist-inspired collages of iconic Beijing sites such as the Summer Palace, near where he lived. His first solo exhibition was held in 1989 in a rented gallery space in the Zhihua Temple complex. The work sold and his career as an independent practitioner was launched.

In Liu's photographs the eye behind the camera guides the viewer to consider a different kind of reality from that manufactured for mass

113 Zhang Hai'er, *Miss Lin from Guangxi, Guangzhou*, 1989, gelatin silver print.

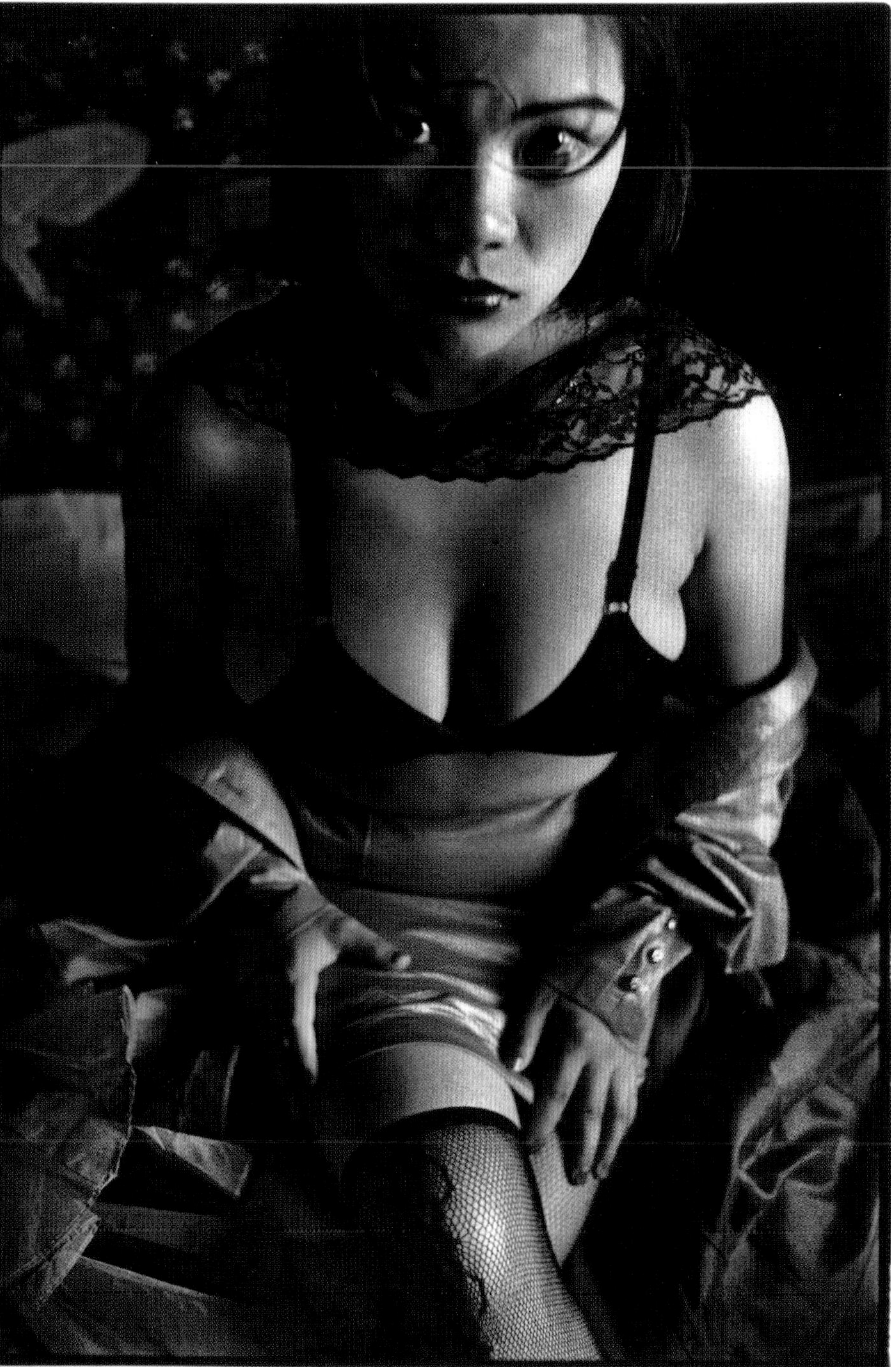

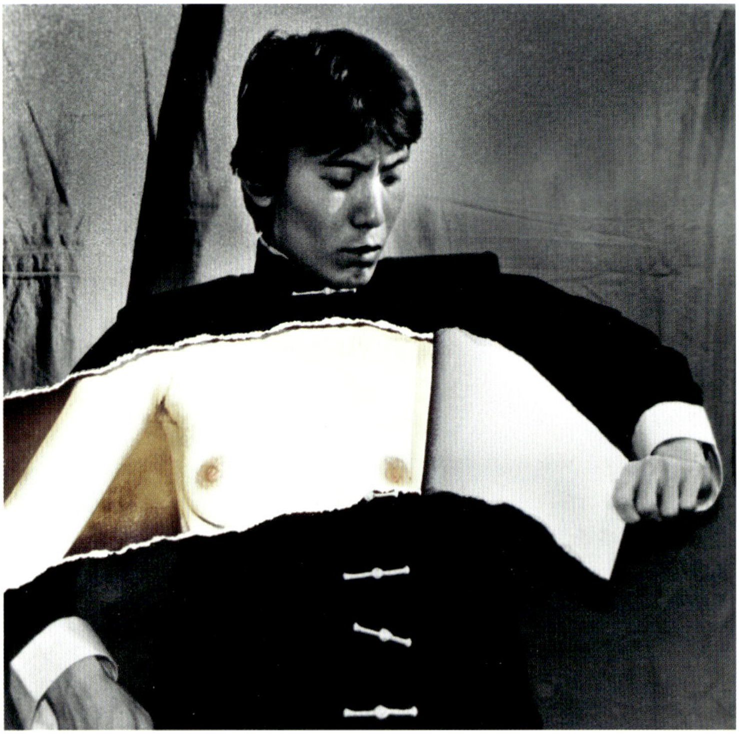

114 Liu Xiao Xian, *Photo #4*, 1990, fibre-based gelatin silver print.

consumption, whether as news, propaganda or art. A Surrealist-inspired image of a man (the model is his brother) tearing open his chest to reveal the naked body of a woman, titled *Photo*, was created in 1989 in the months after Tiananmen. The work, part of a series, is an artistic response to a key word chosen by members of an informal art group who met regularly in Beijing.[6] *Photo* is a carefully constructed image, created before the existence of Photoshop, that questions outward appearances and surface truths, hinting at hidden or private lives to which the state does not have access. This and other early experimental works, none of which were shown publicly in China, have a serious yet playful cerebral dimension.

Mo Yi (*b*. 1958), a photographic artist based in Tianjin, also created moving private works in response to the violence of 4 June 1989. Born in Tibet (he is Han Chinese) and a professional soccer player in Lhasa until the age of 24, he developed an interest in performance and photography as modes of personal expression. His idiosyncratic street works include marching in the street carrying a funerary banner (for which he lost his job and was placed under house arrest), and photographs of himself standing still at busy thoroughfares, titled *Street Face*, witness to time passing. In an attempt to create objective images expressive of the emotional life of the city, he attached the camera to his waist or hung it on his back, pressing the shutter release every five steps.

In a series titled *Tossing Bus* (1989–90), Mo Yi took candid photographs of people travelling with him on public transport. 'It was the autumn and winter of 1989 and China had just come out of [what was officially called] the "6.4 Riot". In the bus, nobody spoke – they were too tired; anyway, it was too cold outside.' The images are blurred or strangely angled, showing expressionless individuals, silhouetted against bus windows that frame views of the street. The bus became a metaphor for the country:

> The nation is like a bus full of querulous passengers. As a Chinese, do you want to get off the bus? But you cannot, because it is your born fate. The driver is not good, the bus is tossing and maybe will overturn at any time, but in spite of anything [that] happens, you have to obey fate . . . These photographs record and symbolize a

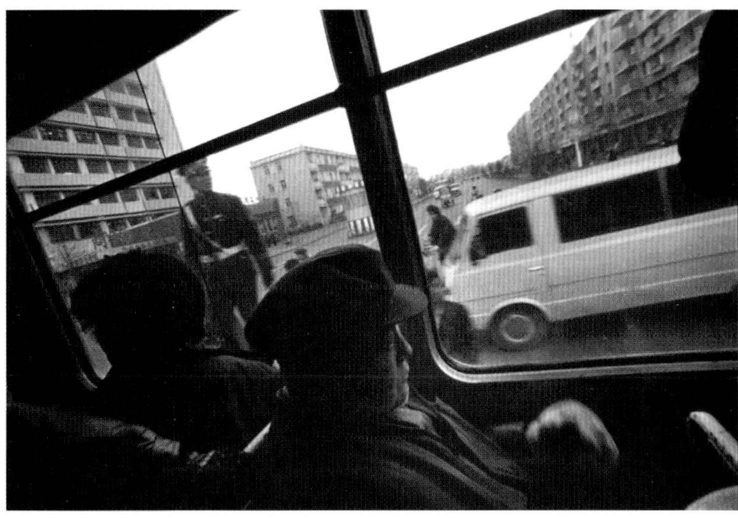

115 Mo Yi, from the series *Tossing Bus – China 1989*, 1989, gelatin silver print.

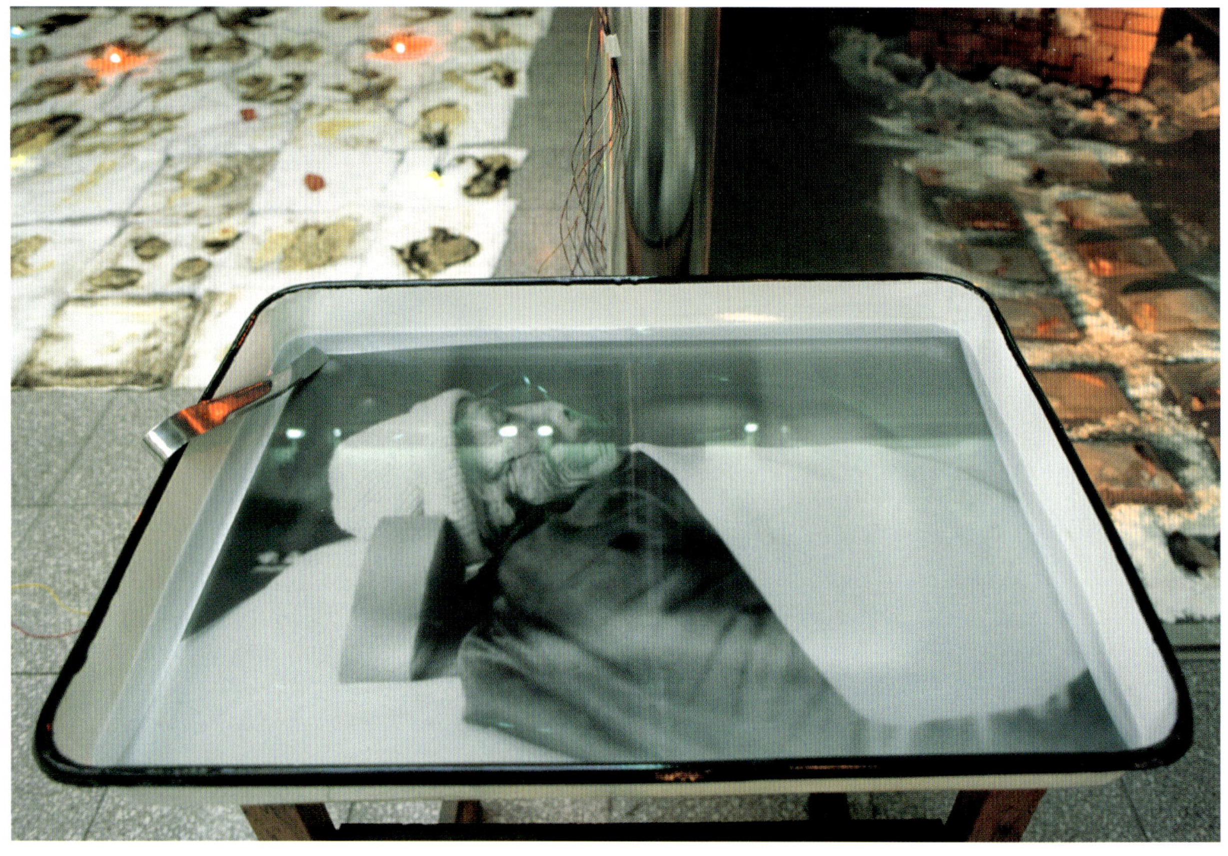

116 Wang Youshen, *Washing: Before and After My Grandmother Passed Away*, 1994, installation.

collective demeanor of a nation at that time . . . And also reflect my own oppressed and helpless emotion and my own spirit.[7]

In the weeks and months after the Beijing massacre of 4 June 1989, many Chinese artists and intellectuals sought safe haven overseas. Wang Youshen visited Australia with the brothers Liu Xiao Xian and Ah Xian for an exhibition in Sydney. He returned to his position at the *Beijing Youth Daily*, however, and went on to create work relating to the media and publishing industry (*Newspaper Series*) and the practice of photography (*Darkroom Series* and *Washing Series*). In *Washing: Before and After My Grandmother Passed Away* (1989–94), Wang used black-and-white film to record the last days of his grandmother's life, photographing her at home (while she was alive); in hospital (after she had died); and as the subject of an art installation (a photograph in a tray of developing liquid). Through the process of washing, the photographic image of his grandmother comes into view, linking the act of photography with the passage of time and the commemoration of life and death. The series prompts the viewer to consider the nature of photography itself, the tension between documentary and conceptual photography, and ideas of public and private, objective and subjective, material and spiritual. A related series from the following year, *Washing: A 1941 Mass Grave in Datong*, refers to atrocities committed by Japan during the Sino-Japanese War. With the cleansing of skulls discovered many years later, the burden of remembering past history through fading images is felt once again.

seven

Performing into the Present

Performance art was another feature of the China/Avant-garde exhibition in 1989 that became pervasive in the 1990s. Acts of spectacle and endurance combining personal expression with social critique were held at short notice in out-of-the-way locations. In a climate of declining opportunities to display contemporary art in public, performance was part of a larger strategy for artists to create and maintain control of their work. One of Beijing's early performance artists was Zhang Huan (*b*. 1965), who lived in a newly formed community of experimental artists in Dashanzhuang, a run-down industrial area on the outskirts of Beijing. He called the area East Village in homage to the famous artist district in New York. On a hot afternoon in June 1994 Zhang Huan sat naked, smeared in honey and fish oil, in a local public toilet. After enduring flies and the stench for an hour, he walked into a polluted pond to 'cleanse' himself. The performance draws on ordinary life to express 'the most essential aspects of being human while also experiencing a kind of contradiction between human nature and the environment in which we live', the artist explains.[1] The body 'is the only direct way through which I come to know society and society comes to know me'.[2]

12 Square Metres was documented in photographs and on video. A torso shot taken by Rong Rong (*b*. 1968) shows Zhang Huan seated naked inside the cavernous public toilet, focused on transcending his physical circumstances. The photograph was reproduced in *The Black Book*, a self-funded artists' publication dedicated to Chinese conceptual art. Edited by artists with connections to New York – Ai Weiwei had recently returned to Beijing following a twelve-year sojourn, and Zeng Xiaojun and Xu

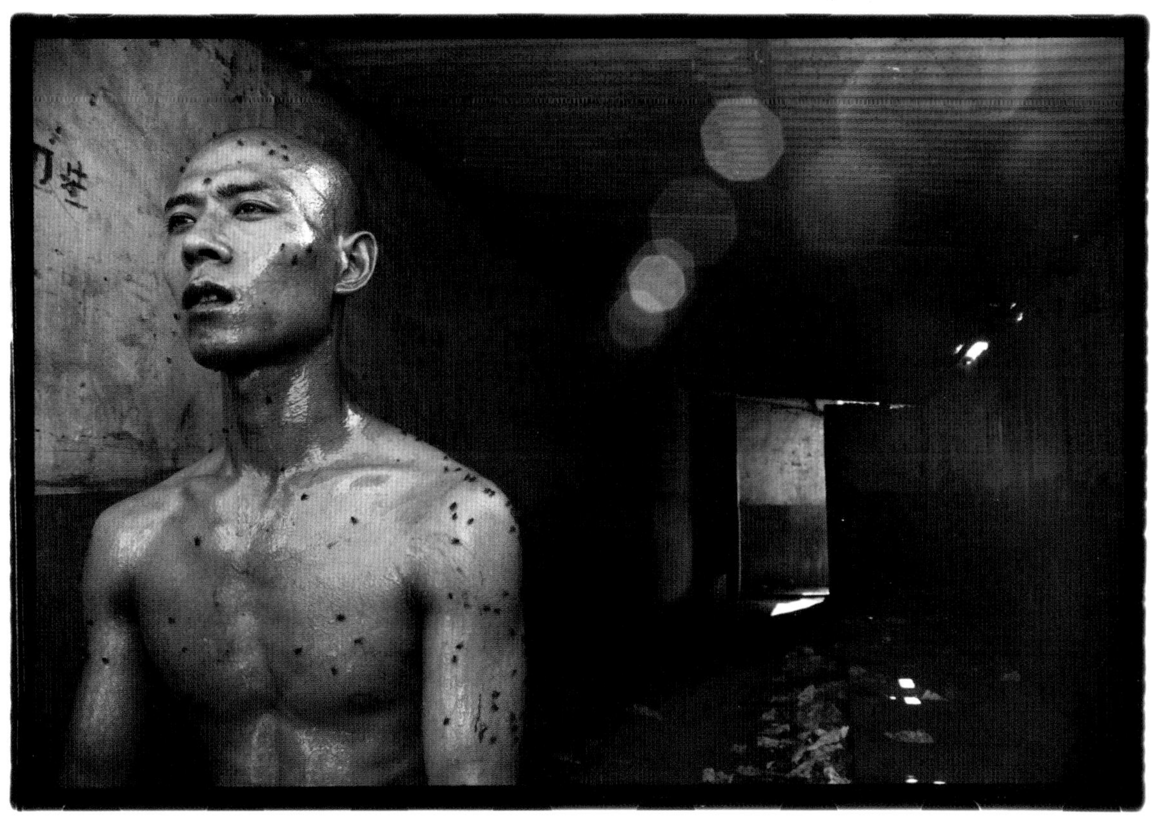

117 Rong Rong, *East Village Beijing No. 20*, 1994, gelatin silver print. Photograph of the performance *12 Square Metres* by Zhang Huan.

Bing, originally from Beijing, were still living in New York – it introduced the work of Duchamp, Warhol, Koons and the Taiwan-born, New York-based performance artist Hsieh Tehching, underlining actual links between the two East Villages.

Another important photographer of Beijing's East Village was Xing Danwen (*b*. 1967), who also trained as a painter. Her staged photographs of Ma Liuming naked, or dressed in women's clothes as his alter ego Fen-Ma Liuming, for the series *A Personal Diary of Chinese Avant-garde Art in the 1990s*, were included in *The Black Book*. They are based on performances by Ma in the wake of a visit to Beijing by British artists Gilbert & George in 1993. The naked body was a powerful and provocative signifier of human individuality and commonality in East Village performances.

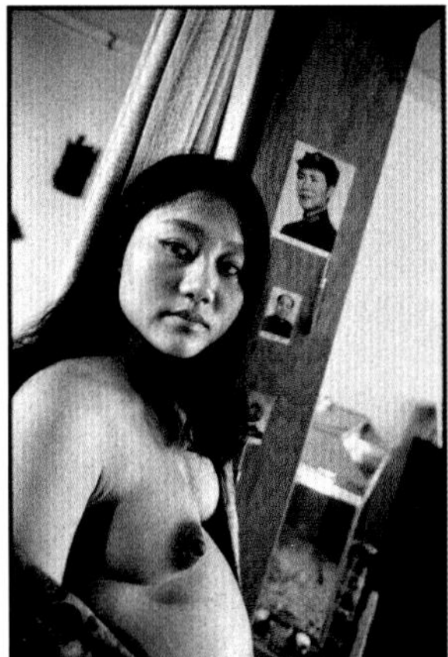
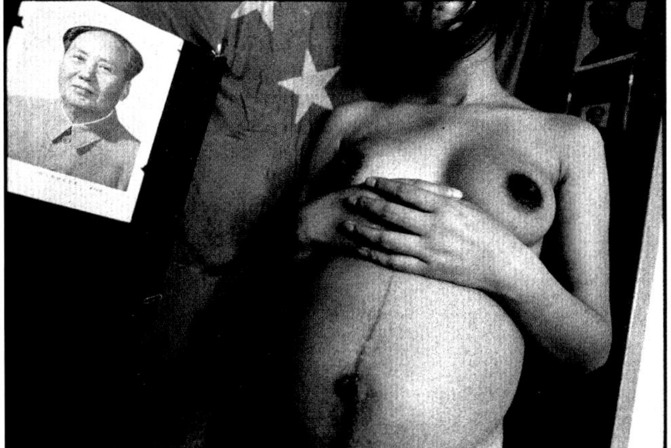
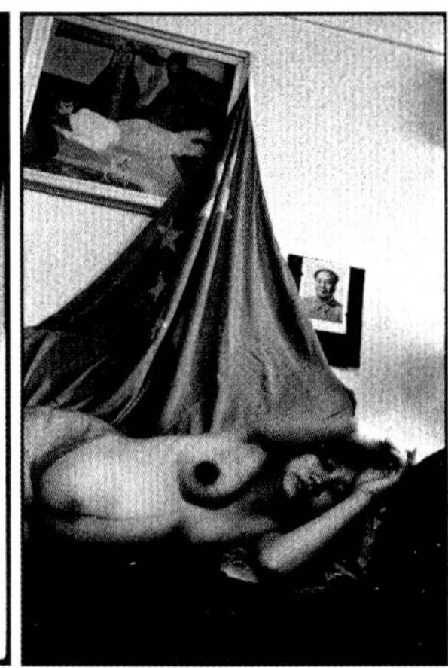

118 Xing Danwen, *Born With the Cultural Revolution*, 1995, chromogenic prints.

The well-known work *To Add One Metre to an Unknown Mountain* (1995, photographed by Lü Nan and others), literally embodied the collective of artists, featuring their naked bodies piled up on top of one another, like sedimentary strata, on a grassy outcrop in mountainous terrain to the northwest of Beijing.

The naked body is the subject of Xing Danwen's series of black-and-white photographs titled *Born With the Cultural Revolution*, 1995. Xing photographed her heavily pregnant friend, who was born in 1966, the year that saw the birth of the Cultural Revolution. Xing describes the woman's body as 'like a landscape within the context of political images'.[3] In the central image of her triptych a mass-produced portrait of Mao Zedong (a print of a painting based on an official photograph taken in 1964 by Zheng Jingkang, 1904–1978) hovers in the background suggesting Mao's ever-present influence on the woman's life. The future into which her child will be born is unknown. It is Mao who engages with the camera, not the woman. In another series of photographs of naked and near-naked women, given the declarative title *I Am a Woman*, Xing creates a realm where the gaze is sympathetic and empowering, informed by gender politics and female desire.

Artists and photographers across the country were attracted to the lives of people on the margins and sought to personalize and humanize the visual record, and in the process elevate their subjects to art. In 1994 Liu Zheng (*b*. 1969) embarked on an epic series called *My Countrymen* as a departure from his work as a news photographer on the *Workers' Daily*. He aimed 'to photograph the most unreal images to be found within reality; to take them into the realm of the ideal, not specific things, but the idealism that exists in people at every moment'.[4] The project was a reaction to his orthodox Party upbringing and strict education. He travelled across the country for seven years creating an archive of more than 10,000 images of people, folk sculpture and museum tableaux representing different states of existence.

Three Elderly Entertainers depicts a group of elderly folk performers (men performing female roles) that Liu came across in a subway station in Beijing. The men were from a coastal town north of Beijing and had

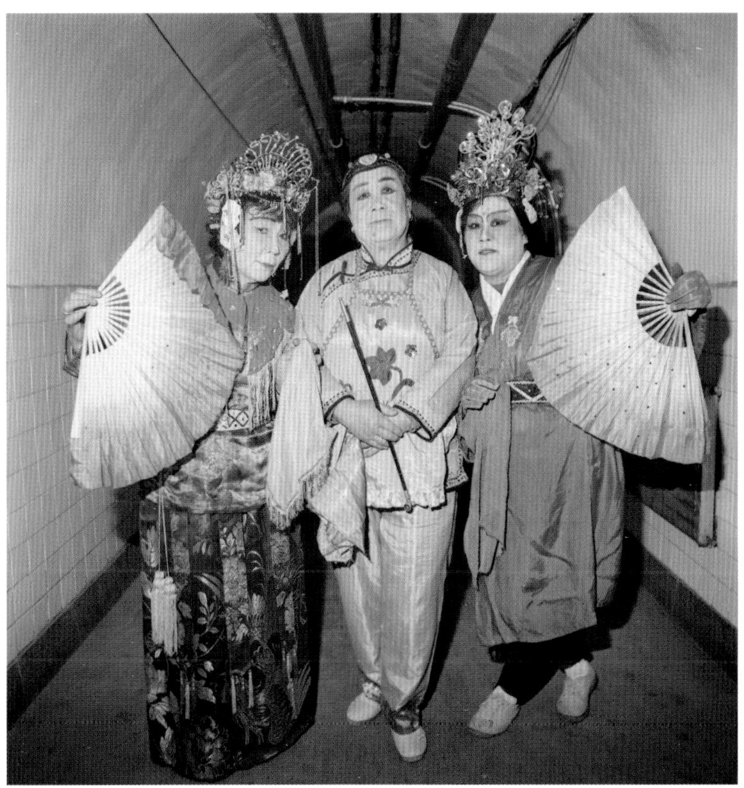

119 Liu Zheng, *Three Elderly Entertainers, Beijing*, 1995, gelatin silver print.

formed a touring troupe after the government brought forward the compulsory retirement age. Liu explains: 'Some low-budget clubs and hotels hire them, because the customers love to see old guys dancing in young girls' outfits . . . Several actors asked me to take their portraits.'[5]

Liu's dialogue with his 'countrymen' as he seeks their permission to photograph them is also a dialogue with his inner self. His subjects, he says, 'are the actors that I have chosen'.[6] In 1995 Liu Zheng and Rong Rong started *New Photo* (four issues, 1996–8), a magazine dedicated to photography that was photocopied and string-bound, with a small circulation. In the penultimate issue the editors highlighted the importance of 'concept' photography: 'When CONCEPT enters Chinese photography, it is as if a window suddenly opens in a room that has been sealed for years. We can now breathe comfortably, and we now reach a new meaning of "new photography".'[7] Hong Lei's colour photograph *Autumn in The Forbidden City, Taihe Hall, East Verandah*, 1997, was reproduced in black and white. A bejewelled dead bird lies on flagstones near the Hall of Supreme Harmony, the grandest and most important building in the Forbidden City where the enthronement of the emperor once took place. The dead bird, a common motif in Hong Lei's work, suggests drama and death at the heart of China's empire. The surreal photograph is handworked, with additional pigment heightening the colour, and the scratched surface echoing the latent violence of the image.

Hong Lei took up photography after studying printmaking at Beijing's Central Academy of Fine Arts. In the mid-1990s he began to reference classical Chinese paintings in his art, altering and subverting their meanings, giving them a critical edge. Photography allowed him to perfect his staged interventions, inspired in part by the small sculptures of Joseph Cornell. In discussing his interest in the past he says: 'I still cannot forget the cultural glory of our ancestors, which I first witnessed as a child. I am troubled and angry about the destruction of this heritage, which I see in my everyday life.'[8]

Changes to economic policy set in motion by reforms introduced by Deng Xiaoping occasioned massive inflows of capital into China, from Hong Kong, Japan, Taiwan and the West, causing the rapid development of cities. Long-term residents were relocated and city blocks razed with

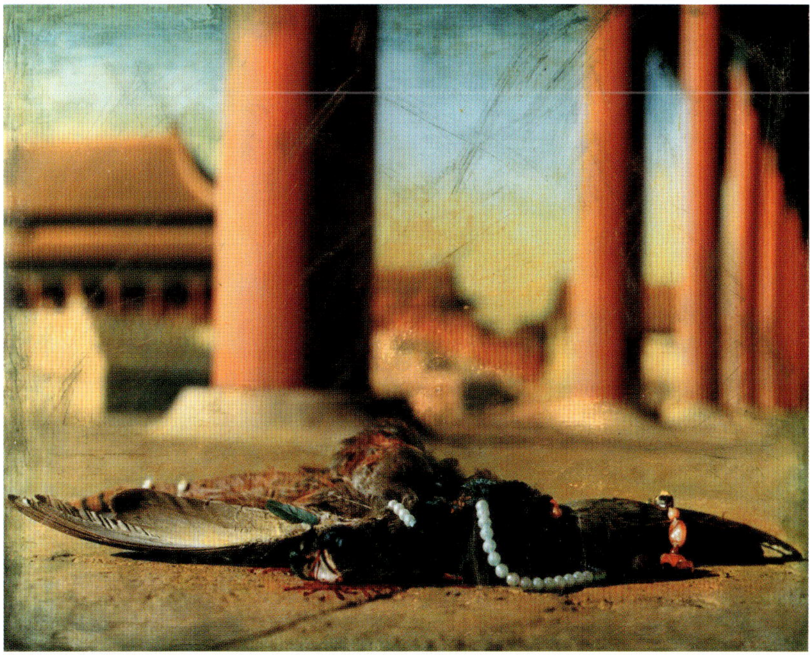

120 Hong Lei, *Autumn in The Forbidden City, Taihe Hall, East Verandah*, 1997, chromogenic print.

breathtaking speed to make way for high-rise office towers, apartments, shopping malls and freeways. During the late 1990s graffiti heads became a ubiquitous sign in the streets and laneways of Beijing. The bald profiles sprayed in black paint remained anonymous until 1998 when the artist Zhang Dali (*b*. 1963) claimed authorship. Zhang Dali had taken up graffiti art in Bologna (he left China in 1989) in response to his sense of alienation, and introduced guerrilla art to the streets of Beijing after his return in 1995. His tough-guy profiles drew attention to ruins, the linear heads acting as witnesses to the destruction of neighbourhoods. Like the developers, Zhang Dali worked under the cover of darkness and returned to take photographs of his heads *in situ*. 'It suddenly dawned on me', he said, 'that the surrounding environment was a natural part of the work. The great changes that were taking place in the Chinese environment provided a stage that was very different from anything I had experienced in any other country. That head is myself, having returned to the source.'[9]

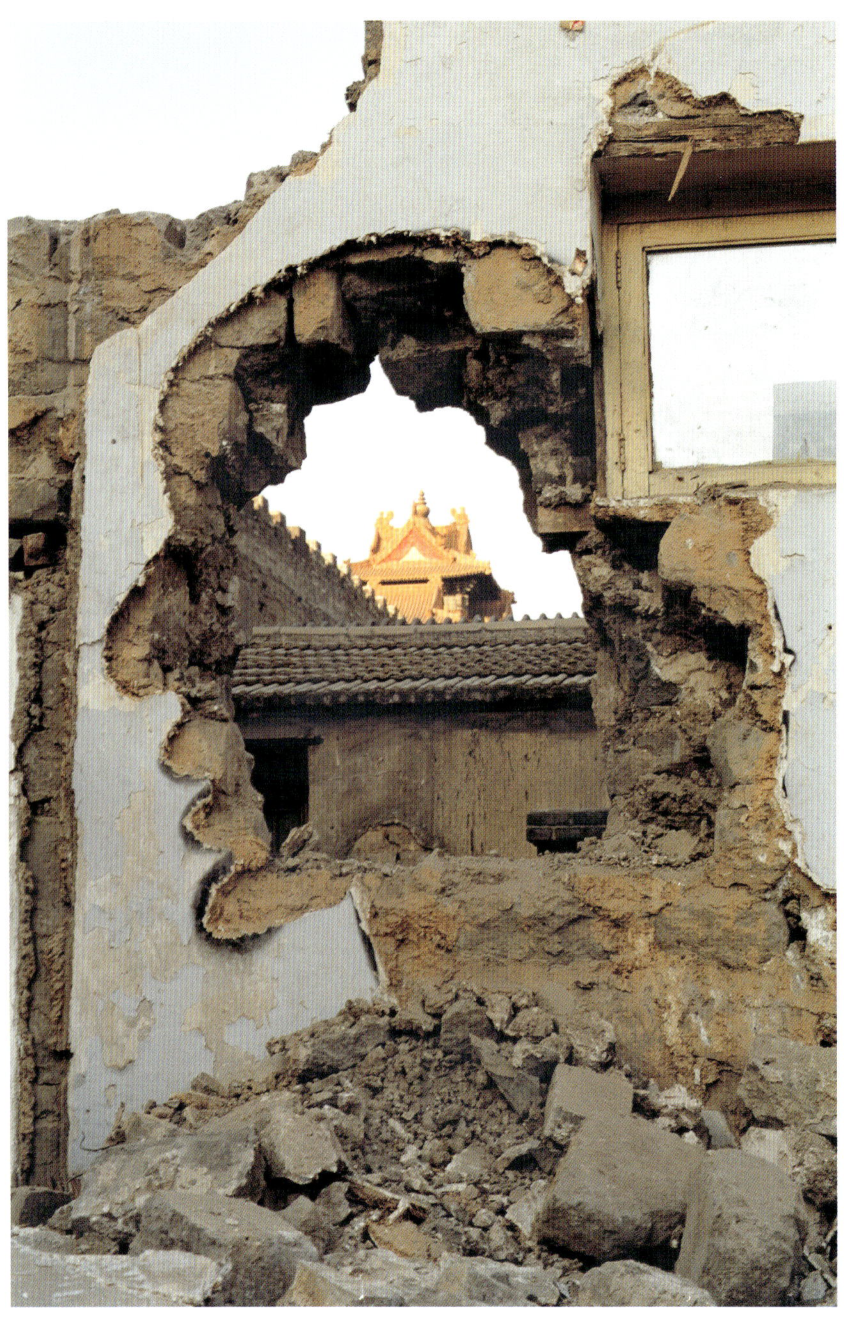

121 Zhang Dali, *Dialogue: Forbidden City*, 1998, chromogenic print.

In *Dialogue: Forbidden City* (1998) Zhang shows destruction close to the ancient imperial heart. By hacking his profile out of the wall of a partially demolished dwelling, Zhang's head becomes a window onto the Forbidden City, drawing attention to the beauty and splendour of the World Heritage Site, and the violence of change.

A Hong Kong artist who sojourned in Italy is Leung Chi Wo (*b*. 1968), a graduate of the Department of Fine Arts at the Chinese University of Hong Kong. Leung was the recipient of an Italian government scholarship and in 1991 he undertook a postgraduate diploma there in the culture of photography. For many years Leung has used a self-made 4 x 5 pinhole camera to capture unusual views of Hong Kong in an attempt to remember the space of the city before sovereignty of the Territory was returned to China in 1997.[10] In a notable series of related works Leung stands at intersections in Hong Kong (he began the series in New York), directing the camera and his gaze upwards, focusing on the sky. Photographs taken at different points of the intersection are cut out and collaged to create a two dimensional work that focuses on the area of void created by the forest of skyscrapers. The sky is transformed into a defined, positive space that also appears threatened. In his *Colour Photo* series he uses filters to print from black-and-white negatives, adding an additional layer of abstraction.

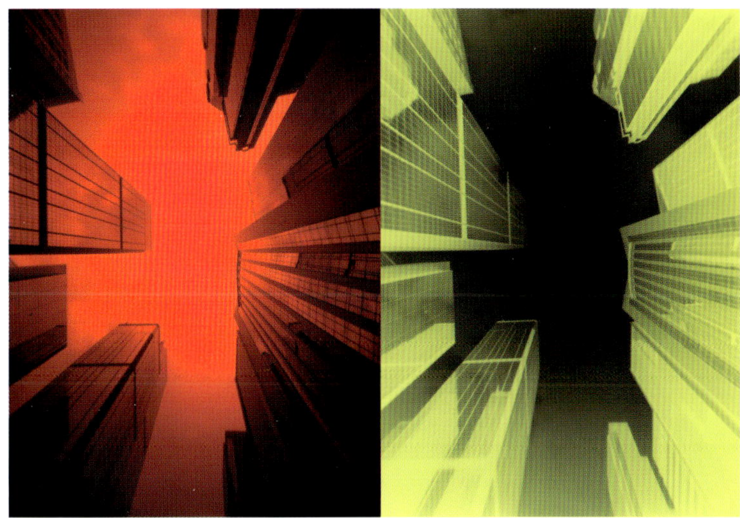

122 Leung Chi Wo, *Gloucester & Gloucester*, 2001, chromogenic print.

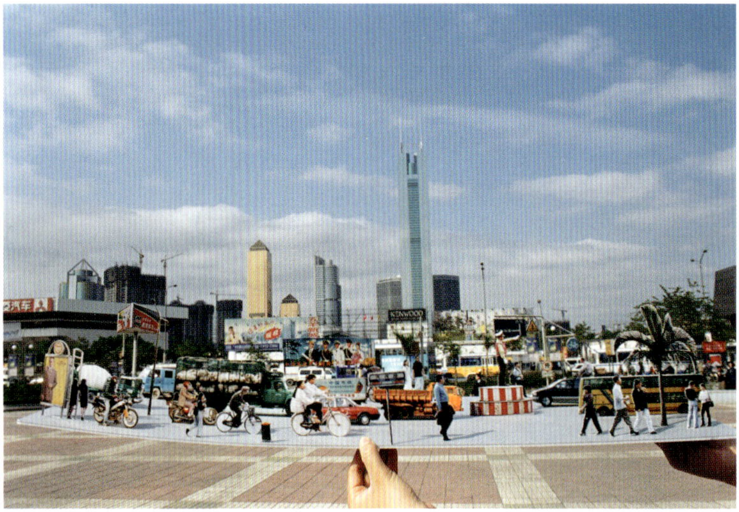

123 Chen Shaoxiong, *Street – 1*, 1997, chromogenic print.

Not far away, in Guangzhou, Chen Shaoxiong (*b.* 1962) turned to photography as a way to combat the feeling of being a tourist in his own city. He embarked on a project to recreate Guangzhou out of photographs, item by item. He developed a method of photographic collage involving a small-scale physical stage onto which he placed the constituent elements of a streetscape, a format that was potentially infinite. In a playful gesture, he took sections of the stage back onto the street and photographed them. While acknowledging the impossibility of keeping up with the rate of change, he says his method 'is certainly much better than traditional photography, that only selects one single thing and leaves out tens of thousands of others!'[11]

The urban environment becomes another kind of theatre in Yang Fudong's staged poster-like photograph series *Don't Worry it Will be Better* and *The First Intellectual* (2000). In these works Yang Fudong adds incongruous slogans to images of young urbanites, but the causes of the drama alluded to in the text occur outside the frame, removing what would normally be the primary subject from the image and defeating any attempt at narrative understanding.

Yang Fudong (*b.* 1971) comes from a small village northeast of Beijing and originally studied oil painting. Today he is best known for his immersive film and video installations. While at art school in Hangzhou, he started to experiment with performance, photography and film – the centre for New Media Art at the China Academy of Art, the first in China, was established in 2001. His first film project, *Estranged Paradise*, was made in Beijing (1997–2002). In need of money to finance his next project, he moved to Shanghai where he worked for UBI, a French video software company. The three images that constitute *The First Intellectual* series were shot in Shanghai's new finance and commerce hub in Pudong where the UBI office was located. Yang cleverly melds elite and popular modes of visual communication to create an ironic portrait of his own generation, suggesting their alienation, confusion and powerlessness in a rapidly changing society.

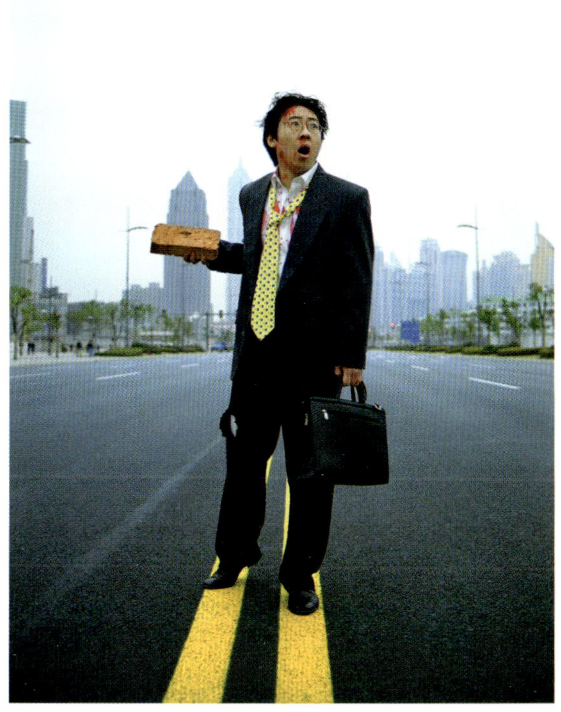

124 Yang Fudong, from *The First Intellectual*, 2000, digital print.

The First Intellectual, which may be understood as an attempt to photograph a state of consciousness, was exhibited in the Fuck Off exhibition. The show, curated by Ai Weiwei and Feng Boyi, coincided with the Third Shanghai Biennale (2000), an official exhibition that claimed to be China's first survey of international contemporary art. Fuck Off (the literal translation of the Chinese is 'Uncooperative Approach') emphasized the independent and critical stance that is basic to art. Ai Weiwei and Feng Boyi explain: 'Allegory, direct questioning, resistance, alienation, dissolution, endurance, boredom, bias, absurdity, cynicism and self-entertainment are aspects of culture as well as features of existence.'[12]

The catalogue opened with a series of works by Ai Weiwei – two black-and-white photographs titled *Perspective* showing a raised hand gesturing with the index finger in front of the White House in Washington, DC (1995) and in front of Tiananmen Square in Beijing (1996). The catalogue is an extension of Ai Weiwei's series of independently published books, the *Black Cover Book* (1994), *White Cover Book* (1995) and *Gray Cover Book* (1997), key sources for understanding the role of

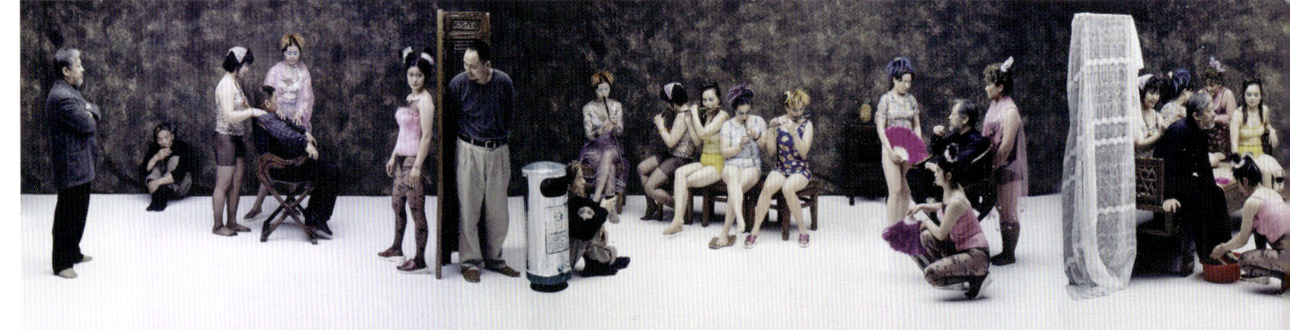

125, 126 (detail) Wang Qingsong, *Night Revels of Lao Li*, 2000, chromogenic print.

photography in its varied applications in the evolution of conceptual art in China.

A striking example of staged photography used to reenact historical images and events and draw attention to social change is *Night Revels of Lao Li* (2000) by Wang Qingsong (*b.* 1966). The work is based on a famous tenth-century painted handscroll, a secret record of the indulgent lifestyle of Han Xizai, a talented but politically impotent scholar-official. Wang Qingsong cast leading avant-garde curator and critic Li Xianting in the role of Han Xizai, creating what he has described as 'a portrait of the current position of intellectuals in Chinese society'.[13] By using art world figures as his actors, Wang alludes to the powerlessness of contemporary intellectuals and their escape into self-contained, self-fulfilling worlds of their own creation.

Wang, who trained as an oil painter at the Sichuan Academy of Fine Arts, is both creator and participant-voyeur. He can be seen in plain clothes seated on the ground, smoking, talking on his mobile phone and peeking at the night revels from underneath the backdrop, reminding us of the power of photography as an art form and a tool of surveillance. *Night Revels of Lao Li* draws painting and history, culture and politics into a complex interplay that uses photography as a performative expression of artistic agency and national critique.

Other important artists who have used staging to very different effect are Zhuang Hui (*b.* 1963), whose large group portraits of villagers or military units, taken with a rotating camera, play on the Chinese tradition of

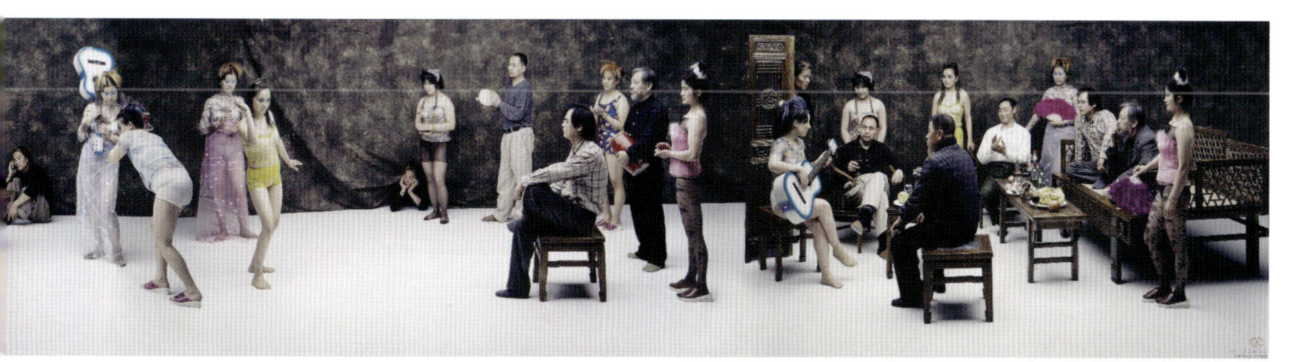

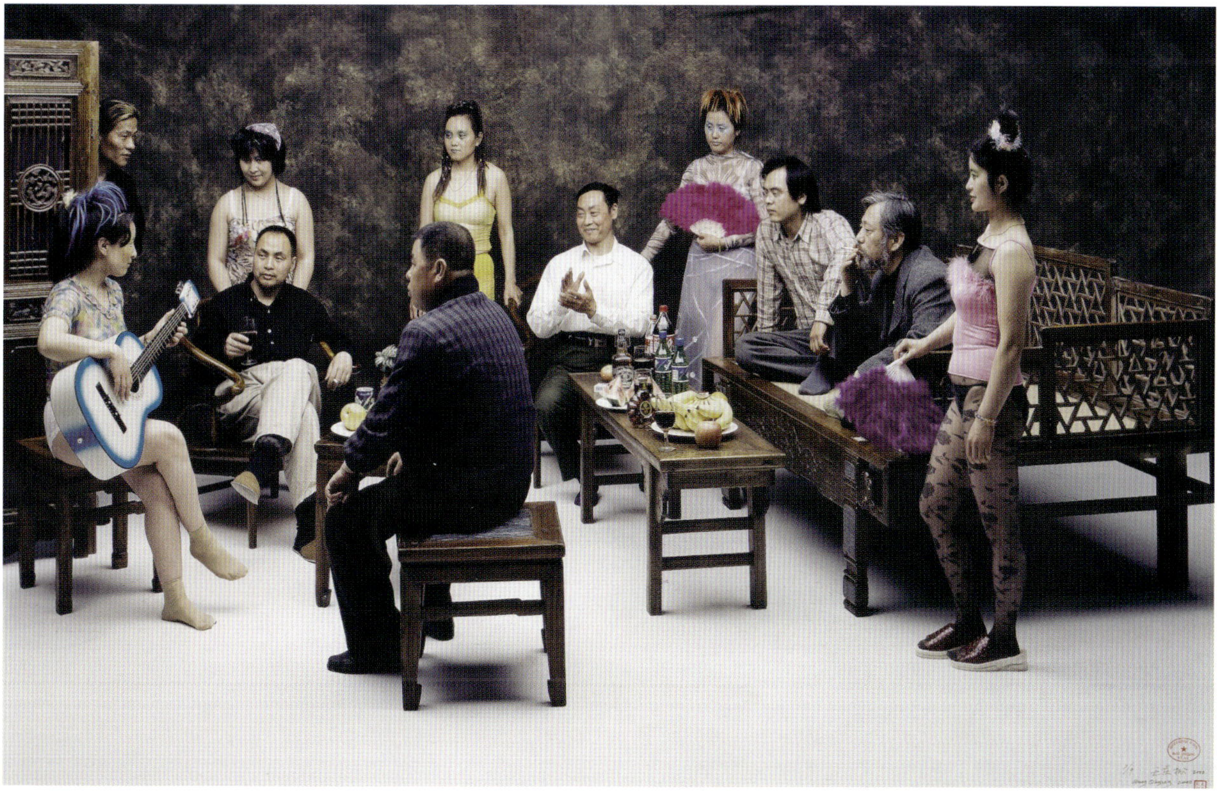

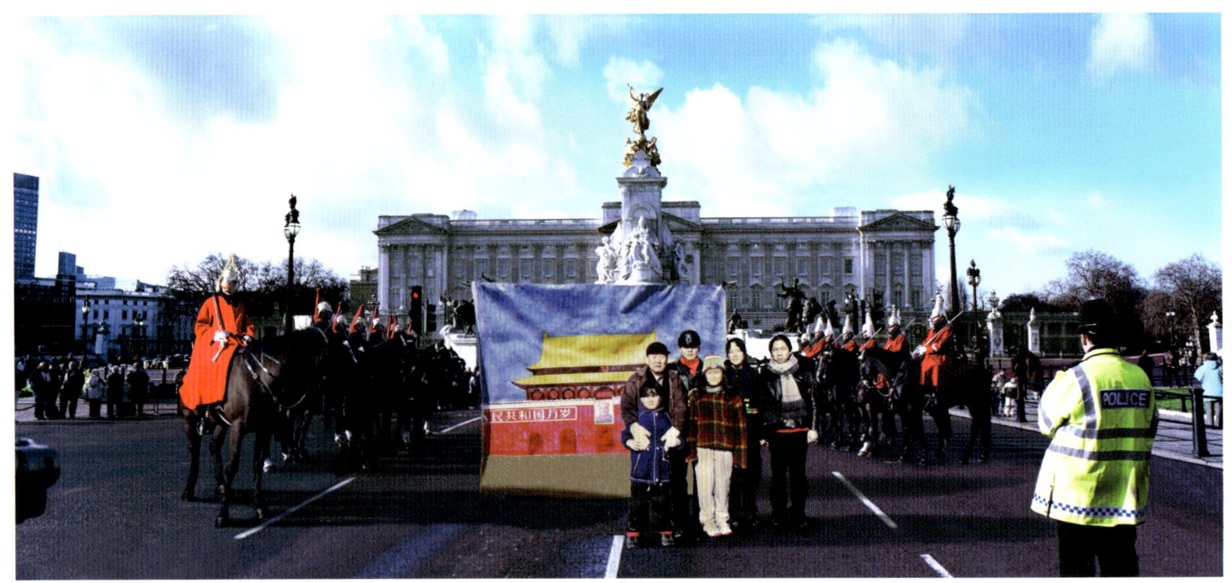

127 Liu Xiao Xian, 'Home-London', from the series *Home*, 2002–3, Lamda print.

the group portrait and collective identity, and Hai Bo (*b*. 1962), who recreates photographs from family albums, drawing attention to those who have survived the vicissitudes of recent Chinese history.

The market for contemporary Chinese art has grown in step with China's booming economy, fuelled by international collectors. With its global currency and inherent contemporaneity, art photography has had particular appeal. Former industrial sites on the outskirts of Beijing and Shanghai have been converted into studio-cum-gallery complexes where artists create works on a scale suited to the grand spaces of contemporary art museums and the curatorial ambitions of international biennales and triennials.

Liu Xiao Xian, who has lived and worked in Sydney since 1990, expresses what many expatriate Chinese artists feel when he says: 'I did not shave my head and thereby renounce my former life, because I have not forgotten my past. The substance of my bones determines that I will always be Chinese.'[14] Since the early 2000s Liu has created artworks in China using materials and workshop facilities that were not available to him in Australia. His photographic and mixed media artworks reflect an interest in understanding his own physical and psychological displacement. A love of optical tricks and a desire to question photographic truth are features of a series of large works begun in 2002 titled *Home*. 'Home-London' shows a Chinese family group posed in front of a painted backdrop of Tiananmen, entry point to the former imperial palace and home of the emperor of China. The backdrop creates a screen between the tourists (an archival photograph of Liu's own extended family) and the postcard view of Buckingham Palace, which has been enhanced with additions of guards on horseback and a blue sky. With its travel snapshot guise and Photoshop perfection, 'Home-London' is a poignant contemporary portrait that comments on blurred boundaries between local and global, past and present, painting and photography, truth and reality.

Miao Xiaochun (*b*. 1964) also used photography to communicate complex feelings of physical and cultural displacement that he describes as a profound 'loss of language'. Having studied German at Nanjing University and then art history at the Central Academy of Fine Arts in Beijing (1986–9), Miao was drawn into the heady world of contemporary art. After working freelance for a number of years he decided to study overseas, in Kassel, Germany, home of the prestigious contemporary art exhibition, Documenta. He immersed himself in the Kunsthochschule Kassel art course, which enabled his first real contact with photography. His graduation work was a series of black-and-white photographs of ordinary German scenes into which he inserted a mannequin dressed as an ancient Chinese scholar. The figure, whose inscrutable staring face is modelled on Miao's own, is stiff and incongruous, disconnected from the surroundings. When he returned to China in 1999, Miao continued the series using digital technology to create large colour images from multiple photographs, some of them eight metres long. While the figure remains the subject, its position within the composition is much less prominent. In *Lingering Under a Lone Pine* (2002), the 'visitor from the past' stands at the base of a pedestrian overpass, facing a lone pine tree, the evergreen symbol of longevity (illus. 128). When, at the end of one day, Miao saw the tree rising from a hole in the pavement (the China Central Television tower is in the distance), he was reminded of a line from the poem 'Returning Home' by the famous poet recluse Tao

Yuanming (365–427): 'Lingering in a spot to caress a lonely pine'.[15] The vertical format of the photograph with a three-point perspective that emphasizes the foreground, middle ground and background, and the small figures used to give a human dimension and sense of scale, are borrowed from Chinese landscape painting.

For these ambivalent monuments to the present, Miao painstakingly stitches multiple photographs together with computer software. His aim is to improve on the camera's inherent technological limitation of single point perspective, allowing the viewer to savour details in the composition in a continuous, revelatory experience similar to slowly unrolling a scroll painting. Miao later taught media arts at the Central Academy of Fine Arts in Beijing and came to use 3D animation and digital ink painting to create imaginary worlds. 'When I deal with photography I am facing reality. I don't want to change many things in the picture', he said. 'But in the digital works, I can do everything. I am facing my dream, facing my imagination. So for me these are two different worlds. One is the real world, the other is a virtual world. They are like day and night.'[16] The digital work is complex and at any given time between one and fifteen assistants might be working with the artist.

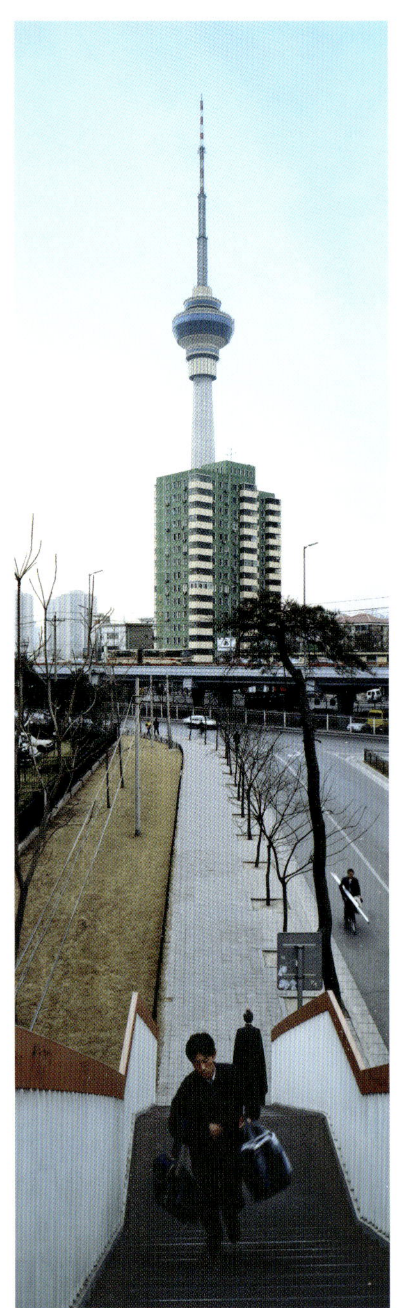

The generation born in the late 1970s and 1980s has no experience of the Cultural Revolution and in most cases individuals were too young for any direct involvement in the events of June 1989. The one-child policy and the booming socialist market economy have defined their lives. From an early age urban youth have had access to a set of ever-expanding consumer choices. Mobile phones and computers provide access to real and fantasy worlds and have become their constant companions. Photographs are an important feature of web and social networking sites and are used by individuals to report on events not adequately covered in the mainstream media, often forcing an official response. Circulating in cyberspace, these images, which are easily transferred from mobile phones to websites, have become a powerful force. At the time of writing there were some 500 million 'netizens' in China.

From the outset Cao Fei's (*b*. 1978) staged photographic works gave expression to generational concerns of what the artist calls 'lostness'.

128 Miao Xiaochun, *Lingering Under a Lone Pine*, 2002, archival pigment print.

129 Cao Fei, 'A Mirage', from the *Cosplayers* series, 2004, chromogenic print.

By dressing up her characters and manipulating images, she could experience purpose and power. Her student video (she graduated from the Guangzhou Academy of Arts in 2001) *Imbalance* was included in Fuck Off. *Imbalance*, she says, 'is a contemporary experience, an uncommon experience that is shared among college students in China. It restricts us and changes us, but at the same time it enables us to expand and be flexible.'[17] Her eight-minute video *Cosplayers* (2004) is inspired by subculture fantasy (linked to technology-based youth entertainment emanating from Hong Kong, Taiwan, Japan and South Korea), and by the gritty photos of street life by the *Guangzhou Evening News* photojournalist Ye Jianqiang. The action takes place against the backdrop of the city and features

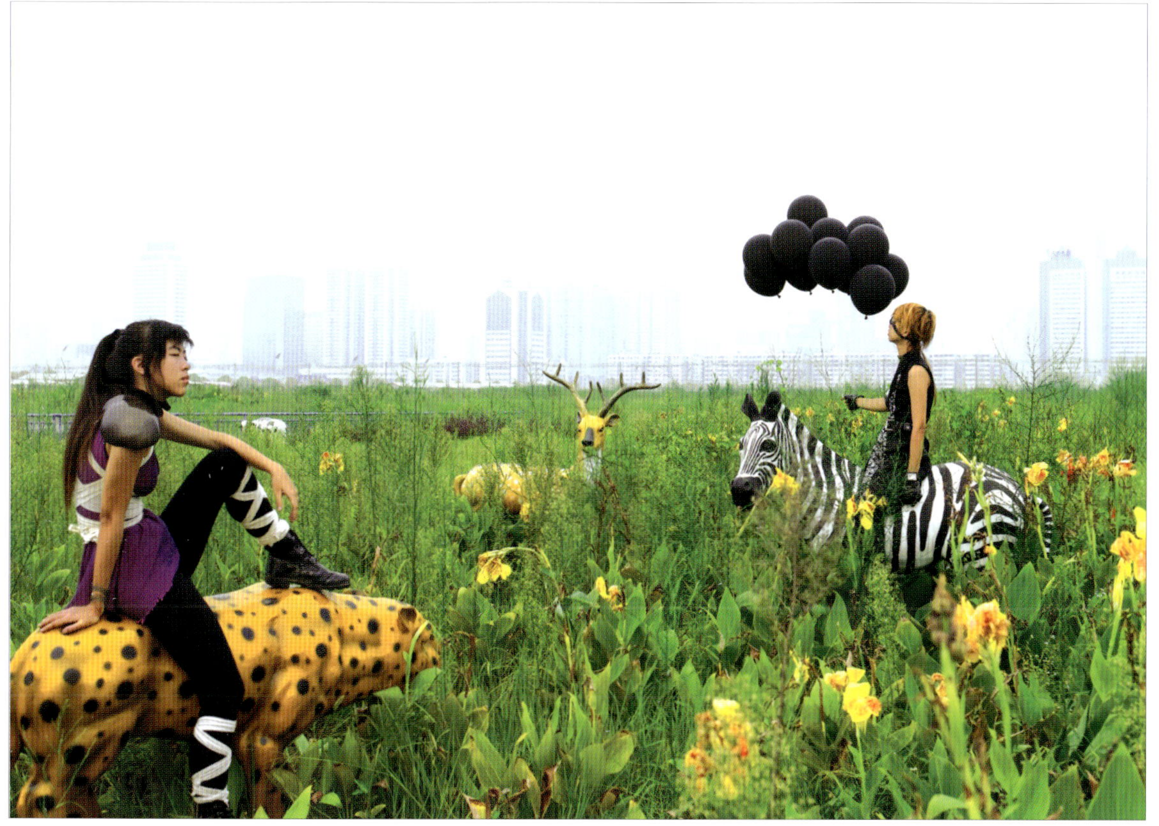

young people dressed as game characters whose costumes empower them to transcend reality. In still photographs, taken by Zhang Hai'er, the forest of office and apartment towers on the horizon shimmer like a mirage, pushed into the distance by the intense colour and absurdity of the paddock where the Cosplayers enjoy an idle moment. A startled deer stares directly at the camera, while A. Ming lounges on a prowling leopard, and Nada, whose outfit teams with the zebra, like camouflage, is fixated on his posy of black balloons. The video ends with daylight as the city begins another working day (illus. 129).

Across the Taiwan Strait, young Taiwanese artists also created virtual worlds as a way of communicating feelings of anxiety about the future. After martial law was lifted in 1987 and the first democratic elections were held in 1996, Taiwan became a prosperous, sophisticated, pluralistic society. Yet it remains in the shadow of mainland China. Kuo I-Chen (*b*. 1979), who represented Taiwan in the 2005 Venice Biennale, creates multimedia interactive installations in which photography and video play a prominent role. '33.5°N, 35.3°E' (2007), is a monumental print from the *Survivor* series, named after a miniature robot-dog that trains its sensor-driven surveillance camera eyes over a post-apocalyptic scene of urban destruction in search of life. Beyond a fragile earth that hovers in space looms the presence of another planet. To create the work Kuo used web images of natural and human-induced catastrophes, including 9/11, Hurricane Katrina, the Iraq War, aeroplane crashes, earthquakes and tsunami, extracting details and stitching them together. He refers to the work as a 'prophecy of the future/past'.[18] By using fragments of real imagery he suggests larger contexts of existence, and the fragile interrelationship between human beings and their physical environment.

A contrasting genre of 'personal photography' emerged in Guangzhou in the early 2000s influenced by the work of photographers such as Noboyuki Araki, Wolfgang Tillmans, Nan Goldin, Sally Mann and Terry Richardson. Strongly autobiographical, though without a conventional narrative, this new style of photography emphasizes self-expression and private experience, described by Gu Zheng as making 'public something that is usually non-accessible, often to a wide and unknown audience'.[19] Many practitioners of 'personal photography' work

130 Kuo I-Chen, '33.5°N, 35.3°E', from the series *Survivor*, 2007, digital print.

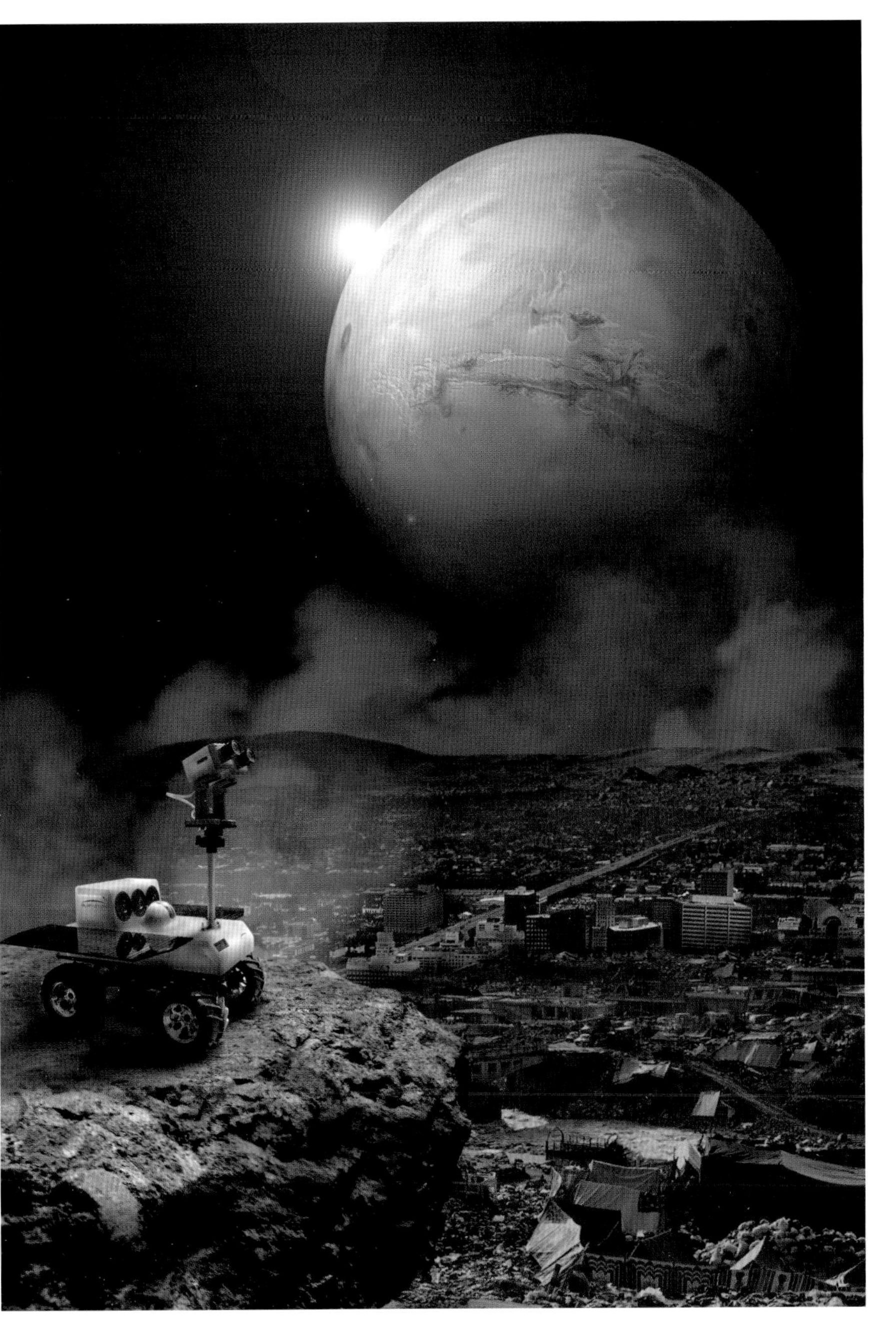

for magazines and newspapers by day and create their own highly personal images at night, participating across the spectrum of a new, image-rich culture. Lin Zhipeng (Zhi Peng, *b*. 1979, known online as 223) explains: 'When I photograph, I don't use the methods of documentary or realistic expression. I merely use the lens in place of real life. Sometimes I photograph my own life; sometimes I take snaps of personal friends, objects and things that are close by. There is no difference between me and anyone else who uses the camera to photograph life.'[20] Identity is expressed through acts of choice made in framing, editing and compiling images.

The work of Birdhead, a Shanghai-based two-person collective established in 2004 by Ji Weiyu (*b*. 1980) and Song Tao (*b*. 1979) explores the urban fabric of Shanghai through snatched fragments of city life. The photographers appear in many of their images, underlining their dual identity and the diary-like nature of their endeavour. While Ji was studying graphic design in London's Central Saint Martins College of Art and Design (2000–2004) and Song was living in Shanghai, they exchanged personal photographs over the internet (they first met at the Shanghai College of Arts and Crafts). Since Ji's return to China they have created numerous 'albums' containing casual-looking snapshots taken in locations across Shanghai, directing the viewer's eyes toward scenes of construction and destruction. For Birdhead and other young practitioners, photography is a primary 'language' for personal expression. Their images are part of a dialogue with themselves and like-minded shooters, who come across each other's images on the internet rather than in the physical space of a gallery or a publication.

In 2009 Sun Yanchu (*b*. 1978), a photographer who lives and works in Zhengzhou, Henan, one of China's interior agricultural provinces, was a finalist in an inaugural award for photographic creation initiated by the Three Shadows Photography Art Centre, founded in Beijing in 2007 by Rong Rong & inri. The award attracted some 300 submissions by Chinese photographers. Gu Zheng, one of the judges, commented on the young photographers' lack of interest in grand narratives and a concern instead with subject matter that was directly related to their everyday lives.[21]

Sun Yanchu's story is typical of many young photographers in remote parts of China whose 'personal' work, which first developed a following on the internet, is now being exhibited in non-commercial and commercial galleries in influential art centres in China and overseas. Sun Yanchu initially supported himself by working in restaurants and in advertising, before entering a local photographic studio as a bridal photographer. After taking portrait photographs for ten years (elaborate bridal photography is core business for many commercial studios), he left his job in 2006 in order to concentrate on his own work, posting photographs on Internet blogs and on photo sharing sites including Flickr.

In 2010 Sun self-published a booklet and CD of black-and-white images from a series begun in 2004 titled *Obsessed*. The cover features a close-up of a woman's buttocks – she wears hotpants and black stockings – astride the railing of a balcony. Other photographs inside include a close-up of a lion in a zoo behind bars; labourers asleep at construction sites; a brassiere abandoned in a park; victims of a hit-and-run accident; stray dogs; a staircase blocked with barbed wire; and the pattern of tyre tracks on a muddy road. Sun's images are not explained, pointing to a lack of interest in directing or fixing meaning. His photographs stand confidently unencumbered, like emotive clues to the photographer's heart and mind.

A haunting colour photograph of a wintry park was taken in Zhengzhou in 2006 during one of his regular photographic outings to counter boredom; it is part of his *In the Park* series (2006–7) (illus. 131). 'When I am bored', he says, 'I ride my bike or go for a walk, plunging into the wilderness or the vast suburbs.'[22] From a high vantage point Sun looks down onto an ugly two-storey building on a road that is bound on both sides by high fences that seem out of place in a park. The road is suspended in space, hovering between the past and the future. The blue-green dusk light evokes old slide film and landscape painting. An electricity wire cuts diagonally through the image like a scratch or a violent gesture, reminding us of the present.

In an artist statement published in the Three Shadows Award catalogue, Sun poses the question: 'How much truth and thought can one photograph really express?':

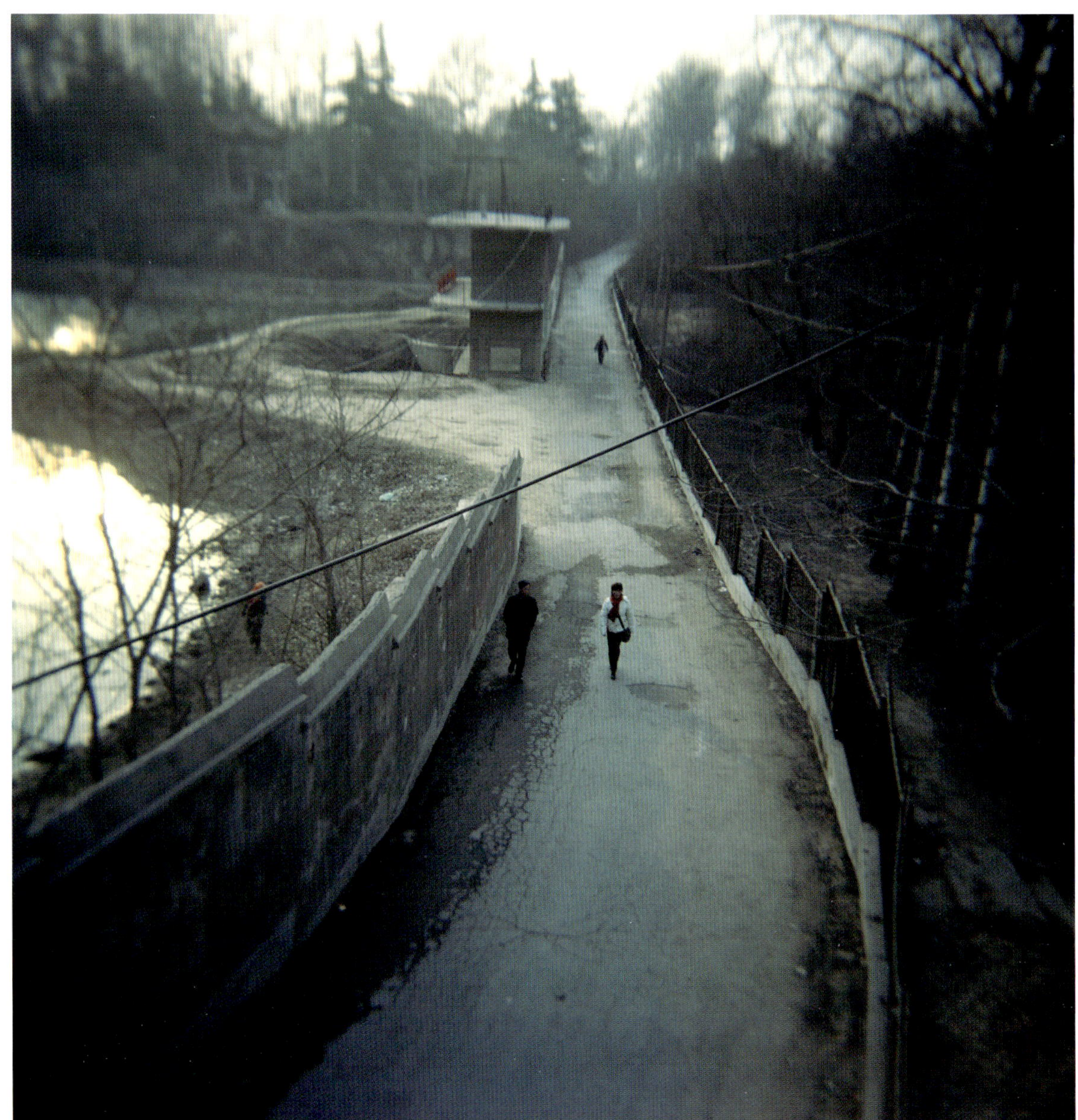

131 Sun Yanchu, *In the Park – 18*, 2006, inkjet print on fine art paper.

> I don't know. I only know that I don't want to stop taking photographs. In this world where the real and the illusory converge, I've pressed the camera shutter countless times, in search of a chance encounter between my spirit and something else, which will give me a momentary high and a chance to escape. I continue to indulge in it . . . the photos are all instances of my collision with reality, a trace of my heart's vibration . . .[23]

Sun Yanchu's camera is always strapped to his waist. It has become an extension of his body, an instrument for seeing and feeling his world, and capturing transient moments that resonate for him. The camera is an enlivening device, a medium through which he experiences possibilities of transformative awareness within mundane reality. It is his tool for mediating a difficult world, 'a link', he says, 'between my heart and my eyes'.[24] And our eyes too.

In 2011 SH Contemporary, the Asia Pacific Contemporary Art Fair in Shanghai (one of a number of influential commercial events in the region), inaugurated a photography prize. The organizers described the medium as 'extremely important' and 'widely used by young Asian artists' with the potential of 'reaching out to a new, younger audience'.[25] The winner, Chen Wei (*b.* 1980), was chosen by an international panel of judges for his 'original language – constantly engaged in a dialogue with the tradition of staged photography'.[26]

Chen works by making a sketch, inspired by a concept, or a line from a novel or newspaper, then builds the scene and photographs it. After developing the image he scans it to a computer and manipulates colour and exposure to achieve the desired affect. His staged self-portrait *A Lighthouse was Winking in the Far Distance* (2010), with its nihilistic and iconoclastic undertones, is a paradox (illus. 132). A blinding light erases the photographer's face making it impossible to determine the person's identity. For Chen it is an image that marks his 30th year, a time of transition, uncertainty and mystery. 'We live, work moving forward on life's trajectory, often because that ray of light beckons us on, but we do not know what lies ahead.'[27] Chen plays with the camera's unique ability to create images that are both real and uncanny:

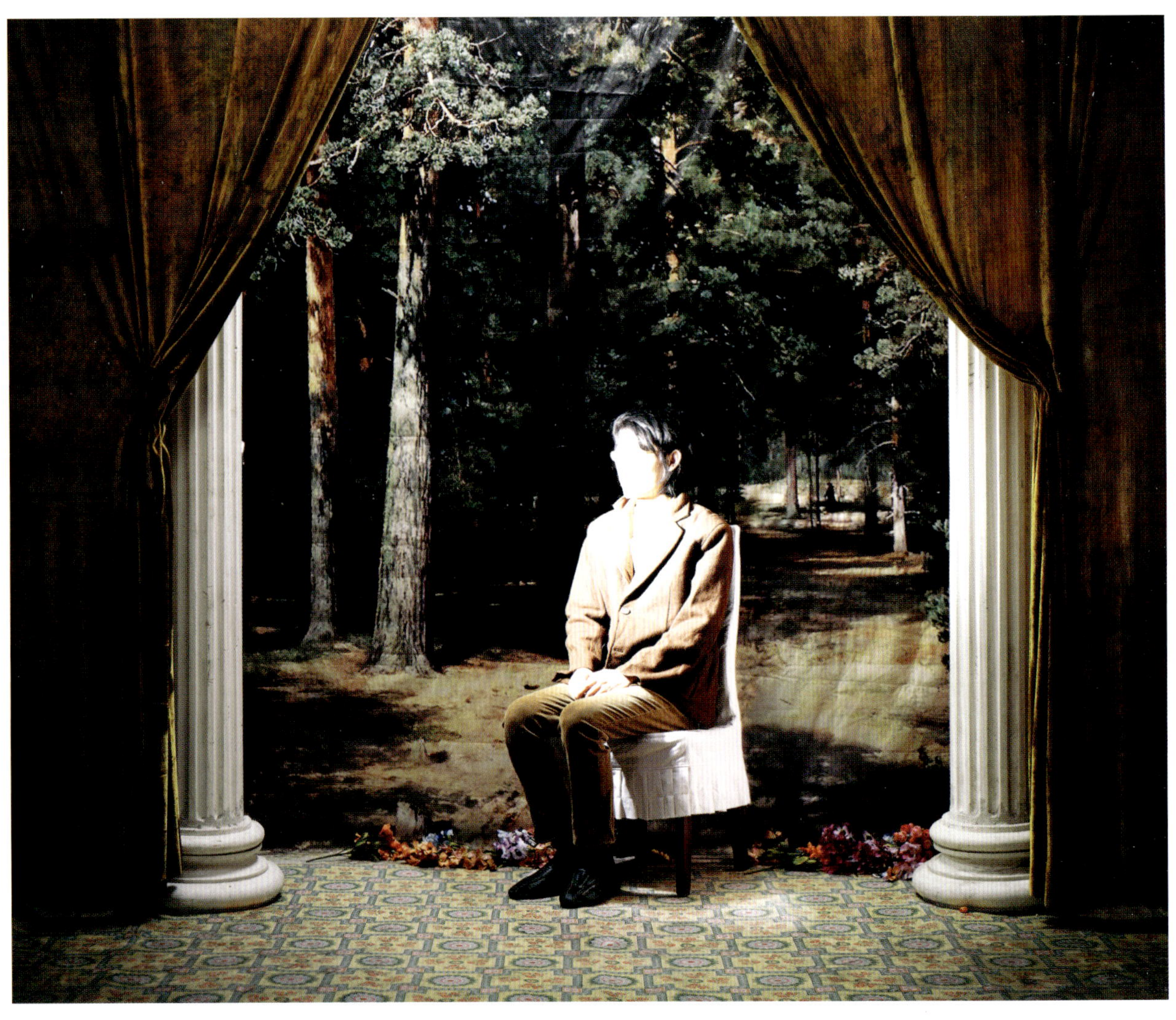

132 Chen Wei, *A Lighthouse was Winking in the Far Distance*, 2010, archival inkjet print.

> I attempt to present fragments that exist outside history, or those strange things that it is impossible to include in official histories. If photography is about truth then it is my hope that the theatricality of everyday fantasy that is present in my works will continue to live in the minds of others.[28]

This enigmatic image of a sitter in a faux photographic studio that connects staged art photography to the tradition of commercial portraiture is a fitting place to leave this account of photography and China. Its unshuttered future is as indistinct, perhaps, as the void surrounding the shadowed face of the imperial official who, in 1844, in one of the earliest surviving photographs of China, gazed into the mysterious scrutiny of an uninvited record. The difference is that the people behind the camera today are young Chinese photographers – professionals and amateurs, photojournalists, photographers of the people, and artists – conjuring images from darkness and light in an attempt to make sense of their worlds.

Glossary of Chinese Names and Terms

'A Nun Seeks Love' 尼姑思凡
Afong, Lai Afong 華芳，賴阿芳
Ai Weiwei 艾未未
An Ge, Peng Zhenge 安哥，彭振戈
Art Life 美術生活

Bannong on Photography 半農談影
Bi Jianfeng 畢建鋒
Birdhead 鳥頭
Black and White Pictorialist 黑白影集
Black and White Society 黑白影社

Cai Ming 蔡铭
Cai Shangxiong 蔡尚雄
Cao Fei 曹斐
'capture a shadow image' 摄影
Central Academy of Fine Arts Student Photography Group 中央美術學院學生攝影協會
Central Office for National News 國家新聞總署
Chang Shan Tzu, Zhang Shanzi 張善子
Chang Tsai 張才
Chang Yee Lau studio, Fuzhou 福州南台塢尾街像儀樓
Chen Baosheng 陳寶生
Chen Chuanlin 陳傳霖
Chen Fan 陳凡
Chen Gongzhe 陳公哲
Chen Juanmei 陳娟美
Chen Shaoxiong 陳劭雄
Chen Shichao 陳士超
Chen Shuxia 陳淑霞
Chen Tiesheng 陳鐵生
Chen Wanli 陳萬裡
Chen Wei 陳維
Chen Yiyi 陳以益
Chen Yongpeng 陳勇鵬
Chen Zhenqing 陳正青
China Film School 中華電影學校
China Photography 中國攝影
China Pictorial 中華圖畫雜誌
Chin Woo Athletic Association 精武體育會
Chin-san Long, *see* Long, Chin-san
China Photography Association 中華攝影學社, 華社
China Photography Brigade 中華寫真隊
chuanshen 傳神
Chung Hwa studio, Shanghai 中華照相館
Commercial Press 商務印書館

Ding Song 丁悚

Eastern Miscellany 東方雜誌
Eastern Times 時報
Eighth Route Army Military and Politics Journal 八路軍軍政雜誌
Erwo Xuan studio, Hangzhou 二我軒照相館
Eternally Red Photography Studio, Beijing 永紅照相
Everybody Photography Society 人人影會

Farewell to My Concubine 霸王別姬
Five in One group 五個一群體
Fu Sheng Photography Studio, Tianjin 福升照相館
Fuchikami Hakuyō 淵上 白陽
Fung Tai Photographer, Beijing 豐泰照相館

Gao Jianfu 高 劍 父
Gao Qifeng 高 奇 峰
Gao Yuan 高源
General Knowledge of Photography 攝影常識
Gu Daxiang 谷大象
Gu Zheng 顧錚
Guang Ji Xuan studio, Shanghai 光霽軒

Hai Bo 海波
He Danshu 何丹書
He Hui 何慧
He Yanguang 賀延光
Heavenly Horse Art Society 天馬會
Hing-Qua John & Co. studio, Shanghai日成廣東路
Hong Hao 洪浩
Hong Lei 洪磊
Hou Bo 侯波
Hou Dengke 侯登科
Hu Boxiang 胡伯翔
Hu Die 胡蝶, Hu Ruihua 胡瑞華
Hu Wugong 胡武功
Huang Bohui 黄伯惠
Huang Yanpei 黄炎培
Huang Zhenyu 黄振玉

Ji Weiyu 季炜煜
Jiang Xiande 蒋先德
Jinghua Daily 京話日報
Journal of the National Essence 國粹學報

Kang Youwei 康有為
Kung-Chin Hui 共進會
Kung Tai Photography Studio公泰照相楼
Kuo I-Chen 郭奕臣
Kwang Wa studio, Shanghai 光華
Kwong Hwa studio, Nanjing 光華

Lee Ming-diao 李鳴鵰
Leung Chi Wo 梁志和
Li Bozhen 李伯貞
Li Jiangshu 李江树
Li Mingzhi 李明智
Li Shixiong 李世雄
Li Tu 李途
Li Xiaqing 李霞卿
Li Xiaobin 李晓斌
Li Zhensheng 李振盛
Liang Shitai, See Tay 梁時泰
Light Society 光社
Lin Cao 林草
Lin Zhi Peng 林志鹏
Ling Fei 凌飛
Lion Art 雄獅美術
Liu Bannong, Liu Fu 劉半農, 劉復
Liu Heung Shing, H. S. Liu 劉香成
Liu Shizhao 劉世昭
Liu Xiao Xian, Liu Xiaoxian 劉曉先
Liu Zheng 劉錚
Liu Zhiping 劉志平
Long, Chin-san, Lang Jingshan 朗靜山
Lu Guang 盧廣
Lu Shifu, K. C. Lu Siefug 盧施福
Lü Nan 呂楠
Lü Tianzhou 呂天洲, 呂頤壽
Lü Xiangyou 呂相友
Luo Guangda 羅光達
Luo Xiaoyun 羅小韻
Luo Yili 羅以禮
Luo Zhenyu 羅振玉

Mao Songyou 毛松友
Mei Lanfang 梅蘭芳
Meng Zhaorui 孟昭瑞
Miao Xiaochun 缪晓春
Miscellaneous Notes on Guangdong 廣東雜述
Mo Yi 莫毅
Modern Miscellany 時代畫報
Modern Photography 現代攝影
Modern Photography Salon 現代攝影沙龍

National Glories of Cathay 神州國光集
New Photo 新摄影
News photography 新聞攝影
News Photography Bureau 新聞攝影局
Nie Guangdi, Candie K. T. Nieh 聶光地
North China People's Liberation Army Pictorial 華北解放軍畫報
North of the River Alliance 北河盟
Northeast Pictorial 東北畫報
Notes on a Mechanism for Capturing Images 攝影之器記

On the Principles and Practice of Photography 脫影奇觀
Ouyang Shizhi 歐陽石芝

People's New Film Company 民新影片公司
People's photography 民間攝影
People's Pictorial 人民畫報
Photography 摄影
Photography Newspaper 攝影報
Pow-Kee Photography Studio 寶記照相館
Pun-Lun studio, Hong Kong 濱綸影相
Puyi, Aisin-Gioro Puyi 愛新覺羅, 溥儀

Qiying 耆英
Qiu Jin 秋瑾

'Rainbow Pass' 虹霓關
Rong Rong 榮榮
Rongchang Photography Studio, Hankou 榮昌照相館
Ru Suichu 茹遂初
Rupture Group 裂變群體

Scenic China 中國名勝
School of Spiritual Light, Fuzhou 靈光書院
Science Updates 格術補
Sha Fei, Situ Chuan, Situ Huan, H. Szeto 沙飛
'shadow image' 影相
Shanghai Sketch 上海漫畫
shashin 寫真
sheying 攝影
Shi Panqi 石盤棋
Shi Qiang 施強
Shi Shaohua 石少華
Shih Dai Photography studio, Fuzhou 時代照相
'small portrait' 小照
snapshot 速影
Song Tao 宋涛
Songstress Red Peony 歌女紅牡丹
spontaneous shot 抓拍
Square City Photography Group 四方影會

State Office of News and Publishing 國家新聞出版總署
Su Sanxing, Chow Kwa studio 蘇三興照相
Summer Palace 頤和園
Sun Yanchu 孫彥初
Sze Yuen Ming studio, Shanghai 施潤明

Taifang Photography Studio, Beijing 太芳照相館
Tai Kang True Face Photography Studio, Beijing 泰昌真容照相館
Tan Jingtang 譚京堂
'take a likeness' 照相
Teng Nan-kuang 鄧南
Three Shadows Photography Art Centre 三影堂攝影藝術中心
Tong Sheng Photography Studio, Shanghai 同生照相館
Tongwen Guan 同文館
Torch studio, Beijing 火炬
True Record 真 相 畫 報
Tsang Hin Wah, Arthur Tsang Hin Wah 曾顯華
Tung Hing studio, Fuzhou 同興畫樓
Tung Hua Studio, Beijing 東華

Wang Jingyao 王晶垚
Wang Miao 王萬
Wang Qingsong 王慶松
Wang Wenlan 王文瀾
Wang Yaodong 王耀東
Wang Youshen 王友身
Wang Yuhuai 王鈺槐
Wang Zhiping 王志平
War Scenes of the Chinese Revolution 大革命寫真畫
Wei Dezhong 魏德忠
Weng Naiqiang 翁乃強
West Lake Landscape 西湖風景,西湖個景
Whampoa, Huangpu 黄浦
Wong, H. S., Wang Xiaoting 海升, 王小亭
Worker, Peasant, Soldier Photographer, Beijing 工农兵照相
Worker, Peasant, Soldier studio, Qiqihar 工農兵, 齊齊哈爾
Workers' Daily 工人日報
'writing the truth' 寫真
Wu Jialin 吴家林
Wu Peng 吴鹏
Wu Yinxian 吴印咸
Wu Xingxuan 吴杏軒
Wu Zhonghang 吴中行

Xiao Chi 肖弛
xiaozhao 小照
Xie Fen 謝芬
Xie Ping 謝平
xiezhen 寫真

Xinhua News Agency 新華社
Xing Danwen 邢丹文
Xu Xilin 徐锡鳞
Xu Xiaobing 徐肖冰
Xu Zhuo 許琢
Xunling 勳齡

Yamamoto Sanshichiro 山本贊七郎
Yang Fudong 楊福東
Yang Jun 楊君
Yang Shaoming 楊紹明
Yao Hua Photography studio, Shanghai 耀華照像
Ye-Chung, Yee Cheong Photography Studio 宜昌照相樓
Ye Jianqiang 葉建強
Ye Jinglü 葉景呂
Ye Qianyu, Yeh Chen-Yu 葉淺予
Yih Shenge studio, Beijing 怡生
Ying Cheong studio, Shanghai 英昌
yingxiang 影像
You Zexiong 尤澤宏
Young Companion 良友
Youzheng Publishing House 有正書局
Yu Xiaoyang 於曉洋
Yu Yinchu 余寅初
Yuan Dongping 袁冬平
Yuan Kewen 袁克文
Yuan Ling 袁苓
Yuan Shikai 袁世凱
Yung Wing, Rong Hong 容閎

Zhang Dali 張大力
Zhang Hai'er 張海兒
Zhang Huan 張洹
Zhang Shuhe 張叔和
Zhang Yaxin 張雅心
Zhang Yimou 張藝謀
Zhang Zudao 張祖道
zhaoxiang 照像
Zhenxiang huabao 真相畫報
Zheng Jingkang 鄭景康
Zhonghua huabao 中華畫報
Zhou Shouchang 周壽昌
Zhou Yuedong 周躍東
Zhu Jiaqing 朱稼青
Zhuang Hui 莊輝
Zou Boqi 鄒伯奇
Zou Jiandong 鄒鍵東

References

one: China Exposed

1 Larry Schaaf, 'Henry Collen and the Treaty of Nanking', *History of Photography*, VI/4 (October 1982), pp. 353–66.

2 Quoted in Mary Warner Marien, *Photography and Its Critics: A Cultural History, 1839–1900* (Cambridge, 1997), p. 3.

3 Jules Itier, *Journal d'un Voyage en Chine en 1843, 1844, 1845, 1846* (Paris, 1848), vol. I, pp. 325–6.

4 Joseph Burnichnon, S. J, *La Compaigne de Jésus en France. Histoire d'un Siècle 1814–1914, vol. 3 1845–1860* (Paris, 1919), pp. 290–1. See also Kiang-nan (Vicariate Apostolic) in *The Catholic Encyclopedia* (1914), www.newadvent.org/cathen/08633b.htm, accessed 21 January 2010.

5 Based on images and information consulted at the Jesuit archive in Vanves, the photograph identified as Languillat in Terry Bennett, *History of Photography in China, 1842–1860* (London, 2009), p. 80 is another of the early Jesuits in China, not Languillat.

6 Aug. M. Colombel S. J., *Histoire de la Mission du Kiangnan: Troisieme Partie II, L'Épiscopat de Mgr Languillat, 1865–1878* (n. p., n.d.), opening image.

7 See Régine Thiriez, 'Photography and Portraiture in Nineteenth-Century China', *East Asian History*, 17/18 (1999), pp. 77–102.

8 Oliver Moore, 'Zou Boqi on Vision and Photography in Nineteenth-Century China', in *The Human Tradition in Modern China*, ed. Kenneth J. Hammond and Kristin Stapleton (Lanham, MD, 2008), pp. 33–53.

9 See Jeffrey W. Cody and Frances Terpak, *Brush & Shutter: Early Photography in China* (Los Angeles, 2011), p. 21.

10 Conversation with Cheng Cunjie, Guangzhou Museum, 10 December 2010.

11 ww.ce.cn/cysc/tech/sm/dv/200811/19/t20081119_17426782.shtml (in Chinese), accessed 25 January 2010.

12 Chen Shen et al., *Zhongguo sheying shi, 1840–1937* [The History of Photography in China, 1840–1937] (Taipei, 1990), p. 41.

13 My thanks to Régine Thiriez for sharing this information and providing evidence of photographic portraits with similar tables.

14 David Harris, *Of Battle and Beauty: Felice Beato's Photographs of China* (Santa Barbara, CA, 2000), pp. 19, 140.

15 For example, the album with photographs relating to Dent & Co. in the Howell collection (Howell was an employee of Dent & Co.), Royal Asiatic Society, London.

16 Quoted in Roberta Wue, *Picturing Hong Kong: Photography, 1855–1910* (New York, 1997), p. 134.

17 Wue, *Picturing Hong Kong*, p. 81.

18 John Thomson, 'Hong-Kong Photographers' (1872), quoted in Wue, *Picturing Hong Kong*, p. 134.

19 *Colonial and Indian Exhibition 1886 Official Catalogue* (London, 1886), p. 369.

20 In 1833 Delano worked for Russell and Company and was acting counsel during the Opium War. He returned briefly to America in 1843 to marry, returning with his wife with whom he lived in Macao until 1846. Delano lost much of his fortune during the economic downturn of 1857 and returned to China in 1859.

21 Another print of a related photograph of the same people, taken on the same occasion, features in an album in the Peabody Essex Museum, Salem (PH 34), that belonged to Elizabeth Quincy Huntington. The photograph is captioned 'English [clerks] of Russell & Co, Hong Kong 1885' with people identified as: 'Chinese compradore, Mr Forbes, Mr Huntington, Mr Tomes, Paul Forbes, Mr Potts, Mr Sherwell.'

22 See Tong Bingxue, 'A Review of Photography in Foochow', in *Yi zhan yi zuo yi sheng: Yige Zhongguoren 62 nian de yingxiang zhi* [Six Decades of a Chinese Life in Photographs] (Shanghai, 2010), pp. 203–5; Zhang Wei, 'Wan Qing min chu de haishang yinglou', *Zhongguo sheying* (Chinese Photography), XII/1 (2011), pp. 60–69.

23 See Régine Thiriez, 'Ligelang: A French Photographer in 1850s Shanghai', *Orientations*, 32/9 (2001), pp. 49–54, and Zhang Wei, 'Wan Qing min chu de haishang yinglou'.

24 PEM, PH36 (C915.1 B955) from an album titled 'Actual Photographs of China'. The Sze Yuen Ming studio may not have taken these photographs originally. With thanks to Barbara Kampas for archival assistance.

25 See Régine Thiriez, 'William Saunders, Photographer of Shanghai Customs', *Visual Resources*, XXVI/3 (September 2010), pp. 325–40.

26 For example, see the Liang Shitai advertisement in *Shenbao*, 29 May 1876, in Cody and Terpak, *Brush & Shutter*, p. 39, and *Huazi ribao*, 12 March 1894. For a similar *Huazi ribao* advertisement, dated 31 January 1895, see Wue, *Picturing Hong Kong*, pp. 56–7.

27 For a detailed discussion of this work see Gu Yi, 'What's in a Name? Photography and the Reinvention of Visual Truth in China, 1840–1911', *Art Bulletin* (forthcoming).

28 The album is part of the Wharton Barker (1846–1921) archive, originally presented through the offices of the China Merchants' Steam Navigation Company, Shanghai, now in the collection of the Library of Congress, Washington, DC.

29 Der Ling, *Two Years in the Forbidden City* (New York, 1911), p. 216.

30 Lin Jing, *The Photographs of Cixi in the Collection of the Palace Museum* (Beijing, 2002), p. 16.

31 With thanks to David Hogge, archivist, Freer Gallery and Arthur M. Sackler Gallery, Smithsonian Institution, Washington, DC, for drawing this to my attention and showing me the glass negatives in the collection.

two: The True Record

1 See Geremie R. Barmé, 'Prince Gong's Folly', in *The Great Wall of China*, ed. Claire Roberts and Geremie R. Barmé (Sydney, 2006), pp. 240–48.

2 John Fryer, Xu Shou, *Se xiang liu zhen, Zhaoxiang luefa* (Shanghai, 1896). Originally published in vols IX–XII of Fu Lanya (John Fryer), ed., *Ge zhi hui bian* [Chinese Scientific and Industrial Magazine] (Shanghai, 1880).

3 With thanks to Régine Thiriez for information about Henry Everitt and his work in Hong Kong.

4 Album 337/2, British Library, and an album in a private collection.

5 Jeffrey W. Cody and Frances Terpak, 'Through a Foreign Glass: The Art and Science of Photography in Late Qing China', in *Brush & Shutter: Early Photography in China*, ed. Cody and Terpak (Los Angeles, 2011), p. 56.

6 Alan Chong and Noriko Murai, *Journeys East: Isabella Stewart Gardner and Asia* (Boston, MA, 2009), pp. 206, 212–13, 230.

7 An album of Mencarini's photographs taken in Fuzhou is in the collection of the Harvard–Yenching Library. With thanks to Régine Thiriez for information about Mencarini.

8 Yung Wing, *My Life in China and America* (New York, 1909), pp. 195–6.

9 Amy I. Wilkinson, letter to Margaret Griffiths, 26 February 1910, cited in Ian Welch and Ellen Hope, 'Amy Oxley: Letters from China. An Australian Missionary Nurse of the Church Missionary Association of New South Wales, Fujian Province, China 1895–c1920' (ANU Missionary History Archives Project, 2004), published online at www.anglicanhistory.org/asia/china. With thanks to Madeleine Newell for drawing this to my attention.

10 James L. Hevia, 'The Photography Complex: Exposing Boxer Era China (1900–1901), Making Civilization', in *Photographies East: The Camera and its Histories in East and Southeast Asia*, ed. Rosalind C. Morris (Durham, NC, 2009), pp. 79–119.

11 A printed page with the names of the people in the photograph is attached to the back of the mount board. G. E. Morrison collection, State Library of New South Wales.

12 *Shenbao* (15 July 1876). The railway, said to have been unauthorized, was acquired by the Chinese authorities and demolished the following year.

13 *Shenzhou guoguang ji* (*National Glories of Cathay*), IV (1908).

14 *Shenzhou guoguang ji*, X (1909).

15 *Jinghua ribao* (29 March 1906).

16 It was finally agreed by both sides that Jiang had slit his own throat 'in a fit of anger'. See Ernest P. Young, 'The Politics of Evangelism', in *Christianity in China: From the Eighteenth Century to the Present*, ed. Daniel H. Bays (Stanford, CA, 1996), pp. 91–113.

17 Chen Shen et. al., eds, *Zhongguo sheying shi, 1840–1937* [The History of Photography in China, 1840–1937] (Beijing, 1987), p. 85. See advertisement in *Shibao* (12 June 1904).

18 *Shenbao* (26 June 1904). With thanks to Wang Cheng-hua for drawing this to my attention.

19 Li's studio is said to have been torched by the army of Feng Guozhang and all of his work destroyed. Chen Shen et al., eds, *Zhongguo sheying shi, 1840–1937*, p. 105.

20 Lu Hanchao, *The Birth of a Republic: Francis Stafford's Photographs of China's 1911 Revolution and Beyond* (Seattle, 2010), pp. 48–9.

21 Based on the success of Erwo Xuan – the album won medals at the Nanyang Exposition (1910) and the Panama-California Exposition (1915). Other studios in Hangzhou produced similar books, for example Yueh Chi studio's *Views of West Lake Hang Chow* (Xihu shengjing), and Da Fangbo studio's *Complete Views of West Lake* (Xihu quanjing).

22 Huang Yanpei, *Huang Yanpei kaocha jiaoyu riji* [Diary of Huang Yanpei's Investigation of Educatiion] (Shanghai, 1914), vol. I, pp. 185–6.

23 *Zhongguo mingsheng, di yi zhong. Huangshan* [Scenic China, Series 1, Huangshan, Anhui] (Shanghai, 1914); *Zhongguo mingsheng, di er zhong. Lushan* [Scenic China, Series 2, Lushan, Jiangxi] (Shanghai, 1915).

24 Shanghai Tushuguan, ed., *Shanghai tushuguan cang lishi yuanzhao* [Historic Photographs in the Collection of the Shanghai Library] (Shanghai, 2007), vol. II, pp. 311–13.

three: China Modern

1 Wen-hsin Yeh, *Shanghai Splendour: Economic Sentiments and the Making of Modern China* (Berkeley, CA, 2007), p. 56.

2 See Ye Xiaoqing, *The Dianshizhai Pictorial: Shanghai Urban Life, 1884–1898* (Ann Arbor, MI, 2003).

3 Ye Xiaoqing, *The Dianshizhai Pictorial*, p. 15.

4 For a profile of Star Talbot and his business activities see Hong Zaixin, 'An Entrepreneur in a "Adventurer's Paradise": Star Talbot and His Innovative Contributions to the Art Business of Modern Shanghai', in *Looking Modern: East Asian Visual Culture from Treaty Ports to World War II*, ed. Jennifer Purtle and H. B. Thomsen (Chicago, IL, 2009), pp. 85–105.

5 See Song Dynasty album leaf in the National Palace Museum in Taipei, and Castiglione's painting 'Tranquil Spring', a double portrait of Qianlong as a young and old man, which uses the phrase *xiezhen* for portrait, in Howard Rogers and Sherman E. Lee, *Masterworks of Ming and Qing Painting from the Forbidden City* (Landsdale, PA, 1988), cat. 55, pp. 89, 182–3.

6 'Erh wo hsieh chen kuan'. See Chien Yun-Ping et al., *In Sight: Tracing the Photography Studio Images of the Japanese Period in Taiwan* (Taipei, 2010), p. 90.

7 *Eastern Miscellany*, VIII/4 (20 June 1911).

8 Su Su, *Qian shi jin sheng* [The Past in the Present] (Shanghai, 1996), pp. 11–12.
9 See www.kaixin001.com/repaste/130942345_6511424785.html, accessed 9 April 2012.
10 Tong Bingxue, *Six Decades of a Chinese Life in Photographs* (*Yi zhan, yi zuo, yi sheng: Yige Zhongguo ren 62 nian de sheying zhi*) (Shanghai, 2010)
11 Tarzan, hero of the jungle, was created by American writer Edgar Rice Burroughs in 1912.
12 Chen Gongzhe's photograph was published in the group's tenth anniversary publication *Jingwu benji* (1919), p. 109 and in the group's pictorial magazine *Jingwu huabao*, IX (15 Dec 1927).
13 For a detailed discussion of this and other early twentieth-century photography groups see Hsueh Sheng Chen, 'Art Photography in China before 1949: The Continuation and Transformation of an Elite Culture', PhD thesis, University of Melbourne (2010).
14 In 1923 the group changed its name to Yishu xiezhen yanjiu hui (Research Association for Art Photography).
15 Liu Bannong, *Bannong tan ying* [Bannong on Photography] (Beijing, 2000), p. 54.
16 The China Camera Club (Zhongguo sheying xuehui) was established in 1925 by Lin Zecang and others as a group for amateur enthusiasts and appealed to a broad national membership. The group published the *China Camera Club Pictorial Weekly* (*Zhongguo sheying xuehui hua bao*), promoting the work of members, international photographers, the results of competitions and activities, and relevant news.
17 Lu Shifu, in *Hei bai ying ji* [The Black and White Pictorialist], I (1934), p. 8.
18 For a discussion of this phenomenon see Chen, 'Art Photography in China before 1949', pp. 181–4.
19 Lydia H. Liu, *Translingual Practice: Literature, National Culture, and Translated Modernity. China, 1900–1937* (Stanford, CA, 1995), pp. 25–6.
20 Chin-san Long, 'Technique of the Composite Picture', second lecture delivered at the Moomba Pacific Photography Fair, Melbourne, Australia, 4 March 1967; and his lecture delivered at the Wilson Hicks International Conference on Communication Arts, University of Miami, Florida, 29 April 1971, in *Photographic Works of Chin-San Long* (Taipei, 1972), n.p.

four: War and Propaganda

1 *Life*, III/14 (4 October 1937), pp. 102–3.
2 *Look*, XXII (21 December 1937), pp. 52–3, published five related images with the headline 'A Chinese Baby Survives an Air Raid'.
3 John Faber, *Great News Photos and the Stories Behind Them* (New York, 1978), pp. 74–5.
4 Gu Zheng, 'Zhanzheng yingxiang yu jiyi de zhengzhixue: Riben dangdai shijue wenhua zhong de jiyi, shenti, zhongzu yu shehui xingbie', in Gu Zheng, *Xiandai xing de di liu zhang miankong: dangdai shijue wenhua yanjiu* [The Sixth Face of Modernity: Research on Contemporary Visual Culture] (Shanghai, 2007), pp. 210–12.
5 Bu Qingqong and Qiu Feng, *Meng kaishi de defang: Wu Yinxian sheying* [Where Dreams Begin: The Photographs of Wu Yinxian], pp. 14–16.
6 *Balujun junzheng zazhi* [Eighth Route Army Military and Politics Journal], II/8 (25 August 1940).
7 Gao Qin, ed., *Touguo xiaoyan de jingtou, 1937–49*: *Zhongguo zhandi sheyingshi fangtan* [Lenses that Penetrated the Smoke of Gunpowder, 1937–49: Interviews with Chinese War Photographers], pp. 16–17.
8 Gu Di, ed., *Zhongguo hongse sheying shilu* [A Historical Record of China's Red Photography] (Taiyuan, 2009), vol. I, p. 320.
9 Ibid., vol. I, p. 439; vol. II, p. 663.
10 Mao Songyou, 'Xinwen sheying gailun', *Hei bai ying ji* [The Black and White Pictorialist], III (1936–7), pp. 81–3.
11 Mao Songyou, *Xinwen sheying* [News Photography] (Shanghai, 1953), pp. 3–4.
12 See notice of 2008 retrospective of Zhang Zudao's photography, www.tsinghua.org.cn/alumni/infoSingleArticle.do?articleId=10019122&columnId=10005594 (in Chinese), accessed 3 January 2012. Dong Cunrui is said to have blown himself up in order to bring down a bridge and thereby prevent the onslaught of Nationalist troops.
13 *Di san jie quanguo sheying yishu zhanlan zuopin xuan* (Shanghai, 1961), p. 1.
14 See http://blog.voc.com.cn/blog_showone_type_blog_id_650668_p_1.html (in Chinese), accessed 8 May 2010.
15 Conversation with Weng Naiqiang, Beijing, 5 December 2010.
16 Jie Li, 'Virtual Museums of Forbidden Memories: Hu Jie's Documentary Films on the Cultural Revolution', *Public Culture*, XXI/3 (2009), pp. 539–49.

five: Reportage and New Wave

1 Bao Kun, 'Bu de bu shuo de Li Xiaobin', in Li Xiaobin, *Biange zai Zhongguo, 1976–1986: Sheying Li Xiaobin* [Reform in China, 1976–1986: The Photographs of Li Xiaobin] (Hangzhou, 2003), pp. 10–21.
2 Li Xiaobin, 'Guan yu "Shangfangzhe"', in *Biange zai Zhongguo* [Reform in China], pp. 42–5, 48–9.
3 Li Anding, 'Yi ban shi yunqi, yi ban shi zhihui', in *Wang Wenlan: Ouran* [Wang Wenlan: Chance], ed. Chen Xiaobo (Beijing, 2007), p. 14.
4 Chen Xiaobo, 'Jingjing paishe: Wang Wenlan fangtan', in *Wang*

Wenlan: Ouran [Wang Wenlan: Chance], p. 211.

5 He Yanguang, 'Shidai gei wo jiyu'. See www.rmhb.com.cn/chpic/htdocs/china/200812/news/p64-wenzi.html, accessed 8 May 2010.

6 Liu Heung Shing, *China After Mao: Seek Truth From Facts* (Hong Kong, 1983), p. 8.

7 Ibid., pp. 8–9.

8 Wang Wenlan, 'Zi pai', in *Wang Wenlan: Ouran*, p. 237.

9 Preface to the Nature. Society. Man exhibition, cited in Geng Hai, ed., *Yongyuan de siyue* [Eternal April] (Hong Kong, 1999), pp. 88–9, n. 5.

10 With thanks to Juliane Noth for bringing this to my attention.

11 See Bao Kun, 'Bu de bu shuo de Li Xiaobin', in Li Xiaobin, *Biange zai Zhongguo* [Reform in China], n.p.

12 Ibid.

13 An Ge, 'Congqian you zuo shan: An Ge de gushi', *Shenghuo zai Deng Xiaoping shidai: Shijue 90 niandai* [Living the Deng Xiaoping Era: A Visual Record of the '90s] (Guangzhou, 2001), p. 281.

14 Zhongguo xiandai sheying shalong, ed., Introduction, in *Shi nian yi shunjian* [Flashback – A Decade of Changes], ed. Yu Shing-tak and Yang Shaoming (Beijing, 1986).

15 Hu Wugong, Preface, in *Hu Wugong: Yanhuo ren jian, 1966–2009* (Guangzhou, 2009), n.p.

16 Zhang Yimou, interview with Kwok-Kan Tam, 1996, in *Zhang Yimou Interviews*, ed. Frances Gateward (Jackson, FL, 2001), p. 108.

17 Wu Jialin, quoted in *FotoFest 2008 China: Photography from China, 1934–2008*, ed. Wendy Watriss (Houston, TX, 2008), p. 79.

18 Wu Jialin, 'Postscript', in *Mountain Folks in Yunnan: Selected Photographs of Wu Jialin* (*Yunnan shan li ren: Wu Jialin sheying ji*) (Kunming, 1993), n.p.

19 Wu Jialin, quoted in *FotoFest 2008 China*, ed. Watriss, p. 80.

20 David Cohen, ed., *A Day in the Life of China* (San Francisco, 1989), pp. 86–7, 188–9.

21 Ibid., pp. 206–7.

22 Conversation with Lü Nan, 15 January 2012.

23 Lü Nan, quoted in *FotoFest 2008 China*, ed. Watriss, p. 86.

24 Hu Wugong, 'Yingxiang zhong de renwen Zhongguo', in *Humanism in China: A Contemporary Record of Photography*, ed. Wang Huangsheng and Hu Wugong (Guangzhou, 2006), pp. 12–13.

six: U-Turn

1 Zhongyang meishu xueyuan xuesheng sheying xiehui, 'Women de hua: Zhongyang meishu xueyuan xuesheng sheying xiehui zuopin xuan', *Sheying bao* [Photography Newspaper] (13 August 1987), p. 4.

2 Gu Zheng, 'Quan li ti sheng Zhongguo sheying jie' (4 November 2010). See http://vision.xitek.com/004002/article-53824-1.htm, accessed 9 April 2012.

3 Yang Xiaoyan, 'Pai she zhege dongzuo . . . yu Zhang Hai'er duihua', *Sheying*, I (August 1988), p. 43.

4 Ibid., pp. 44–5.

5 'Kaitou de hua', *Sheying*, XIII (1988), p. 1.

6 The group included Ah Xian, Guan Wei, Wang Youshen and Yang Yongqiang (Nicholas Jose and Bronwyn Thomas were regular observers). The gatherings occurred regularly in each other's homes and were also social occasions.

7 Mo Yi, 'Tossing Buses 1989–1990' and 'Your fate is so bad, Tossing Bus 1989, China', in Mo Yi, *Memories from 1989*, Sanying tang (Three Shadows Photography Arts Centre), limited edition, n.p. See also Wu Hung, 'Mo Yi: An Ethnographer in Contemporary Chinese Art', ibid.

seven: Performing into the Present

1 Zhang Huan, '12 Square Metres', in *Contemporary Chinese Art: Primary Documents*, ed. Wu Hung (New York, 2010), p. 214.

2 In Melissa Chiu, *Breakout: Chinese Art Outside China* (Milan, 2007), p. 15.

3 In 'History and Memory', Haus der Kulturen Welt, www.hkw.de/en/programm/2006/cultural_memory/texte_2/History_and_Memory.php, accessed 25 March 2011.

4 Liu Zheng, 'Zi shu', *Liu Zheng*, ed. Li Mei and Ruan Yizhong (Beijing, 2004), p. 12.

5 Quoted in Wu Hung, 'Photographing Deformity: Liu Zheng and his Photo Series *My Countrymen*', in *Wu Hung on Contemporary Chinese Artists* (Hong Kong, 2009), p. 76.

6 Liu Zheng, 'Zi shu', p. 12.

7 Wu Hung, *Between Past and Future: New Photography and Video from China* (Chicago, 2005), p. 25.

8 Hong Lei, in 'Artists' Statements', quoted in Wu Hung, *Between Past and Future*, p. 205.

9 Zhang Dali, 'Zi shu', *1990 nian yilai de Zhongguo xianfeng sheying* [Chinese Avant-garde Photography since 1990], ed. Zhu Qi (Changsha, 2004), p. 226.

10 Hitomi Iwasaki, 'Leung Chi Wo: Something About City Sky', in *Leung Chi-Wo City Mapping: Rough Cuts*, exh. cat., Lee Ka-sing Gallery, Toronto (Toronto, 2003), n.p.

11 Chen Shaoxiong, in *Chinese Artists, Texts and Interviews: Chinese Contemporary Art Awards (CCAA), 1998–2002*, ed. Ai Weiwei, (Beijing, 2002), pp. 94–8.
12 Ai Weiwei and Feng Boyi, 'About "Fuck Off"', in *Fuck Off (Bu hezuo fangshi)*, exh. cat., Eastlink Gallery, Shanghai (Shanghai, 2000), p. 9.
13 Wang Qingsong, 'Artist's Statement', in Wu Hung, *Between Past and Future*, p. 213.
14 [Liu] Xiao Xian, 'Guanyu wode "guandian"', *Zhongguo sheying bao* (13 June 1997), p. 5.
15 See 'Wu Hung in Conversation with Miao Xiaochun', in *Miao Xiaochun*, ed. Uta Grosenick and Alexander Ochs (Cologne, 2010), p. 176, and pp. 172–8.
16 'Miao Xiaochun pushes limits of digital art', *Art Radar*, posted 1 December 2010. At http://artradarjournal.com, accessed 29 March 2011.
17 Cao Fei, 'Cao Fei', in *Fuck Off (Be hezuo fangshi)*, p. 16.
18 See www.kuoichen.net, accessed 31 March 2011.
19 Gu Zheng, 'A Theory of Chinese Personal Photography', in *3030: New Photography in China*, ed. John Millechap (Hong Kong, 2006), p. 17.
20 Gu Zheng, 'A Theory of Chinese Personal Photography'. Translation modified after consulting the original, Gu Zheng, 'Zhongguo si sheying lun', *Shehui kexue*, XII (2006), p. 101.
21 Gu Zheng, 'Investigating Reality in Order to Discover the Self', in *Points of Impact: China Through the Eyes of Young Photographers: The Exhibition of 2009 Three Shadows Photography Award*, exh. cat., Three Shadows Photography Art Centre (Beijing, 2009), p. 182.
22 Sun Yanchu, see http://next.kunstlicht.sh/artists/sun-yan-chu, accessed 8 May 2011. My thanks to Karen Smith for drawing my attention to the work of Sun Yanchu.
23 Sun Yanchu, quoted in *Points of Impact*, p. 102.
24 Sun Yanchu, *Obsessed*, artist statement on CD cover, 2010.
25 Press release, SH Contemporary, The Asia Pacific Contemporary Art Fair, Shanghai (12 September 2011).
26 Press release, 'The First Asia Pacific Photography Prize Goes to Artist Chen Wei' (15 September 2011).
27 Communication with Chen Wei, 7 November 2011.
28 Chen Wei, 'The Fabulist's Path', in *Sightings: Searching for the Truth: 2009 Guangzhou Photo Biennial*, ed. Wang Huangsheng (Nanchang, 2009), p. 226.

Select Bibliography

Acret, Susan, ed., *A Strange Heaven: Contemporary Chinese Photography*, exh. cat., Asia Art Archive, Hong Kong (Hong Kong, 2003)

Ai Weiwei, Feng Boyi and Hua Tianxue, eds, *Bu hezuo fangshi* [*Fuck Off*], exh. cat., Eastlink Gallery, Shanghai (Shanghai, 2000)

Albertini, Andrea and Primo Marella, *Out of the Red: The New Emerging Generation of Chinese Photographers*, exh. cat., Marella Arte Contemporanea, Milan (Milan, 2004)

An Ge, *Shenghuo zai Deng Xiaoping shidai: Shijue 80 niandai; Shijue 90 niandai* [Living the Deng Xiaoping Era: A Visual Record of the '90s], 2 vols (Guangzhou, 2001)

Bao Kun, ed., *Sheying Zhongguo: Zhongguo sheying 50 nian* [Photographing China: Highlights of 50 Years of Chinese Photography] (Beijing, 2006)

——, *Guan kan zai guan kan: Dangdai yingxiang wenhua* [Look and Look Again: Contemporary Photography Culture] (Beijing, 2009)

Bennett, Adrian Arthur, *John Fryer: The Introduction of Western Science and Technology into Nineteenth-Century China* (Cambridge, MA, 1967)

Bennett, Terry, *History of Photography in China, 1842–1860* (London, 2009)

——, *History of Photography in China, 1861–1879* (London, 2010)

Berghuis, Thomas J., *Performance Art in China* (Hong Kong, 2006)

Cameron, Nigel, *The Face of China As Seen by Photographers and Travellers, 1860–1912* (Millerton, NY, 1978)

Capa, Cornell, ed., *Behind the Great Wall of China: Photographs from 1870 to the Present*, exh. cat., Metropolitan Museum of Art, New York (New York, 1972)

Cartier-Bresson, Henri, *China in Transition: A Moment in History* (London, 1948)

Chen Hsueh Sheng, 'Art Photography in China before 1949: The Continuation and Transformation of an Elite Culture', PhD thesis (University of Melbourne, 2010)

Chen Shen, Hu Zhichuan, Ma Yunzeng, Qian Zhangbiao and Peng Yongxiang, eds, *Zhongguo sheying shi, 1840–1937* [The History of Photography in China, 1840–1937] (Beijing, 1987)

Chen Zhi'an and Ding Wenfang, eds, *Zhongguo sheyingjia cidian* [A Dictionary of Chinese Photographers] (Ji'nan, 1985)

Chong, Alan, and Noriko Murai, *Journeys East: Isabella Stewart Gardner and Asia*, exh. cat., Isabella Stewart Gardner Museum, Boston (Boston, MA, 2009)

Cody, Jeffrey W., and Frances Terpak, *Brush & Shutter: Early Photography in China*, exh. cat., J. Paul Getty Museum, Los Angeles (Los Angeles, 2011)

Duan Yuting, ed., *Yingzi de lianjinshu: Di san jie Lianzhou guoji sheying nian zhan* [The Alchemy of Shadows: Third Lianzhou International Photo Festival], exh. cat. (Shanghai, 2008)

——, ed., *Guancha yu bei guancha: 2006 Lianzhou guoji sheying nian zhan* [Between the Observer and the Observed: 2006 Lianzhou International Photo Festival], exh. cat. (Shanghai, 2006)

Duan Yuting and Jiang Wei, eds, *Wode zhaoxiangji: Di si jie Lianzhou guoji sheying nian zhan* [My Camera: Fourth Lianzhou International Photo Festival], exh. cat. (Shanghai, 2009)

Gao Qin, ed., *Touguo xiaoyan de jingtou: 1937–1949 Zhongguo zhan di sheying shi fangtan* [Interviews with Chinese War Photographers] (Beijing, 2009)

Grosse-Aschhoff, Angelus, *The Negotiations Between Ch'i Ying and Lagrené* (New York, 1950)

Gu Di, ed., *Zhongguo hongse sheying shi lu* [A Historical Record of Red Photography in China], 2 vols (Taiyuan, 2009)

Gu Yuan, ed., *Guangdong sheying yishu zhi, 1843–2006* [A Record of Photographic Art in Guangdong, 1843–2006] (Guangzhou, 2008)

Gu Zheng, *Xiandai xing de di liu zhang miankong* [The Sixth Face of Modernity] (Shanghai, 2007)

Gu Zhenqing, ed., *Right Here: Photographs by Chin-San Long*, exh. cat., Zhu Qizhan Art Museum, Shanghai (Shanghai, 2006)

Guoli lishi bowuguan, ed., *Huishou Taiwan bainian sheying youguang* [A Retrospective of One Hundred Years of Taiwan Photography], exh. cat., National Museum of History, Taipei (Taipei, 2003)

Harris, David, *Of Battle and Beauty: Felice Beato's Photographs of China*, exh. cat., Santa Barbara Museum of Art (Santa Barbara, CA, 2000)

Hevia, James L., 'The Photography Complex: Exposing Boxer Era China (1900–1901), Making Civilization', in *Photographies East: The Camera and its Histories in East and Southeast Asia*, ed. Rosalind C. Morris (Durham, NC, 2009), pp. 79–119

Hong Kong Museum of History, *The Road to China's 1911 Revolution*, exh. cat. (Hong Kong, 2011)

Hong Zaixin, 'An Entrepreneur in an "Adventurer's Paradise": Star Talbot and His Innovative Contributions to the Art Business of Modern Shanghai', in *Looking Modern: East Asian Visual Culture from Treaty Ports to World War II*, ed. Jennifer Purtle and H. B. Thomsen (Chicago, IL, 2009), pp. 85–105

Hu Wugong, *Zhongguo yingxiang geming: Dangdai xinwen sheying yu jishi sheying* [The Revolution in Photography: Contemporary News Photography and Documentary Photography] (Beijing, 2005)

Huang Shaofen, *Shanghai sheying shi* [A History of Photography in Shanghai] (Shanghai, 1992)

Huang Tsai-Lang, ed., *Ri zhi shiqi xiezheguan de yingxiang zhuisun* [In Sight: Tracing the Photographic Studio Images of the Japanese Period in Taiwan] (Taipei, 2010)

Jiang Jiehong, *Shi nian baoguang: Zhongyang meishu xueyuan yu Zongguo dangdai yingxiang* [A Decade-long Exposure: The Central Academy of Fine Arts and Chinese Contemporary Photography], exh. cat. (Shanghai, 2010)

Jiang Qisheng, Shu Zongqiao and Gu Di, eds, *Zhongguo sheying shi, 1937–1949* [The History of Photography in China, 1937–1949] (Beijing, 1998)

Jin Yongquan, *Hongqi zhaoxiangguan: 1956–1959 nian Zhongguo sheying zhengbian* [Red Flag Studio: Debates on China's Photography, 1956–1959] (Beijing, 2009)

Kuo, Jason C., ed., *Visual Culture in Shanghai, 1850s–1930s* (Washington, DC, 2007)

Lacoste, Anne, *Felice Beato: A Photographer on the Eastern Road*, exh. cat., J. Paul Getty Museum, Los Angeles (Los Angeles, 2010)

Lai, Edwin K., Régine Thiriez, Ko Tim-Keung et al., *First Photographs of Hong Kong, 1858–1875*, exh. cat., Hong Kong Photographic Culture Association (Hong Kong, 2010)

Lai, Kin-keung Edwin, 'The Life and Art Photography of Lang Jingshan', PhD thesis (University of Hong Kong, 2000)

——, 'Hong Kong Art Photography: From its Beginnings to the Japanese Invasion of December 1941', M.Phil thesis (University of Hong Kong, 1996)

Lau, Grace, *Picturing the Chinese: Early Western Photographs and Postcards of China* (San Francisco, 2008)

Li Jie, 'Virtual Museums of Forbidden Memories: Hu Jie's Documentary Films on the Cultural Revolution', *Public Culture*, XXI/3 (2009), pp. 539–49

Liu Beisi and Li Yihua, eds, *Gugong jiu cang renwu zhaopian ji* [A Selection of Historic Figure Photographs from the Forbidden City] (Beijing, 1990)

Liu Heung Shing, *China After Mao: Seek Truth From Facts* (Hong Kong, 1983)

——, ed., *China in Revolution: The Road to 1911* (Hong Kong, 2011)

Liu Heung Shing and Karen Smith, *Shanghai: A History in Photographs, 1842–Today* (London, 2010)

Long Chin-San, *Photographic Works of Chin-San Long* (Taipei, 1972)

Lu Hanchao, *The Birth of a Republic: Francis Stafford's Photographs of China's 1911 Revolution and Beyond* (Seattle, 2010)

Lü Peng, *A History of Art in Twentieth Century China* (Milan, 2010)

Lütgens, Annelie, and Gijs van Tuyl, *The Chinese: Contemporary Photography and Video From China*, exh. cat., Kunstmuseum Wolfsburg (Ostfildern, 2005)

Millichap, John, ed., *3030 New Photography in China* (Hong Kong, 2006)

Moore, Oliver, 'Zou Boqi on Vision and Photography in Nineteenth Century China', in *The Human Tradition in Modern China*, ed. Kenneth J. Hammond and Kristen Stapleton (Lanham, MD, 2008), pp. 33–53

Pearce, Nick, *Photographs of Peking, China, 1861–1908: An Inventory and Description of the Yetts Collection at the University of Durham: Through Peking with a Camera* (Lewiston, NY, 2005)

Pinney, Christopher, and Nicholas Peterson, eds, *Photography's Other Histories* (Durham, NC, 2003)

Pledge, Robert, and Li Zhensheng, *Red-Color News Soldier: A Chinese Photographer's Odyssey Through the Cultural Revolution* (London, 2003)

Purtle, Jennifer, and H. B. Thomsen, eds, *Looking Modern: East Asian Visual Culture from Treaty Ports to World War II* (Chicago, 2009)
Renmin de daonian lianhe bianji zubian, ed., *Renmin de daonian* [The People's Mourning] (Beijing, 1979)
Shanghai sheyingjia xiehui and Shanghai daxue wenxueyuan, eds, *Shanghai sheying shi* [History of Photography in Shanghai] (Shanghai, 1992)
Shanghai tushuguan, ed., *Shanghai tushuguan cang lishi yuan zhao* [Historic Original Photographs in the Collection of the Shanghai Library], 2 vols (Shanghai, 2007)
Shen Jiawei, ed., *Old China Through Morrison's Eyes*, 3 vols (Fuzhou, 2005)
Silbergeld, Jerome, *Humanism in China: A Contemporary Record of Photography* (New York, 2009)
Spence, Jonathon D., and Annping Chin, *The Chinese Century: A Photographic History of the Last Hundred Years* (New York, 1996)
Su Zhigang, Lin Li, Liu Ning and Zhou Zheng, eds, *Zhongguo sheying shilüe* [A Brief History of Chinese Photography] (Beijing, 2009)
Suchomel, Filip, and Marcela Suchomelová, . . . *and the Chinese cliffs emerged out of the mist: Perception and Image of China in Early Photographs* (Prague, 2011)
Thiriez, Régine, *Barbarian Lens: Western Photographers of the Qianlong Emperor's European Palaces* (New York, 1998)
——, 'Ligelang: A French Photographer in 1850s Shanghai', *Orientations*, XXXII/9 (November 2001), pp. 49–54
——, 'William Saunders, Photographer of Shanghai Customs', *Visual Resources*, XXVI/3 (September 2010), pp. 325–40
Tong Bingxue, *Yi zhan yi zuo yi sheng: Yige Zhongguoren 62 nian de ying-xiang zhi* [Six Decades of a Chinese Life in Photographs] (Shanghai, 2010)
Wallace, Keith, ed., *Action–Camera: Beijing Performance Photography*, exh. cat., Morris and Helen Belkin Art Gallery, Vancouver (Vancouver, 2009)
Wang Huangsheng, ed., *Di san jie Guangzhou guoji sheying shuangnian zhan: Kan zhen D.com* [2009 Guangzhou Photo Biennial. Sightings: Searching for the Truth] (Nanchang, 2009)
——, ed., *Zuo you shi xian: 2007 Guangzhou guoji sheying shuangnian zhan* [Evolution: 2007 Guangzhou Photo Biennial], exh. cat. (Guangdong, 2007)
—— and Hu Wugong, eds, *Zhongguo renben: Jishi zai dangdai* [Humanism in China: A Contemporary Record of Photography], exh. cat., Guangdong Museum of Art, Guangzhou (Hong Kong, 2003)
Wang Wenlan, ed., *Bai ming sheying jizhe jujiao Zhongguo, 1949–2009* [One Hundred Photojournalists Focus on China, 1949–2009] (Beijing, 2009)
Wang Yan, ed., *Sha Fei sheying quanji* [The Complete Photographs of Sha Fei] (Guangzhou, 2005)
Wang Zhiping and Li Xiaobin, eds, *Ziran. Shehui. Ren* [Nature. Society. Man], exh. cat., Sun Yat-Sen Park, Hong Kong (Hong Kong, 1979)
Watriss, Wendy, ed., *FotoFest 2008: Photography from China, 1934–2008*, exh. cat., FotoFest International, Houston (Houston, TX, 2008)
Worswick, Clark, *Sheying: Shades of China, 1850–1900* (Madrid, 2008)
——, and Jonathon D. Spence, *Imperial China: Photographs, 1850–1912* (New York, 1978)
Wu Hung, *Wu Hung on Contemporary Chinese Artists* (Hong Kong, 2009)
——, *Contemporary Chinese Art: Primary Documents* (New York, 2010)
Wu Hung and Christopher Phillips, *Between Past and Future: New Photography and Video from China*, exh. cat., Smart Museum of Art, University of Chicago (Chicago, IL, 2005)
Wue, Roberta, *Picturing Hong Kong: Photography, 1855–1910*, exh. cat., Asia Society, New York (New York, 1997)
Xu Yun, ed., *Wu Jialin sheyingji: Yunnan shanli ren* [Selected Photographs of Wu Jialin: Mountain Folks in Yunnan] (Kunming, 1993)
Yang Rae, *China: Fifty Years Inside the People's Republic*, exh. cat., Asia Society, New York (New York, 1999)
Yang Xiaoyan, *Xin Zhongguo sheying 60 nian* [Photo 60 Years in China] (Shijiazhuang, 2009)
Yapelli, Tina, *Zooming into Focus: Contemporary Chinese Photography and Video from the Haudenschild Collection*, exh. cat., San Diego State University Art Gallery (San Diego, CA, 2003)
Yeh, Catherine Vance, *Shanghai Love: Courtesans, Intellectuals and Entertainment Culture, 1850–1910* (Seattle, 2006)
Yeh, Wen-Hsin, *Shanghai Splendour: Economic Sentiments and the Making of Modern China, 1843–1949* (Berkeley, CA, 2007)
Yu Shing-tak and Yang Shaoming, eds, *Contemporary Chinese Photographs by Members of the China Modern Photo Salon 1985* (Beijing, 1985)
Zhang Xiaoqiang, ed., *Tupian: Zhongguo bai nian shi* [Photographs: A History of One Hundred Years in China] (Jinan, 1994)
Zheng Lunan, *Junzhong lao zhaopian: Lao zhaopian beihou de gushi* [Old Military Photographs and the Stories Behind Them] (Beijing, 2010)
Zhongguo guojia bowuguan, ed., *Zhongguo guojia bowuguan cang wenwu yanjiu congshu: Lishi tupian juan* [Research Series of the Collection of the National Museum of China: Historical Photographs Volume] (Shanghai, 2006)
Zhongguo guojia bowuguan and Daying tushuguan, eds, *1860–1930 Yingguo cang Zhongguo lishi zhaopian* [Western Eyes: Historical Photographs of China in British Collections, 1860–1930], 2 vols (Beijing, 2008)
Zhongguo sheying, ed., *Geming yangban zuopin juzhao xuanji* [A Selection of Photographic Stills from the Model Revolutionary Operas] (Beijing, 1976)
Zhongguo sheyingjia chubanshe, ed., *Jianzheng: Gaige kaifang sanshi nian* [China's Thirty Years] (Hong Kong, 2009)
Zhu Qi, ed., *1990 nian yilai de Zhongguo xianfeng sheying* [Chinese Avant-garde Photography Since 1990] (Changsha, 2004)

Acknowledgements

The project was first suggested to me by Geremie R. Barmé, Australian Research Council Federation Fellow and Professor of Chinese History at The Australian National University, with whom I worked as a research fellow from 2006 to 2009. The opportunity to work with Michael Leaman and Reaktion Books has been a privilege and a pleasure. I extend particular thanks to Harry Gilonis, Aimee Selby and the anonymous readers of the manuscript. Much of the research was carried out when I was a research fellow at the Radcliffe Institute for Advanced Study, Harvard University, from 2009–10, and at the Harvard–Yenching Institute, working with Dr Raymond Lum, curator of historic photographs in the Harvard–Yenching Library, in 2011. The generosity of friends and colleagues at the Radcliffe Institute and Yenching Library were central to the research and shaping of the book.

Many friends, colleagues and associates in China, Australia, North America, Europe and elsewhere have contributed to this undertaking. The insightful conversations with An Ge, Nancy Berliner, Chen Xiaobo, Helen Ennis, Gu Yi, Li Xiaobin, Li Xin, Lü Nan, Raymond Lum, Sang Ye, Régine Thiriez, Eugene Wang and Winnie Wong have given me particular pleasure.

I sincerely thank the photographers and their family members or representatives for their support, including permission to reproduce photographs. This book has been generously supported by numerous institutions that provided reproductions of photographs in their collections including: Terry Bennett Collection; Chinese Photographers Association, Beijing; Guangzhou Museum, China; Harvard–Yenching Library, Harvard University, Cambridge; Isabella Stewart Gardner Museum Archives, Boston; Menzies Library, The Australian National University, Canberra; Musée Français de la Photographie, Bièvres; National Gallery of Australia, Canberra; Powerhouse Museum, Sydney; Queensland Art Gallery, Brisbane; Smithsonian Institution, Washington, DC; Tong Bingxue Collection; Wellcome Library, London. I would like to acknowledge Geremie R. Barmé's Australian Research Council Federation Fellowship project 'Beijing as Spectacle', the support of which has added to the visual richness of this book.

I especially acknowledge the help and advice of the following people and institutions: Archives de la Province de France de la Campagnie de Jésus, Vanves: Father Robert Bonfils; Australian National University: Geremie Barmé, Darrell Dorrington, Helen Ennis, Liao Hsin-tien, Sophie McIntyre and Rebecca Wong; Boston Museum of Fine Arts: Jane Portal, Hao Sheng, Ellen Takata and Karen Quinn; British Library, London: Malani Roy and Jennifer Howes; Freer and Sackler Galleries, Smithsonian Institution, Washington, DC: David Hogge; French Museum of Photography, Bièvres: Rémi Calzada; FOTOE: Lin Yuehao; George Eastman House, Rochester: Rachel Stuhlman, Joe Struble, Todd Gustavson and Kathy Connor; Getty Museum, Los Angeles: Jeffrey Cody, Frances Terpak and Ted Walbye; Guangzhou Museum: Cheng Cunhao and Zhu Wanzhang; Harvard University: Joanne Bloom, Amanda Bowen, Robert Burton, Nanni Deng, Maggie Hale, Henrietta Harrison, Jie Li, Madeleine Newell, Ying Qian, Eugene Wang, Sharon Wang, Winnie Wong and Sophia Wong Chesrow; Harvard–Yenching Institute: Elizabeth J. Perry, Elaine Hall Witham and Ruohong Li; Harvard–Yenching Library: James Cheng, Raymond Lum, Xiao-He Ma and Li Yuhua; Hong Kong Maritime Museum: Stephen Davies; International Centre of Photography, New York: Christopher Phillips, Claartje Van Dijk and Matthew Carson; Isabella Stewart Gardner Museum, Boston: Kristen Parker and Joe Saravo; Library of Congress, Washington, DC: Jeff Bridgers; National Gallery of Australia, Canberra: Gael Newton; National Gallery of Victoria, Melbourne: Isobel Crombie; National Museum of Chinese History, Beijing: Chen Lusheng, Wang Fang and Zhang Ming; National Palace Museum, Taiwan: Hans Huang; Palace Museum, Beijing: Chen Lihua, Fu Yiqiang, Yuan Hong and Zhang Ying; Peabody Essex Museum, Salem: Nancy Berliner, Christine Bertoni, Bruce MacLaren and Barbara Kampas; Powerhouse Museum, Sydney: Dawn Casey, Kathy Hackett and Iwona Hetherington; Queensland Art Gallery: Russell Storer; Radcliffe Institute for Advanced Study, Harvard University: Marlon Cummings, Barbara Grosz, Sharon Lim-Hing, Melissa Synott and Judy Vichniac; Royal Asiatic Society, London: Kathy Lazenbatt; Shanghai Library: Wu Jianzhong, Zhang Wei, Chen Guojia, Huang Xiangong, Wang Manxiu and Zhou Qing; Three Shadows Photography Art Centre, Beijing: Rong Rong and Lu Liqing; Wellcome Library, London: William Schupbach and Anna Smith; and Terry Bennett, Chen Ruilin, Shuxia Chen, Chen Xiaobo, Chen Yanyin, Chen Yingfang, Jeremy Clarke, John Clark, Peter Coyne, James Fox, Gao Jisheng, Geng Hai, Geng Ling, Andre Gensburger, Gu Zheng, Guan Wei, Ihab and Sally Hassan, He Cong, Rod Headington, Carma Hinton, Norman Hodgson, Hong Zaixin, Huang Zhuan, Jin Xiong, Joan Lebold Cohen, Serge Kakou, Richard Kelton, Eric Lefebvre, Li Chen, Li Gongming, Li Mei, Li Xiaobin, Li Xin, Richard Kent, Hsinyi Tiffany Lee, Liu Heung Shing, Liu Xiao Xian, Meredith Lue, Sandra Matthews, Meng Sihui, Helen Parker, Susan Perschel, Ruth Phillips, Suhanya Raffel, Daniella Rossi, Sang Ye, Shen Jiawei, Uli Sigg, Karen Smith, Nicholas Standaert, Ann Stephen, Lindsay Stewart, Edward Stokes, Jan Stuart, Sun Jin, Naomi Szeto, Jean-Yves Trehin, Régine Thiriez, Kenji Tierney, Tong Bingxue, Sue Trevaskes, Wang Yan, Wang Youshen, Wang Ziyin, Wang Zhongxiu, Weng Naiqiang, Ellen Widmer, Wu Yanhua, Bob Wyatt, Xing Fei, Xu Hong, Yang Guobin, Catherine Yeh, Yu Deshui, Zeng Huang, Zhang Fei and Zhang Peili.

Heartfelt appreciation also goes to my husband Nicholas Jose, who now knows more about photography and China than he ever thought necessary.

Photo Acknowledgements

The author and publishers wish to express their thanks to the following sources of illustrative material and/or permission to reproduce it:

Courtesy An Ge: 104, 105; Archives de la Province de France de la Campagnie de Jésus, Vanves: 3; from *Beijing Guangshe nianjan*, I (1927): 62; Terry Bennett Collection: 8, 9, 18; courtesy Cai Shangxiong: 80; courtesy the artist (Cao Fei) and Vitamin Creative Space: 129; courtesy the artist (Chen Shaoxiong): 123; courtesy Chen Wei: 132; Chinese Photographers Association, Beijing: 5; from The Commercial Press, *Dageming xiezhen hua* [War Scenes of the Chinese Revolution], 14 vols (Shanghai, 1911), vol. I: 40; from Erwo Xuan Studio, *Xihu fengjing* [West Lake Landscape] (Hangzhou, 1908–10): 43; Freer Gallery of Art and Arthur M. Sackler Gallery Archives, Smithsonian Institution, Washington, DC (gift of Joanna Sturm, 2009): 22; courtesy of George Eastman House International Museum of Photography and Film, Rochester, NY: 69; from Gu Di, ed., *Zhongguo hongse sheyingshi* [A Historical Record of Red Photography in China], vol. I (Taiyuan: Shanxi chuban jituan, Shanxi renminchubanshe, 2009): 79; Guangzhou Museum, Guangdong Province (gift of Mr Zou Mengcai, grandson of Zou Boqi): 4; Harvard-Yenching Library, Cambridge, Massachusetts (photos © President & Fellows of Harvard College, used with permission): 30 (Edwin Bangs Drew collection), 31 (Edwin Bangs Drew collection), 54 (Arthur Holcombe collection), 87, 88, 89, 90; courtesy He Yanguang: 97; from *Hei bai ying ji*, I (1934): 64, 65; from *Hei bai ying ji*, II (1935): 67; courtesy Hong Lei: 120; from Hsiao Yong-sheng, *Hua-yi Chi-chin Long Chin-san* [A Collection of Artworks by Long Chin-san] (Taipei: Xiongshi, 2004): 68; courtesy Hu Wugong: 107; Isabella Stewart Gardner Museum Archives, Boston: 29; The J. Paul Getty Museum, Los Angeles: 7; from *Jin-Cha-Ji Pictorial*, 3 (1943): 73; from *Jinghua Daily*, 29 March 1906: 38; from *Jingwu benji* [Chronicle of the Chin Woo Athletic Association] (Shanghai, 1919): 59, 60, 61; courtesy Kuo I-chen: 130; courtesy the artist (Leung Chi Wo): 122; courtesy Li Jiangshu: 101; courtesy Li Xiaobin: 95, 100, 103; courtesy Li Zhensheng: 92; Library of Congress, Washington, DC (Prints and Photographs Division): 21 (from Liang Shitai [See Tay] album 'Portraits of I-huan, Prince Ch'un, and Views of His Palace at Peking', Wharton Barker Papers); courtesy of Lin Quanxiu: 50; photograph by Liu Heung Shing, all rights reserved: 1; courtesy the artist (Liu Xiao Xian): 114, 127; courtesy of the artist (Liu Zheng): 119; from Chin-san Long, *Jingshan sheying ji* (Shanghai, 1929): 63; courtesy of Eve Long: 63, 68; courtesy Lü Nan, © copyright Lü Nan: 111; courtesy Luo Xiaoyun: 93; courtesy Meng Zhaorui: 85; Menzies Library, The Australian National University, Canberra (Giles Pickford Collection, photos © The Australian National University): 34, 35; courtesy Miao Xiaochun: 128; Mitchell Library, State Library of New South Wales, Sydney (George Ernest Morrison papers – photos State Library of New South Wales, Sydney, Australia – Mitchell Collection): 24 (PX*D 157 / vol. II / 56), 33 (PX*D 156 / vol. II), 39 (PXA 207 / vol. I), 44 (PXA 208), 45 (PX*D 151 / vol. II); courtesy Mo Yi: 115; Musée Français de la Photographie, Bièvres: 2; Museum of Fine Arts, Boston (gift of Sarah Buchan Jewell – photograph © 2012 Museum of Fine Arts, Boston): 23; National Gallery of Australia, Canberra: 6, 27; from *National Glories of Cathay* [Shenzhou guoguang ji], vol. V (October 1908): 37; National Palace Museum, Taiwan: 49; The New York Public Library for the Performing Arts (Astor, Lenox and Tilden Foundations, Billy Rose Theatre Division): 52; courtesy of the Palace Museum, Beijing: 20; courtesy of the Peabody Essex Museum, Salem, Massachusetts: 13, 14, 19, 26; photos courtesy Powerhouse Museum, Sydney: 66 (gift of Alastair Morrison, 1992), 74, 78, 84; Private collection: 47; Collection Queensland Art Gallery, Brisbane, Australia (The James C. Sourris, AM Collection, purchased 2002 with funds from James C. Sourris through the Queensland Art Gallery Foundation – Acc. 2002.013): 125, 126; Research Library, Getty Research Institute, Los Angeles: 15 (2007.R.11), 25 (2006.R.1.4), 28 (2003.R.22), 32 (2005.R.11, gift of Mary C. Stollman); courtesy Rong Rong: 117; Collection of the Royal Asiatic Society of Great Britain and Ireland, London: 10, 12; courtesy Ru Suichu: 81; photos Shanghai Library: 36, 40, 41, 42, 46, 51, 55, 59, 60, 61, 62, 63, 64, 65, 67; courtesy Shi Zhimin/ZM Collections 71, 91; courtesy Sun Yanchu: 131; courtesy S. K. Teng: 75; Régine Thiriez Collection: 48; Tong Bingxue Collection: 16, 17, 56, 57, 58; from *True Record*, I (1912): 41; from *True Record*, III (1912): 42; courtesy Arthur Tsang Hin Wah, © Bettmann/CORBIS: 110; courtesy Wang Huangsheng and Hu Wugong, eds, *Zhongguo renben: Jishi zai dangdai* [Humanism in China: A Contemporary Record of Photography], exh. cat. (Hong Kong, 2003): 80, 81, 82, 83; courtesy Wang Miao: 99; © the artist (Wang Qingsong), reproduced by permission, from the Collection of the Queensland Art Gallery, Brisbane: 125, 126; courtesy Wang Wenlan: 96, 106; courtesy Wang Yan: 70; courtesy of the artist (Wang Youshen): 116; courtesy Wang Zhiping: 98; courtesy Wei Dezhong: 82; Wellcome Library, London: 11; courtesy Weng Naiqiang: 86; courtesy Wu Jialin: 109; courtesy Wu Peng: 94; courtesy Wu Wei/Wu Yinxian Memorial House Museum, www.wuyinxian.com: 72; courtesy the artist (Xing Danwen) and Danwen Studio, Beijing: 118; courtesy Yang Fudong: 124; from *Young Companion*, I (1926): 53; courtesy Yu Deshui: 108; courtesy Yuan Ling: 77; courtesy Zhang Dali: 121; courtesy Zhang Hai'er: 112, 113; courtesy Zhang Yimou: 102; courtesy Zhang Zudao: 83, from *Zhonghua* magazine, 46 (September 1936): 55; courtesy Zou Yi: 76.

Index